IMINGAISHA

IMINGAISHA

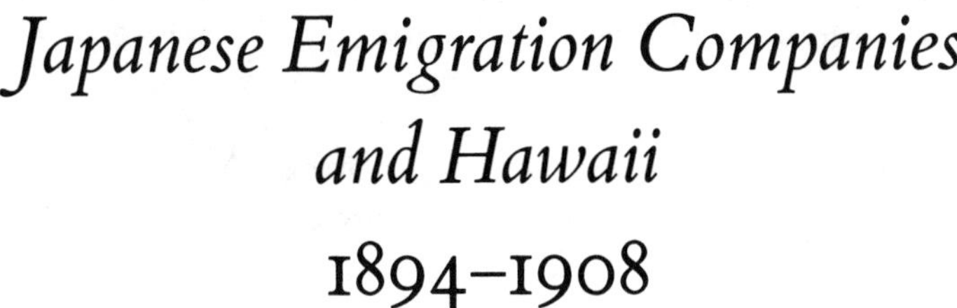

Japanese Emigration Companies and Hawaii

1894–1908

ALAN TAKEO MORIYAMA

UNIVERSITY OF HAWAII PRESS
HONOLULU

Publication of this book was made possible by a generous grant from Mr. and Mrs. Andy M. Ichiki in memory of Andy's father, Masaji Ichiki, who immigrated to Maui circa 1910 from Fukuoka Prefecture and had the good fortune of fulfilling his dream of America for himself and his family. The success the elder Mr. Ichiki enjoyed as the owner and operator of a chain of department and grocery stores on Oahu and Maui could not have occurred but for the supreme confidence he had in his own abilities, his flair for conceiving innovative business ideas and techniques and, probably most significant, the unselfish and unquestioning assistance he received from the devoted and hardworking Hawaii-born girl he chose as his wife.

MANUFACTURED IN THE UNITED STATES OF AMERICA

Library of Congress Cataloging-in-Publication Data

Moriyama, Alan Takeo, 1948–
Imingaisha : Japanese emigration companies and Hawaii, 1894–1908.

Bibliography: p.
Includes index.
1. Japan—Emigration and immigration—History.
2. Japanese—Hawaii—History. I. Title.
JV8721.M67 1985 325.52 85-8694
ISBN 0-8248-1004-X

Whatever intellectual curiosity and
discipline for scholarship I have
I've learned from my father
Sadao Moriyama.

Whatever compassion and gentleness I have
I've learned from my mother
Elaine S. Moriyama.

This book is dedicated to both of them.

Contents

Appendixes

Maps

Tables

Notes on Japanese Terms

1. All Japanese personal names are in Japanese order, surnames first, except for those of authors published in English.

2. Except in familiar place names and names from English-language publications, macrons indicate long vowels.

3. In romanized names and titles of documents written or published before 1945, I have used the word "Nippon" (Japan). For documents that have appeared after that year, I have used "Nihon."

Preface

STUDIES on emigration and immigration are important not merely for students of history but for all of us today. Americans are fortunate enough to live in a multiracial, multiethnic, multigenerational society, and how we view and treat other people depends on what we know about them. Knowing why and how these people came to America and the manner in which they struggled for economic security and political equality can help us to understand and hopefully appreciate them better.

I began this study without any preconceived notion about what particular model, framework, or theory concerning immigration would be most useful. Instead there were only two assumptions that guided my research. The first was that primary Japanese-language materials had to be examined in order to understand this period; fortunately these were available in the archival holdings of the Japanese Foreign Ministry. The second assumption was that if there were models, frameworks, or theories that were applicable to my subject, they would appear as the research progressed. I found this to be true and I feel that in historical studies of this nature, this may be the best approach.

Three professors at UCLA, Fred Notehelfer, Lucie Cheng, and Alex Saxton, guided my graduate studies. The result was a dissertation and subsequently a manuscript, the basis of this book. Professor Itō Takashi of Tokyo University showed me how research is done on its highest level. Professor Kachi Teruko, formerly of Tsuda University, guided my early research efforts in Japan with grace and dignity.

Writing a publishable manuscript is a difficult task; fortunately, there were a number of colleagues and friends who with their comments made this work easier. I am grateful to all of them. In particular I wish to thank Dr. John Liu, the associate editor of *Amerasia Journal.* He was not only very detailed in his comments but he also shared some of the results of his research on Hawaiian plantations. George Akita, professor of history at the University of Hawaii, was a source of encouragement and valuable comments and suggestions from the very beginning of this project. I am indeed fortunate to have met him.

Examining and understanding research materials over the years was only possible with the help and patience of staff members of the Diplomatic Record Office, the National Diet Library in Japan, the Hawaii State Archives, the University of Hawaii Hamilton Library, the UCLA University Research Library, and the UCLA Asian American Studies Center Reading Room. Special thanks go to Ms. Yamada Hiroko of the Diplomatic Record Office and Ms. Mihoko Miki of the UCLA Oriental Library, who both went out of their way to make things easier for me and who also granted me access to a variety of materials.

The Japanese American Postdoctoral Fellowship administered by the UCLA Asian American Studies Center generously provided the funds and the time to turn my dissertation into a publishable manuscript. The funds for this fellowship are part of an endowed chair position in Japanese American Studies at UCLA.

I am grateful to the University of Hawaii Press for publishing this book especially during this, the year in which we celebrate the one hundredth anniversary of Japanese contract workers arriving in Hawaii.

The person who has helped me the most, by commenting on the many drafts of my manuscript, advancing my knowledge of Japanese language materials, encouraging me over the years, and finally by teaching me how to understand many different aspects of modern Japanese history is my wife, Kaneko Sachiko. She is a scholar of Japanese women's history and my best friend.

Introduction

THE scholarly examination of Japanese as emigrants and that of these people as immigrants to the Hawaiian islands and the mainland United States has been conducted in fields of study that are still seeking "homes." The former has never been accepted as a legitimate part of the study of modern Japan and the latter has not been seen as essential for an understanding of the American west. This regrettable state of affairs has come about because of the self-imposed categories and limitations under which scholars in both countries have operated.

There have only been a few attempts by Japan's scholars to study the origins and background of their nation's emigrants, and these examinations have not been done within the framework of the historical development of modern Japan. Thus the experience of these emigrants is often viewed in isolation from significant events that also took place during the Meiji (1868–1912) and Taishō (1912–1926) periods. When presented by historians, emigration appears as an unimportant forerunner to the colonization policies of the 1930s. The emigrants themselves are seen as people who could not succeed in Japan and who had to travel abroad in order to survive. Little attention has been paid to the link between economic and social conditions in the Japanese countryside and the subsequent interest in emigration. Futhermore almost no consideration has been given to the vital role private emigration companies played in this process. Research on this topic using primary language sources can offer insights into the workings of Japan's government, how private ventures developed during the Meiji period, and the ways in which many Japanese viewed the outside world at the time. Most important, such research reveals the specific contributions emigrants made to a growing and changing Meiji Japan, as well as explains why they left Japan.

Studies done in Japan are limited in that they provide only the background of emigrants and the process by which they left their country. By ignoring what happened to these people after they left their homeland, Japanese scholars have presented only half the story. This has been the case for a number of years because of language problems and limited access to historical documents in Hawaii and the mainland United States.

The few American scholars who have studied the Japanese in Hawaii and on the U.S. mainland have generally viewed them as a minority group (in terms of numbers and/or power) achieving success in a larger society. Limited by language problems as well and unable to examine primary documents in Japan, their studies of Japanese Americans begin with the arrival in America, leaving, once again, only half the story of this complex process told. In addition, historians describe the development of the American west (including Hawaii) as having taken place in spite of different racial and ethnic groups rather than because of them. Until very recently, the contributions of Japanese workers to the economic and social development of the American west have been ignored in studies because the workers have been viewed as objects of history rather than as active participants.[1] Thus only a few attempts have been made to present the Japanese experience in America in the context of the political, economic, and social structures of American society.

An examination of Japan's emigration experience must begin with the premise that it involved two different societies and that a link was formed between them by the emigrants and the emigration process. It must, therefore, begin with the origins and background of the emigrants in Japan and end with the period after their arrival—when they settled as immigrants in Hawaii.

In addition to being a link between the sending nation and the receiving one, overseas emigration is also an ongoing process. This means political, economic, and social interaction, both on a national and individual level, over a period of years. Although changes may take place as this continues, the process is institutionalized and becomes a legitimate and acceptable form of interchange.

In Japan the word *imin* refers to those who enter Japan as immigrants, as well as to those who leave it as emigrants. For several reasons only a small number of foreigners entered Japan as settlers, not the least of which was that there a large population was confined to a small chain of islands. The government of the 1615–1867 period, the Tokugawa Shogunate, restricted the entrance of foreigners and virtually isolated the nation from outside influence. As a result, the Japanese people were almost completely homogeneous racially, had a common language, and they generally viewed non-Japanese as being uncivilized if not inferior. This was not a society which freely welcomed outsiders to live and work within its borders.

However, a significant number of Japanese went overseas as imin during the Meiji, Taishō, and early Shōwa (1926–) periods. Although statistics on departing travelers in the early years of the Meiji period are not very reliable, it is estimated that about 776,000 Japanese emigrated abroad between 1868 and the beginning of World War II in 1941.[2]

These Japanese emigrated to different parts of Central and South America, Southeast Asia, Oceania, and North America. They became fishermen in Canada, rice farmers in northern Borneo, and pearl shellers in Australia. They also worked on coffee plantations in Brazil, nickel mines in New Caledonia, and sugar plantations in Cuba. Settlements were established everywhere, from Siberia to Guam to San Francisco. In addition, Japanese colonized different areas of their prewar empire. At least 270,000 of them settled permanently in Manchuria, Taiwan, along the Korean peninsula, and in parts of northern China.[3] Thus over one million emigrants and colonizers went overseas between 1868 and 1941.[4]

The Japanese went in the largest numbers to the Hawaiian Islands—at least 231,206 between 1868 and 1929. The emigrants knew Hawaii as the Kingdom until 1893; as the Republic until 1898; and finally as the United States territory of Hawaii. Many Japanese chose to return home or travel to the U.S. mainland after their contracts had expired. Yet during the prewar period, these islands in the middle of the Pacific Ocean continued to attract hundreds of thousands of villagers who eventually left their homes for work overseas.

The migration of Japanese to Hawaii can be divided into five different periods. During the first, the years 1868 through 1885, emigration was prohibited by the Japanese government. As we will see in chapter 1, at least 147 individuals traveled to Hawaii, under somewhat strange circumstances, in 1868 and it was because of the failure of this venture that further emigration from Japan was prohibited. However, beginning in 1885 emigration was permitted and emigrants—government-sponsored, company, and independent, each of which had a different means to travel abroad—went to Hawaii.

In 1885 the government allowed emigration to Hawaii for ten years but only under strict controls. The total number who arrived in Honolulu aboard the twenty-six ships was 29,069, and they were known as "government-sponsored emigrants."[5]

During the 1894 to 1908 period Japanese workers went to Hawaii using a unique type of middleman, private companies or agents legally known as *toriatsukainin.*[6] Most people, including emigrants, referred to the companies as *imingaisha,* or emigration companies.[7] About 125,000 men and women arrived in Hawaii as "company emigrants" during this fifteen-year period.[8]

After 1908 workers from Japan went to Hawaii as "independent emigrants."[9] That is, the government or a private company did not sponsor those traveling overseas after 1908; rather these emigrants went on their own. From that year until 1924 about 48,000 Japanese migrated to Hawaii, and most of them had relatives and family members waiting for them there.

The fifth period begins with the National Origins Act of 1924, an ordinance that cut off Japanese migration to the United States. Those few who did arrive there after that year did so as American citizens of Japanese ancestry returning to the land of their birth. This period during which Japanese were effectively prevented from entering the United States continued until reforms to the immigration laws were drawn, that is, until after World War II.

Before 1900 most of the emigrants went to Hawaii with labor agreements in hand. They will be referred to as "contract emigrants" and those without contracts, "free emigrants."[10] Government-sponsored workers were always under contract. So were most of those who used private companies (until 1900), although a few of these were free. All of the independent emigrants were free emigrants when they arrived in Honolulu.

When we look at those who migrated to Hawaii, we should remember that, at the time, most Japanese had had no contact with foreigners, even those from urban areas. For example, while thousands of workers were traveling to a foreign country, Tokyo had only 628 foreign residents as of 31 December 1896.[11] This meant that the meeting place for Japan and the west was, to some extent, Hawaii, where farmers and laborers had to adjust to different languages, foreign customs and laws—to what essentially was an alien culture. Thousands of them returned to their homes after years of working in Hawaii. They carried not only substantial sums of money with them but also experiences and memories of a different way of life. Returning emigrants were not teachers, writers, or professional people and therefore they had little impact on the sophisticated circles of Tokyo and Yokohama. However, in small farming and fishing villages in rural areas, they were important not only because they introduced new ideas but also because they instilled in their friends and neighbors hope that they too might achieve success. It was these people living in small villages who dreamed of "earning 400 yen in three years" and of returning home "clad in brocade."[12]

Of the different actors who participated in Japanese overseas emigration, this book will concentrate on the emigration companies for a number of reasons. What little writing has been done in this field has generally focused on either the earlier years of government-sponsored emigration or the later period when the question was less who would leave Japan and more who would be able to enter the United States. However, it was during the relatively short period of 1894 to 1908 that the majority of Japanese emigrants traveled to Hawaii, and for the 125,000 men and women who sought work abroad, the private companies were essential. This study will describe and analyze this period which has heretofore been neglected.

CHAPTER I

The Background in Japan and Hawaii

DURING the chaos of the last days of the civil war ending the Tokugawa Shogunate and the struggle to set up the new Meiji government, foreigners made several requests to have Japanese workers sent abroad. Until May of 1866 the shogunate did not allow *any* Japanese to emigrate;[1] but by November of that year it began offering overseas passports to its citizens.

Before the end of the shogunate Eugene Van Reed, an American merchant who served as the Hawaiian consul in Japan, received permission to send one group of Japanese to work on sugar plantations in Hawaii.[2] After recruiting 141 men and 6 women from the Tokyo and Yokohama areas, Van Reed left Japan aboard the *Scioto* on 17 May 1868—but without the permission of the newly established Meiji government.[3] As a result, the foreign ministry first sent inquiries to the American consul in Japan and complained about Van Reed's activities. It asked for the return of the workers. Later, ministry officials went further and sought help in the negotiations from other governments. At one point the U.S. government agreed help was warranted: "these laborers went without [the Japanese government's] permission and . . . they are badly treated in Hawaii."[4]

The Japanese were expected to work on sugar cane plantations, but many of them came from urban areas around Tokyo and Yokohama and consequently numerous disagreements with their Hawaiian employers over wages, work hours, and the type of labor contracted for by both parties arose. Eventually a number returned, some at government expense, thoroughly dissatisfied with their Hawaiian experience.

A second attempt to send emigrants overseas was made in 1868 by a German company in Japan which sent forty-two workers to farm on the island of Guam. As did the first attempt, this venture met with failure, and in 1871 all of the surviving workers were brought back by the Japanese government.[5]

A year later a Dutchman, Edward Schnell, tried to establish a six-hundred-acre silk and tea settlement in northern California with a group of Japanese from the former Aizu-Wakamatsu domain (Fukushima prefecture). This too failed, and all that remains at the settlement site is a memorial marking the grave of Okei, the first Japanese woman to die in America.[6]

These three undertakings were illegal because the government did not grant permission to their organizers. No passports were issued, yet records of the attempts appear in foreign ministry documents. These Japanese can be seen as the predecessors of later emigrants in the sense that they were the first to be organized to travel and work abroad. In each case, however, they failed to fulfill the terms of their agreements, and legal, organized emigration could not be sustained over an extended period of time. Rather, the government's response to these attempts and to rumors of ill-treatment of its citizens in Hawaii was to suspend overseas emigration for the next sixteen years. Until 1885 only government officials, occasionally businessmen, and a few students traveled abroad legally.

The Background in Japan

Both the Meiji government's attitude toward emigration and its policies did not change until 1885 (one exceptional case in 1883 will be reviewed later in this chapter). There were three series of events that inspired the changes in 1885. The first took place in the Japanese countryside and affected the economic welfare of the average farmer. The second occurred in the Hawaiian sugar cane fields and resulted in attempts by the government of the Kingdom of Hawaii to initiate a treaty that would allow Japanese immigration. Lastly, officials in Tokyo and Yokohama began to receive requests from other countries interested in importing workers.

After 1868 the leaders of the new Meiji government made a commitment to "enrich the country" by welcoming western ideas and technology. However, their decision to industrialize the country placed a burden on the large agricultural sector. In order to finance this move toward modernization, national revenues had to be increased and in 1873 the government initiated a series of land tax reforms.

These reforms made the tax on agricultural land a fixed sum that was determined at the rate of 3 percent of the legal value of the property. In other words, this land tax stayed the same from year to year until the next land adjustment, whether the value of the crops rose or fell. The tax had to be paid in currency rather than in agricultural products (usually rice). In addition, these reforms brought about the establishment of land titles and clarified the basis of the landlord–tenant relationship.[7] These changes enabled the government to make long-term plans and budgets because the income and expenditure quantities were fixed.

On a national level, these changes proved beneficial. They helped to introduce the commodity market into rural areas and freed laborers for work in new industries.[8] The old land tax system, which had brought in only 2 million yen in 1868, was replaced with a system that provided the government with 60.6 million yen in its first year of operation, a sum that was more than 90 percent of all tax revenues and about 70 percent of all fiscal revenues for that year.[9]

From the farmers' point of view, this meant they were at the mercy of market conditions and the changing value of their crops (mostly rice). In other words, if the price of rice rose, they would receive more money for their crops and the fixed taxes would have a lesser effect on their income. On the other hand, if rice prices dropped, farmers not only would get less money for their crops but a larger portion of their income would go to taxes. Therefore they found themselves in a somewhat difficult position because the Tokugawa feudal system had to some extent protected them against crop failures and bad harvests by granting tax reductions and this security was not provided by the new tax system.[10] Furthermore under the Tokugawa system, rent levels charged by landlords were set by domain officials, but the Meiji government eliminated all forms of rent control.[11]

The money from this new land tax accounted for more than half of government revenues until 1900, and it is estimated that throughout this period the tax burden on individuals in agriculture was at least twice that of those in other sectors.[12] The channeling of agricultural surplus into the nonagricultural sector through taxes is a phenomenon often seen in developing countries.[13]

The period following the tax reforms saw government spending and inflation increase and the money supply expand for a number of reasons. During the years 1870 to 1874, the government spent 88.1 million yen on stipends owed former samurai, and over 41 million yen trying to suppress the Satsuma rebellion of 1877.[14] Because Japan isolated itself from other countries for a long time, it faced serious problems in terms of international currency exchange and with foreign imports that were becoming competitive with native products such as cotton, indigo, and coleseed.[15] As can be seen in Table 1, the price of rice more than doubled in the period between 1877 and 1880.

This inflationary period came to an abrupt end in 1881 with the fiscal policies introduced by Finance Minister Matsukata Masayoshi. Under his guidance the government managed to stabilize the economy by decreasing expenditures, issuing less paper money, and establishing a silver exchange.[16] However, a severe deflationary period ensued. What's more, prices in the marketplace fell because a policy of the major rice exchanges—one encouraged by the central government—required that rice be inspected and meet standards established by the exchanges.[17] (The rice price index in Table 1 shows a drop after the changes in 1881, as does the index of another economic indicator in Table 2.)

This deflation brought about a period of hardship, and a sizeable

TABLE 1
Price Index for Rice, 1877–1884

Year	*Price Index*
1877	100[a]
1878	117
1879	156
1880	203
1881	203
1882	178.8
1883	129.5
1884	104.2

Sources: Shindo, "Inflation," p. 46 for the 1877–1881 years and Ike, "Taxation and Landownership," p. 174 for the years 1882 to 1884.

[a]Ike has used 1876 rather than 1877 as the basis for his comparisons.

TABLE 2
Inflation and Deflation, 1877–1885
(Based on the Cost in Paper Money of One Yen Worth of Silver)

Year	*Cost in Yen*
1877	1.033
1878	1.099
1879	1.212
1880	1.477
1881	1.696
1882	1.571
1883	1.264
1884	1.089
1885	1.055

Source: Ōkubo et al., *Kindaishi,* p. 195.

number of farmers found it difficult to survive, given that the price of rice was low and the land tax fixed.[18] Between 1883 and 1890 over 367,000 landholding farmers were dispossessed because they were unable to pay the land taxes.[19] Small landholders became tenant farmers, and the percentage of cultivated land under tenancy increased until it reached 35.9 percent in 1884 and 40.2 percent by 1892.[20] It should be noted that while poverty was not the only reason for the increase in tenancy during this period, a decrease in financial resources certainly contributed to this result. In addition, it must be pointed out that people in debt, as a number of farmers during this time seemed to be, are better off during periods of inflation when their payments are in less valuable money, while the opposite is true during periods of deflation.

Tokyo newspapers in 1885 pointed out the extreme severity of conditions at the time. One newspaper article described how two-thirds of a village of eighty households in Fukuoka prefecture had disposed of their belongings by public auction and were waiting for death.[21]

Such examples are undoubtedly exceptions and do not reflect the overall economic situation in the Japanese countryside. Recent research has shown that certain regions had relatively high rates of agricultural production. Farmers in some areas supplemented their income from rice crops by raising secondary crops. Some also had second businesses: they sold rapeseed oil, tobacco, or they made bean curd or confections. Others operated small stores or eating houses.[22]

Also, families in some rural areas suffered to a considerable extent because of natural disasters, inadequate irrigation systems, poor land, or short growing seasons. There remains today ample written testimony from this period to support this.[23]

One factor which influenced Japanese emigration significantly was the tradition of *dekasegi rōdō,* or temporary work away from home. It began in rural areas early in the Tokugawa period when farmers sought to be less dependent on rice production. As has been mentioned, some families chose to add cash crops to their farms—indigo, cotton, rush—so they would not be at the mercy of price fluctuations in the marketplace, which ruined many farming households. Others relied on cottage industries, particularly during the winter months, to supplement their income.[24] More unfortunate farming families could only rely on members of their households, and thus some parents sold their daughters into prostitution, sometimes to work overseas.[25]

A number of families sent their sons out to seek jobs in urban areas, hoping that there would be some kind of work available. The dekasegi workers from these families expected to return to their villages when conditions improved in the countryside. This type of internal migration relieved the economic pressure in the countryside by reducing the number of people in each household and increasing the chances of acquiring income outside the farm. Research on Tokugawa-period dekasegi workers indicates that most of them were young, single men, although it was not unusual for heads of families to seek temporary work as well.[26]

During the Meiji years, dekasegi workers were common among many farming families, and men were not the only ones to work away from home. As the government relied more on cotton and silk exports to pay for imported industrial goods, the number of textile mills increased in Japan.[27] Textile company agents, with the backing of the Japanese government, went from village to village to recruit female workers (mostly under the age of twenty) for their mills. They promised good meals and high wages to those willing to sign labor contracts. Like other emigrants, these young women helped pay the price of Japan's modernization during the Meiji period.

This option to work away from home was important for farming families particularly in the mid-1880s. One writer has pointed out that "many daughters and younger sons of farming families, precisely that group which in the past has formed the agricultural hired labor force, left their native villages during the Meiji period to work in expanding urban industries or to colonize new land in Hokkaido."[28]

The dekasegi rōdō tradition made the transition to overseas emigration easier by attaching a sense of legitimacy to the idea of acquiring temporary work abroad. Emigration became an acceptable option for farming families who were struggling to survive, and another means of temporarily solving economic problems in the countryside.[29]

The Background in Hawaii

Although relations between the Kingdom of Hawaii and Japan were strained, primarily because of the 1868 fiasco, they began to improve after the signing of the Treaty of Commerce and Friendship in 1871. During the late 1870s and early 1880s the island economy faced a major problem. The king's representatives managed to successfully negotiate the Reciprocity Treaty with the United States, and from 1876 fifteen Hawaiian products—including sugar—entered American markets duty-free. As a result, the sugar planters were determined to increase sugar production to take advantage of their special status. However, this increase was not possible without an adequate cheap labor supply to cultivate the additional acreage of land.

By 1884 the number of native Hawaiians had fallen from approximately 130,000 in 1832 to about 44,000. Although about 14,000 Chinese entered Hawaii between 1878 and 1882, only 5,037 were working on sugar plantations in 1882. At the same time, the sugar industry, which began with one plantation at Koloa in 1835, was increasing its production (see Table 3).[30]

The sugar planters and the Hawaiian government had tried many times to import foreigners for the plantations. Between 1850 and 1885 they recruited workers from many countries, including China, Portugal, Austria, Norway, Germany, and the United States.[31] Agents searched the globe for potential workers, visiting distant, and in some instances unlikely, places such as Siberia, Mongolia, the Azores, Italy, Malaysia, the East Indies, Poland, and Australia.[32]

In the years between 1864 and 1886 the sugar planters spent over $850,000 and the government over $1 million on attempts to attract foreign workers.[33] Despite the *Gannen mono* (first-year emigrants) incident in 1868, the sugar planters continued to look to Japan as a source of plantation workers for a number of reasons. First, Japan was one of

TABLE 3
Sugar Produced in Hawaii, 1868–1885

Year	*Sugar in Tons*	*Year*	*Sugar in Tons*
1868	9,106	1877	12,788
1869	9,151	1878	19,215
1870	9,392	1879	24,510
1871	10,880	1880	31,792
1872	8,498	1881	46,895
1873	11,565	1882	57,088
1874	12,283	1883	57,053
1875	12,540	1884	71,327
1876	13,036	1885	85,695

Source: Watanabe, *Hawai rekishi,* pp. 279–280. Same figures from an HSPA publication as compiled by William Henry Taylor, "The Hawaiian Sugar Industry" (unpublished Ph.D. dissertation, 1935), p. 166.

the few labor markets available in Asia that was not controlled by a major western nation. Second, the sugar planters felt that the average Japanese would accept lower wages than the white worker, and the transportation cost from Japan was much lower than from Europe. Lastly, sugar planters who had employed Japanese in 1868 were particularly pleased with their performance. One Hawaiian foreign office representative wrote in 1874: "our planters and others who have employed Chinese and Japanese, are generally partial to the latter. . . ."[34] Thus representatives from Hawaii began making requests to the Japanese government for workers in 1871.[35]

Requests for Japanese Emigrants

During the 1868 to 1885 period Tokyo officials received a number of requests for Japanese workers from abroad. One of the earliest came in 1876 from Australia and asked for workers willing to travel to the Northern Territory. Japan's response was swift and simple: "all emigration of the Japanese out of the Empire will be resisted by the Government."[36]

In September of 1883 the foreign ministry received a note from one of its representatives overseas reporting that the Dutch government wanted Japanese workers in the West Indies. Foreign Minister Inoue Kaoru replied that he had received similar petitions from Spain and Hawaii but that until the treaty revision procedures were completed, no action concerning sending Japanese abroad would be taken.[37]

The governor of Kanagawa prefecture reported in July of 1884 that he had been asked to supply five hundred workers to help build a railway line on Victoria Island for the Canadian Pacific Railroad Company.[38] About a year later, Deakin Brothers and Co. asked permission to hire Japanese mechanics to work in San Francisco, where it was based.[39] As had been the case with previous requests, permission was not granted by the foreign ministry.

In June of 1885 George Hucker, a British citizen, sought permission to hire Japanese "conjurers and jugglers" to work in Hong Kong, Singapore, Penang, and Java. Later that year, Kanagawa prefectural authorities found that Horace Fletcher of the Japanese Development Company of Chicago needed painters, lacquer workers, ivory carvers, and screen makers to work in the United States for a three-year period.[40]

The governor of Kanagawa prefecture also reported on 11 September 1885 that he had received two petitions, one from Charles Comelli of New York and the other from another American, John Marshall, to allow them to hire groups of Japanese "jugglers, acrobats and performers" to work in the United States.[41] In the post–Civil War period when many Americans began to develop an increasing awareness of foreign cultures, traveling circuses and entertainment shows featuring foreign performers were popular, particularly in areas that had limited access to other forms of popular entertainment.

All of these requests were received through official channels, usually through the Kanagawa prefectural offices because the major port for foreigners, Yokohama, was located in that prefecture. The Japanese foreign minister made the final decision in each case.

There was one exceptional case when permission was actually granted. On 18 October 1883 thirty-seven emigrants departed from Japan to work as pearl shellers and pearl divers on Thursday Island, just north of the Australian continent.[42] Permission to recruit these workers was granted to John Miller, a British citizen. Some writers have claimed that a small number of Japanese went there as early as 1876, and there is some evidence that supports this claim.

By late 1885 the Japanese government had to decide whether or not to allow overseas travel for ordinary citizens. How should it respond to the increasing number of appeals for workers? What was the safest method of allowing overseas emigration? The latter was an important concern of Japanese government officials because above all they did not want a repeat of the Gannen mono incident in which their citizens were treated poorly in Hawaii and consequently had to be transported back at the government's expense.

Meanwhile from 1871 Japanese officials felt pressure from their Hawaiian counterparts. Three important Hawaiian officials visited Japan in the late 1800s to plead Hawaii's case. The reigning monarch of the Kingdom, King Kalakaua, visited Japan in 1881. Although he pointed out the need for foreign workers in Hawaii, no action was taken by the Japanese government, partly because several European nations made it clear they did not want Japan to begin renegotiating treaties. Renegotiations, they felt, would have affected their own relations with Tokyo. During the following year, a diplomatic mission headed by John M. Kapena arrived from Honolulu with a specific proposal for a labor convention between the two countries.[43] Finally in 1884 a high government representative, Colonel Curtis Piehu Iaukea, presented another set of proposals for the importation of Japanese workers to Hawaii on a regular basis. In the end, the Itō Hirobumi cabinet decided to accept the idea of a labor convention but only under strict governmental supervision.

The person most responsible for this change in Japan's policy was Robert Walker Irwin who, through contacts in government and business circles, had established himself as a "legitimate friend" of Japan.[44] He had worked as an adviser for Mitsui Bussan, which later became one of the major *zaibatsu* (financial groups) in Japan. During his seven years with that company Irwin became close friends with both Masuda Takashi, the man who eventually became head of Mitsui Bussan, and Foreign Minister Inoue.[45] These two ties with the Japanese establishment played a crucial role in not only starting emigration to Hawaii but also in influencing subsequent decisions made in this regard. Irwin served as the official representative of the Hawaiian government during the delicate negotiations for a treaty covering Japanese immigration to Hawaii.

Thus Tokyo authorities were persuaded to change their "no emigration" policy for several important reasons. The economic condition of the average farmer in the countryside had worsened after 1881, and the central government took action. Also, the foreign ministry had received a number of requests from abroad, particularly from Hawaii, for workers. However, before it agreed to allow its citizens to work overseas, it wanted to see if a properly supervised system could succeed over a period of time.[46] Therefore the Hawaiian officials' proposal for a labor convention supervised by both governments was appropriate. This labor convention, which governed emigration from Japan to Hawaii between 1885 and 1894, was signed in Tokyo on 28 January 1886.

CHAPTER 2

The Government-Sponsored Emigration Period

ALTHOUGH the Japanese government revealed that it would allow overseas emigration to Hawaii in an announcement in 1884, the actual signing of the labor convention proposed by Hawaiian government officials did not take place until early in 1886.[1] By this time the first two ships carrying contract workers had already arrived in Honolulu. As stipulated in the first article of the agreement, this convention applied to Japanese workers already in Hawaii as well as to those intending to emigrate.

Between the years 1885 and 1894, the period of government-sponsored emigration, twenty-six ships carried Japanese to Hawaii.[2] According to the records of the Japanese consulate in Honolulu, 29,995 emigrants were transported, the ships making an average of three or four landings a year.[3] Hawaii's Bureau of Immigration documents, however, show different data; the dates of arrival of several ships are not those shown in the consulate's report and the total it gives is 28,957.[4]

The Japanese who were sent during this period were referred to as government-sponsored emigrants because the two governments involved were responsible for them. The labor convention read in part: "the Hawaiian Government shall assure all the responsibilities of employer toward the emigrants, and shall . . . be responsible for due and faithful performance of all conditions of such contracts."[5] A U.S. commissioner of labor commented some time later: "The [Hawaiian] Government thus became a . . . bureau through which the plantations were supplied with labor. This gave the Japanese Government a responsible party with whom it could deal directly in all matters relating to the condition of its emigrant citizens in Hawaii, while the Planters . . . were convenienced by thus using the state as a recruiting organization."[6]

Provisions of this convention outlined the Hawaiian government's promise to provide free passage to Hawaii for all emigrants in "first class passenger steamers," for "a sufficient number of Inspectors and Interpreters who shall be able to speak and interpret the Japanese and English languages," and lastly for a "sufficient number of Japanese physicians to attend the emigrants."[7]

The Japanese government kept firm control of this system to the point of preventing private interests from entering this field. In 1886 one Paul Bohm established an office in Honolulu and advertised that he had "made arrangements to bring from Japan experienced ladies' maids, housemaids, childrens' nurses, house and stable boys, gardeners and general servants, agricultural and general laborers, sailors, etc." Bohm claimed he had lived in Japan for sixteen years and was able to recruit Japanese workers. The responses from Hawaii's representative, Robert Irwin, and Foreign Minister Inoue came quickly. In his letter to the foreign minister in which he discussed Bohm, Irwin used these words: "fraud," "prevent any abduction of Japanese unlawfully taking place," and "the fast character of Mr. Bohm." The Japanese government's response was to restrict private emigration by withholding passports because, as Inoue wrote, "His Imperial Majesty's Government regards the matter as prejudicial to the successful maintenance of all the stipulations contained in the emigration convention . . . ."[8]

The emigrants who traveled to Hawaii under this convention signed three-year contracts and thereby promised to work twenty-six days a month, ten hours a day in the fields or twelve hours in the sugar mill (see Appendix 1 for full text of contract). Initially men were guaranteed wages of fifteen dollars a month (nine dollars for work wages and six dollars for a food allowance) and their wives ten dollars (six dollars for work wages and four dollars for food). Besides these wages, the Japanese received passage to Hawaii, a place to live, medical care, and fuel. The basic contract underwent slight modifications in 1887 and 1891. Minimum wage was increased and emigrant ships had to obtain approval from Japanese authorities.[9]

These immigrants came to a multiethnic society that had almost no Japanese residents. Records show that in 1882 only 15 Japanese were employed on the sugar plantations.[10] By the end of the government-sponsored emigration period in 1894, that number had risen to

12,631.[11] Japanese made up more than 64 percent of the total number of plantation workers employed at that time.

The Government-Sponsored Emigrants

What kind of people traveled thousands of miles to work in a country where alien customs, foreign clothing, strange foods, and incomprehensible languages awaited them? From documents of this period (1880s) it is clear that first of all, most of them came from areas in southwestern Japan, in particular, Hiroshima, Yamaguchi, Kumamoto, and Fukuoka prefectures (see Map 1). They made up 67 percent of those going to Hawaii on the first shipment, 82 percent on the second, and 94 percent on the third.[12] This trend continued over the years. For example, of those who left Japan—from the eighth shipment until the last, the twenty-sixth shipment—36 percent were from Hiroshima.[13] Residents from Yamaguchi made up 34 percent; Kumamoto, 20 percent; and Fukuoka, 8 percent. One historian has written that up to 96 percent of all the government-sponsored emigrants during this ten-year period came from these four prefectures.[14]

The people who were attracted to working abroad sought a chance at economic success and living circumstances better than what they found in Japan. Farmers in the four prefectures discussed, whether they owned property or were tenant farmers, worked small plots of land.[15] For example, in Hiroshima prefecture 70 percent of its farmers worked on property of less than 1.96 acres each.[16]

Villages in Hiroshima generally had, in addition to smaller plots of cultivated land, a higher population density rate and more labor-intensive and wet-land farming than villages of other prefectures.[17] Although they grew alternative crops such as cotton, indigo, sweet potatoes, and rush, farmers still found themselves at the mercy of market fluctuations. These villages also had few cottage industries, a decreasing number of self-employed farmers and thus an increasing number of tenant farmers. Furthermore, situated along the Inland Sea coast or in the delta areas of major rivers, these villages were vulnerable to the sudden ocean storms and seasonal floods which plague most of Japan. Several historians have pointed to the fact that a large number of emigrants were from villages that suffered natural disasters between 1884 and 1886.[18]

There were also many emigrants to Hawaii from villages on the

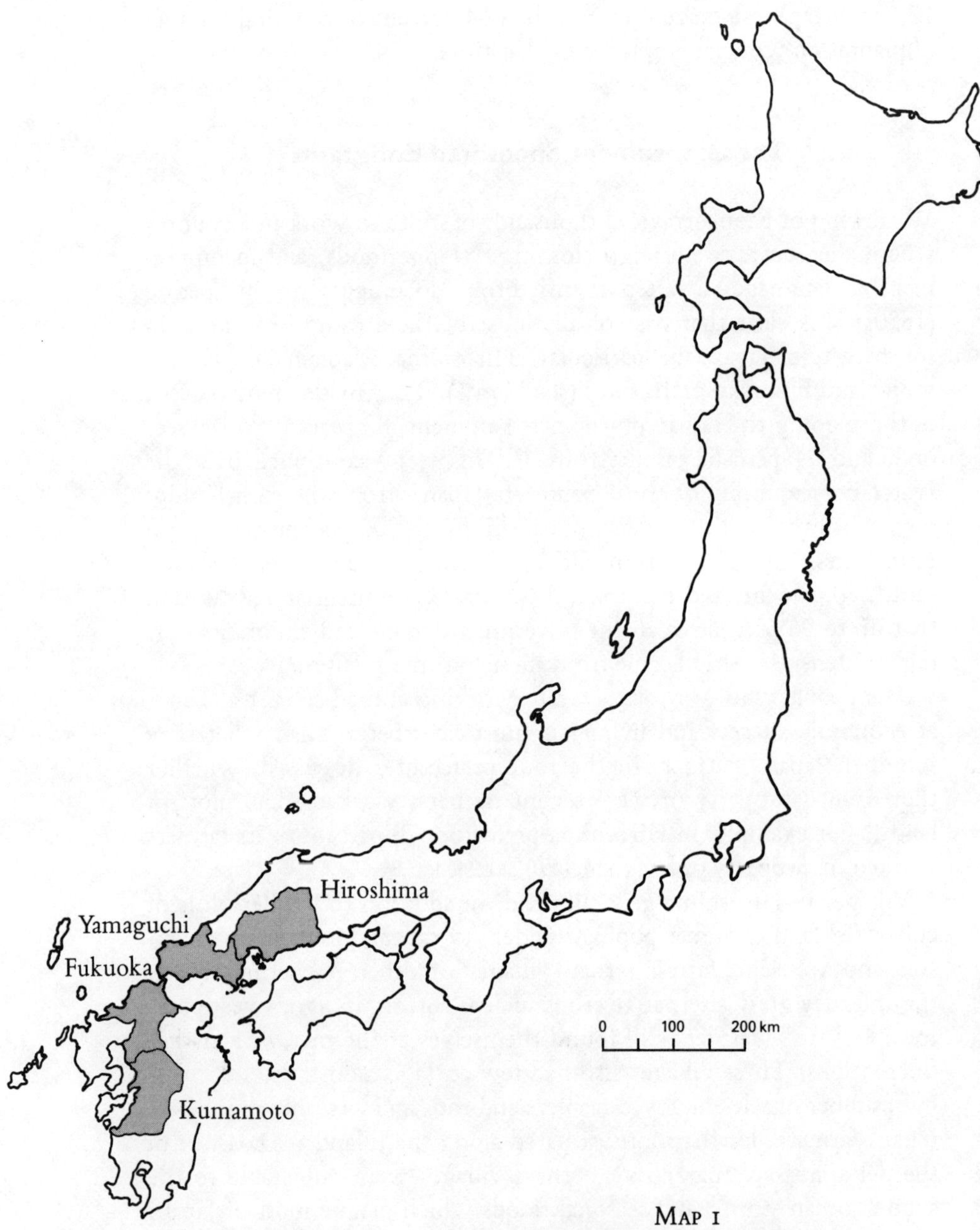

MAP 1
Four Emigrant Prefectures in Southwestern Japan

eastern half of the island of Ōshima in Yamaguchi prefecture. Why was this so? This particular area had poor soil conditions and farmers here could only cultivate sweet potatoes. The western half of the island had rice paddy fields under cultivation and was more prosperous. The population density rate was also higher in the eastern part of the island, and farmers there had an earlier tradition of dekasegi work beginning in the Tokugawa period. During the Satsuma rebellion (1877), the forces of Saigo Takamori burned most of the city of Kumamoto on the west coast of the island of Kyushu. As a result, Ōshima residents (mainly from the eastern half of the island) went there as temporary construction workers in order to rebuild the city, a task which took several years. Finally, local officials on that part of the island went out of their way to issue notices on the possibility of working in Hawaii. They also set up a series of public lectures on Hawaii featuring Hino Norisuke (?), a speaker hired by the prefecture.[19]

Although these "emigrant villages" in Hiroshima and Yamaguchi prefectures are representative of the others in southwestern Japan that sent many of their residents overseas, there were villages such as these all around Japan; thus the question of why emigrants came from these particular four southwestern prefectures has still not been adequately answered. However, an examination of early recruitment practices might suggest one reason.

In 1886 Irwin found himself in charge of recruitment in Japan and also a special agent of the Hawaiian Bureau of Immigration. It was also at this time that he became involved with Masuda and Inoue. His ties with these men were such that on occasions when Irwin had to travel abroad, Masuda was put in charge of handling emigration matters. These ties even extended into his private life, as the fact that Inoue had served as the go-between for Irwin and his Japanese wife indicates.[20]

Inoue and Masuda were originally from the domain of Chōshū (Yamaguchi prefecture) and so it would be easy to assume that both were concerned about the state of the economy there. It is believed that Inoue used his influence and suggested that with regard to recruitment of emigrants emphasis be placed on Yamaguchi, Hiroshima, and Kumamoto prefectures.[21] According to a written history of Mitsui Bussan, Masuda directed company employees to go to Yamaguchi, Hiroshima, Kumamoto, and Fukuoka to help with recruitment.[22] In his autobiography Masuda states that he suggested Irwin sign up workers in Hiroshima and on Ōshima Island in Yamaguchi prefecture.[23]

The recruitment of emigrants in southwestern Japan was in keeping with instructions the Hawaiian government sent Irwin: it specifically asked that he recruit workers from the countryside who had previous experience in farming.[24] The final result was that Irwin went first to Yamaguchi and Hiroshima in his quest to find workers for the Hawaiian sugar cane plantations.

During this and the later emigration company period, the recruiters had to consider carefully where they would sign up workers. For example, while large numbers of emigrants were being sent from prefectures in southwestern Japan to Hawaii, Japanese textile mills were sending agents to Nagano, Yamanashi, Gifu, Niigata, and Toyama prefectures in central Japan.[25] As a result, women from central Japan made up the large majority of workers in the Meiji-period textile mills. The agents found it convenient and less costly to enlist groups of young women from this region and then lead them across the snow-covered mountains to the mills.

Because of the instructions sent to Irwin from Hawaii, emigrants recruited in Japan tended to be from farming families. The president of the Bureau of Immigration asked that the recruits be chosen as follows: "The laborers shall be young, able bodied, healthy, agricultural laborers only, [and] they shall be men who have heretofore habitually engaged in agricultural pursuits, and shall under no circumstances be taken from the inhabitants of towns or cities, or be from among persons engaged or trained in pursuits other than agricultural."[26]

Recent research has shown that in some cases farmers made up 73 percent of the Hawaii-bound travelers.[27] The Hawaiian government claimed that the first shipment of emigrants in 1885 were "all tenant farmers and have not heretofore been laborers in the ordinary sense of the word."[28]

Another characteristic of the early shipments was that they were mainly of male workers.[29] A number of works on the history of the Japanese community in Hawaii have mentioned the small number of females as compared to males in the Japanese community in Hawaii. As can be seen in Table 4, it took decades before the ratio of men to women reached appropriate proportions, and in the meantime the small population of women caused, among other things, the "picture bride" phenomenon and the late development of a second generation of Japanese in Hawaii.

TABLE 4
Population of Japanese in Hawaii, by Sex, 1890–1930

Year	*Male*	*Female*
1890	10,219	2,391
1896	19,212	5,195
1900	47,508	13,603
1910	54,784	24,891
1920	62,644	46,630
1930	75,008	64,623

Source: Yamato, *Japanese*, pp. 31–32.

From 1885 through 1892 men made up 80 percent of the immigrants arriving in Hawaii.[30] The reason for this was that the Honolulu officials had insisted that women make up no more than 25 percent of the total. In 1887 the Bureau of Immigration passed a resolution which read in part: "Resolved that the president be authorized to instruct the agent of the [bureau] in Japan that not exceed 25% of women will be acceptable to the [Bureau] of Immigration."[31] The sugar planters felt that women were necessary for only a limited number of jobs on the plantations. Many women worked as cooks and laundry helpers for the large number of single men living in the plantation camps. Also, according to the official emigrant lists, all women who arrived in Hawaii were emigrants' wives or daughters (indicated on the lists as *tsuma* and *musume* respectively). In all of the cases they were referred to only by their given names.

Recent studies have shown that most of the men were quite young when they left Japan, meeting one of the criteria set by the Bureau of Immigration. Anywhere from 64 to 71 percent were under the age of thirty at the time of departure.[32] An announcement issued by the governor of Hiroshima prefecture stated that the age range of prospective emigrants was between twenty and thirty.[33] Although teenagers as well as men in their forties went to Hawaii, overall the vast majority were in their twenties.

One issue which has puzzled historians has been the "successor" or "nonsuccessor" status of emigrants. Although a number of writers have argued that the second and third sons were more likely to go abroad, recent evidence has indicated, particularly with regard to the government-sponsored emigrants, that nonsuccessor sons made up only 6 to 30 percent of the total.[34] Most of those leaving Japan were heads of families, wives, or eldest sons. This is further evidence that many intended to return to Japan after a short period, since heads of households and eldest sons were necessary to legally carry on the family line. It could be argued here that the intention to return after a stay abroad is both a characteristic of the dekasegi rōdō system and an indication that perhaps economic conditions in rural areas were not so severe as to discourage emigrants from coming back home. The Japanese conscription system (which is discussed in detail in chapter 5) may have also been a contributing factor to the large number of firstborns being sent abroad. By offering exemptions to emigrants as well as to "heirs and lineal grandsons," the conscription law created a loophole by which a family could send its firstborn, of conscription age, abroad and designate a younger son as heir, and thereby "protect" two sons from military service.

Some of the traits the government-sponsored emigrants held in common came about because of the "selective recruitment" carried out in Japan. Men of a specific character were chosen to work in Hawaii. In a report to the Hawaiian minister of the interior in 1891, a Bureau representative wrote: "The local authorities [in Japan] take upon themselves the care, that the permit to go to the Hawaiian Islands, is given only to men of good character, and those who are law abiding and industrious. This system is carried out with such scrupulous attention, that even among the great numbers who have come here . . . under the convention, few turbulent men and no known violators of law and peace can be found."[35]

What attracted almost all of the Japanese to work in Hawaii was the $15 a month they could earn. The rate of exchange was about 85¢ to a yen, and so Japanese workers could earn 17.65 yen a month (see Appendix 6 for exchange rate during this period).[36] This was a large amount of money for the average Japanese farmer and worker in 1885, as can be seen in the examples of wages for several types of occupations in Table 5 (1 yen equals 100 sen). And of course, those who went to Hawaii were also given a place to live free of charge and a contract promising employment for at least three years.

Workers going to Hawaii would say, "400 yen in three years," meaning that they intended to save this amount out of their salaries during the contract period and return to Japan.[37] Of course, this was

TABLE 5
Wages in Japan, 1885

Occupation	*Daily Wages (in Sen)*	*Monthly Wages (in Yen)*
Roof tile maker	26	7.8
Printing typesetter	21	6.3
Carpenter	21	6.3
Day worker	16	4.8
Silk mill worker (female)	11	3.3
Farmer (female)	10	3.0

Source: Kaigai ijū jigyōdan, *Kaigai ijū,* p. 5.

overly optimistic since they'd have to save 11 yen out of an income of less than 18 yen per month. Yet it was certainly more realistic to attempt that in Hawaii than in Japan, as Table 5 also shows. The day worker in Japan would have to work almost seven years and the silk mill worker ten years without spending any of their earnings in order to accumulate a total of 400 yen.

Statistics on daily wages earned by several types of workers in Hiroshima prefecture show an even lower income level for stonemasons, carpenters, sake brewery workers, woodcutters, and sawmill workers, who earned between 15 and 19 sen daily in 1884 but only between 13 and 16 sen in 1885.[38] The same survey estimated that male farmers earned an average of 14.48 yen annually in 1884 and 9.98 yen the following year. In the same two years, female farmers made 7.40 yen and 4.98 yen, respectively. This drop in wages in almost all categories of workers during this two-year period took place just as overseas migration to Hawaii began. Another survey taken in January of 1885 of wages in one county in Yamaguchi prefecture shows similar patterns. Farmers there averaged 10.7 sen a day, while woodcutters, stonemasons, and metal workers earned between 15 and 16.3 sen.[39]

In a report on workers' wages in 1891, the *Japan Weekly Gazette* pointed out that the only workers in Japan who earned wages higher than that offered in Hawaii (not including food allowance) were first-class carpenters, plasterers, stonemasons, *tatami* (rice straw mats) makers, tailors (of foreign clothing), and lacquerers.[40] Common laborers earned about 9 yen a month.

In addition to the economic incentive, other means were used to recruit potential emigrants. Leaflets advertised Hawaii as a paradise, as a place where people were gentle in nature and where the Japanese language could be spoken and understood.[41] Its climate was said to suit Japanese; also rice and other familiar foods were available there.

Articles that appeared in local newspapers encouraged workers to go abroad. For example, in a Yamaguchi prefectural paper, *Bōchō Shinbun* (Bōchō Newspaper), the following appeared in November of 1884: "Workers for Hawaii! Processing for workers bound for Hawaii has been taking place at Shōkyōsha [company name]. Working on behalf of the Hawaiian consul, we are recruiting married couples and single men."[42]

"Village-to-village" recruiting also took place, and employees of emigration companies later refined this practice. Paid agents went from one village to another to sign up those who were willing to work in Hawaii. Until now, the theory that this type of direct recruiting had taken place was only conjecture without evidence. However, emigrant lists submitted to the Japanese foreign ministry support this theory. A close examination of the names and addresses of those who left on the first shipment sailing on the *City of Tokio* bears this out. Of the 944 emigrants aboard, 420 came from Yamaguchi prefecture.[43] Of these 420, 305, or 32 percent, of the *entire* shipment came from the island of Ōshima.[44] The list of these passengers shows that village-to-village recruitment took place from the eastern end of the island. (See Map 2).

The first eight individuals on the list came from Ihota-*son* (village).[45] The next thirty-five were residents of Yuu-son, which is a short distance to the southwest of Ihota-son. A road links both, and recruits from other villages along this road appear on the lists in the following order: three emigrants from Kodomari-son, ten from Hirano, and then eighteen from Wasa. Obviously, one or more recruiters started in Ihota-son and slowly moved west along the major road on the island, signing up emigrants along the way.

That a village name does not appear again on the lists indicates one-time village-to-village recruitment. The only other possibility is that whoever compiled these lists in Yokohama knew the geography of the islands in Yamaguchi prefecture and decided for some reason to put them in geographic order, but this is unlikely. As we will see later, this village-to-village recruiting appears again during the emigration company period when more complete records were kept.

The significance of this is that in addition to different methods of "passive" recruitment—advertising through pamphlets and notices

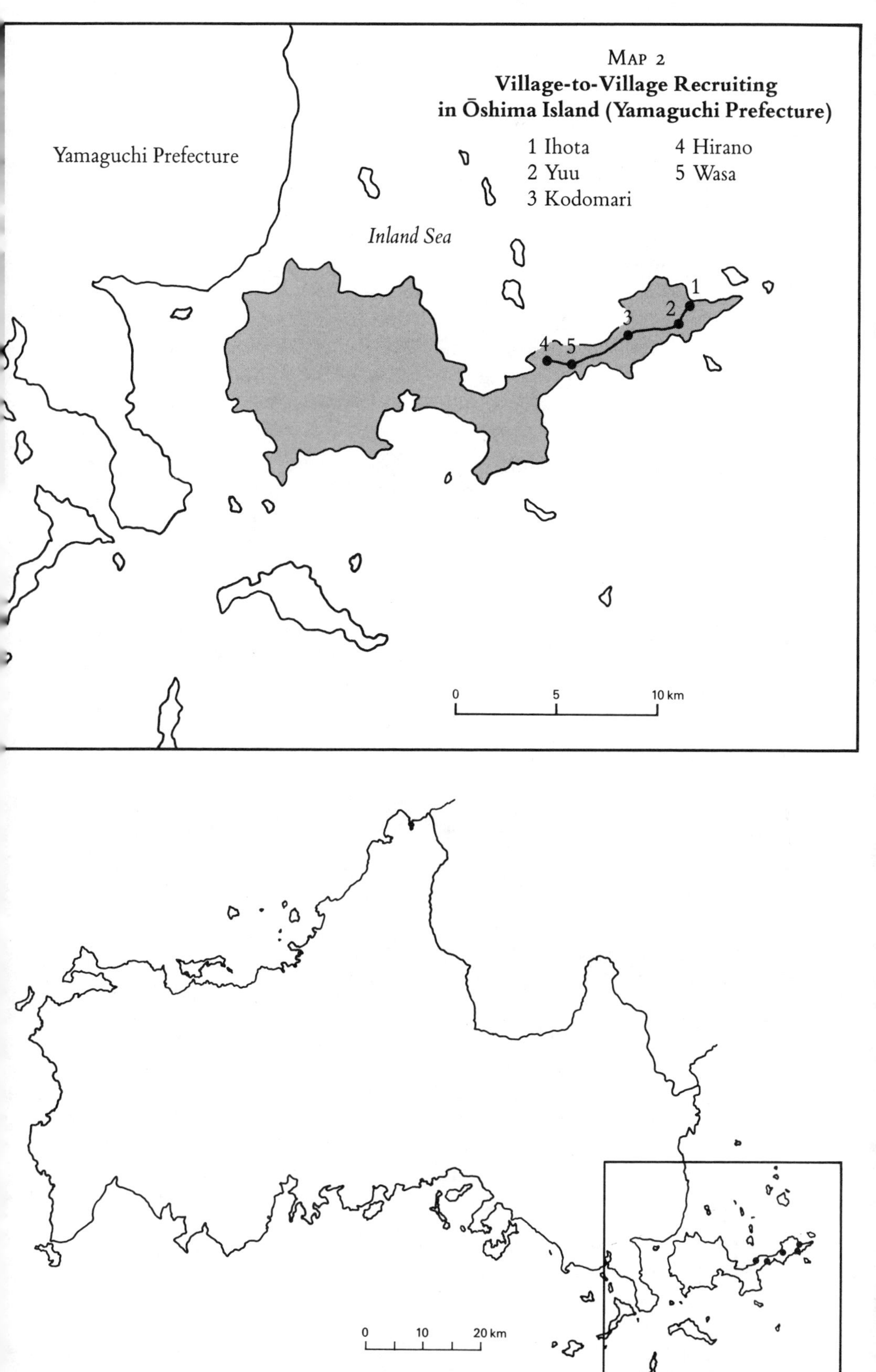
Map 2
Village-to-Village Recruiting
in Ōshima Island (Yamaguchi Prefecture)
1 Ihota
2 Yuu
3 Kodomari
4 Hirano
5 Wasa
Yamaguchi Prefecture
Inland Sea
1
2
3
4
5
0
5
10 km
0
10
20 km

and holding meetings with local officials, active campaigning from village to village took place in different areas of the country. As a result, when the Japanese government tried to fill 600 emigrant slots on the first ship to Hawaii, it received over 28,000 applications from around the country.[46]

Correspondence between Irwin and the Japanese government in October of 1887 reveals that the Hawaiian government had to advance an estimated $75 for each emigrant going to Hawaii.[47] As it turned out, however, the cost was much less. According to the Japanese consulate in Honolulu, it cost $50 to bring one worker to Hawaii in 1888.[48] The breakdown of this cost is shown in Table 6. Early in this period emigrants paid between $8 and $9 for the doctors and interpreters who worked in the port facilities of Japan and Hawaii, but this was discontinued after many workers complained about it.[49]

Although the labor convention of 1886 (Article 5) specified that workers were to have their ship passage provided for by the sugar planters, attempts were made to change this in 1887.[50] Feeling that the cost of importing workers was too high, the Hawaiian government asked that the emigrants repay the planters for the passage fare over the term of their contracts. This new policy was carried out for two years from 1888 until the end of 1890. However, at the Japanese government's insistence, the planters once again assumed most of the cost of passage fare from 1891.

TABLE 6
Emigrants' Expenses, 1888

Expenses	*Amount*
Passage fare from Yokohama to Honolulu	$23.00
Registration, handling, and commissions	3.50
Expenses after arriving in Hawaii	1.25
Relief fund for needy persons	1.25
Expenses in Japan, government commission	5.00
Fee for doctors and interpreters	8.00
Miscellaneous expenses in Hawaii	5.00
Miscellaneous expenses in Japan	3.00
Total	$50.00

Source: Report from the Consulate to the Foreign Ministry, 30 December 1888, *JFMAD 3.8.2.3,* vol. 7.

Life for the Japanese in Hawaii

In this early period Japanese left for Hawaii from the port city of Yokohama in Kanagawa prefecture. After approximately a two-week voyage, they landed in Honolulu. There they were examined by doctors and remained in quarantine under the supervision of the Bureau of Immigration.

Before leaving their homes Japanese immigrants signed labor contracts that specified which Hawaiian plantation they would be working on. Thus, after arriving in Honolulu they went with family members and friends to the same plantations.

Since most recruiters worked in one area at a time, emigrants tended to leave Japan in groups based either on family or geographic (village) ties.[51] These groups were kept intact after arrival in Hawaii, and because of the labor contracts many workers ended up on plantations based on their geographic background *(shusshinchi)* in Japan.[52] For example, among those arriving in Honolulu on 8 February 1885, fifteen men, six women, and ten children, all from the island of Ōshima, traveled by boat to one of the plantations in Hamakua connected with F. A. Schaefer. Another group consisting of twenty-five men, thirteen women, and eleven children, all former Hiroshima residents, was sent to Kohala plantation. A third party of twenty-five who were from the Kuga district in Yamaguchi went to Ookala plantation. Five men and one child from Tokyo were grouped with twenty men, one woman, and two children from Wakayama prefecture and sent to Hilo plantation. Another group, thirty-three men previously of Okayama prefecture, was sent to Lihue on the island of Kauai. This pattern can be seen in later shipments as well.

It is difficult to say whether or not the sugar planters had made a conscious decision to hire workers from specific local areas in Japan to fulfill their labor needs. Certainly they had no hand in the initial recruitment carried out in Japan by Irwin other than to suggest that it be done in rural areas. However, as time passed, some may have realized that when people from the same village or local area were allowed to live together on the plantation there was more stability in their camp, communication problems because of differences in regional dialect were prevented, and workers performed better.

Emigration under this labor convention system worked fairly well, though on a larger scale than expected by both the Hawaiian and Japanese governments. In a letter to Inoue in 1886, Irwin wrote: "The

Japanese Emigration is an *absolute* success. The people are happy and well treated. All (or nearly all) work very hard and are regular misers. The *real* character of the true Japanese farmer is a hard working thrifty man. Nearly every Planter is entirely satisfied with Japanese laborers."[53] (Emphasis in original.) Arguing that "this scheme is now thoroughly organized," he urged a continuation of the convention.

Two years later, Irwin was still very positive about all aspects of this emigration process. This is apparent in the following excerpts from a letter Irwin wrote to Foreign Minister Ōkuma Shigenobu:

> We found [everywhere] that the laborer was satisfied with his employer and that the Planter considered the Japanese laborer as a rule superior to the Chinese and Portuguese.
>
> We found universal prosperity among the laborers, many of them receiving higher wages than stipulated in their contracts.
>
> [The workers'] health was generally good . . . and the death rate was lower than in Japan.[54]

The emigration of Japanese to Hawaii can also be considered a success because the expectations of the workers were met. Most went to Hawaii to earn as much money in as short a time as possible. Records exist of the amounts of money they sent back to their families and villages. One of the reasons Inoue encouraged emigration was that he hoped overseas workers would remit money to Japan.[55] (See Table 7.)

The total amount sent by the Japanese workers during the ten-year

TABLE 7

Money Remitted to Japan from Hawaii, 1889–1894

Year	*Amount Remitted*
1889	$ 159,709
1890	233,960
1891	298,425
1892	338,456
1893	319,476
1894	459,778
Total	$1,809,804

Source: Irie, *Hōjin hattenshi,* vol. 1, p. 80.

period of government-sponsored emigration came to more than $2,640,000.[56] This sum—3,826,086 yen (at a rate of 69¢ per 100 yen)—was more than half of the total revenue Japan received from its leading export in 1892, processed tea products.[57] Remittances were the eighth leading source of overseas revenue in that same year. Since money from abroad was sent through the Japanese consulate, the $2,640,000 did not include funds emigrants carried with them when they returned. There is evidence that returning workers were carrying at times more money than they had sent as remittances. A study of seven returning Hiroshima residents between 1886 and 1889 shows that they carried an average of 273.7 yen on their arrival.[58]

Surveys taken in the late 1880s show how emigrants from the Kuga district in Yamaguchi prefecture used their money when they returned from Hawaii.[59] One shows that of thirty-nine returnees, twenty had purchased land, ten paid off debts and established new households, and the remaining nine either lent their money out or put it in savings accounts to earn interest. Another survey of 302 returnees revealed 151 were paying off debts, 86 earning interest from their money, and 65 buying land.

There is also a study of thirty emigrants from Hesaka village, located just north of Hiroshima city.[60] In 1892 they sent back to their families a total of 1,620.91.9 yen, or an average of 54 yen per emigrant. Although some of the receiving families either used the entire amount to pay back loans or saved it, on the average, 32.5 percent of the sum was saved, 9.3 percent was spent on land or tools, 27 percent paid off debts, and the remainder was used for miscellaneous purposes. Of the thirty families, twenty-seven showed a distinct improvement in their standard of living as a result of these remittances, while the remaining three families experienced no change in their lives as a result of receiving money from overseas.

Most of those who remitted funds to Japan sent small amounts on a regular basis rather than one large sum. For example, a survey of over 3,400 Hiroshima emigrants who sent 270,000 yen and over $700 during 1891 shows that over 75 percent remitted less than 100 yen each and over 43 percent less than 50 yen each.[61] Fifty-five individuals each sent more than 300 yen and only seven, more than 500 yen. In terms of how this money was used in the countryside, the same survey reported that 30 percent was saved, 13 percent was used to buy land or tools, and the remainder was earmarked for loan payments and other purposes.

The survey went on to point out that in 1891, 579 returning

Hiroshima residents brought 170,000 yen with them. Of this amount, 33 percent was used to buy land or tools, 26 percent was saved, and the remainder used for loan payments and other purposes. In another case, the money remitted to one district in Yamaguchi prefecture in 1886 totaled $178,913. That particular district spent only the equivalent of $80,465 in total expenditures during that same year.[62]

This new source of wealth that was spread among farming families benefited areas in southwestern Japan economically and also popularized overseas emigration. The following is an account about one individual who sent back a large sum of money to his family:

> Iwase Kansuke, a forty-five year old resident of Ōshima in Yamaguchi prefecture, emigrated to Hawaii on the first ship. On November 27, 1886 he sent back the sum of 129 yen 24 sen 8 rin. This money was sent by way of the town office. . . . At that time rice sold for 3 yen 80 sen per sixty kilogram bag . . . and yet one man, in less than ten months, was able to send back almost 130 yen. This was an accomplishment beyond the imagination of the other people of the island. Rumors quickly spread throughout the island; everyone's imagination was seized with the idea of emigration to Hawaii to make money.[63]

Although exceptional, this case points out how rumors of newly found wealth, whether based on fact or fiction, contributed to popularizing the idea of working in Hawaii.

Though the Japanese workers may have achieved a semblance of economic success, they encountered various problems on the plantations. A number of the workers were dissatisfied with wages and working conditions, and this led to desertions and labor disputes. The first strike by Japanese workers consisted of a walkout of sixteen workers on Papaiko plantation on the island of Hawaii.[64] They had arrived on the first shipment to Hawaii in February of 1885 and struck on 7 April. They complained that many had to labor longer hours than was stipulated in their contracts and that even the sick were forced to work.

Other walkouts took place that same year. Workers on the Paia and Haiku plantations complained about a lack of medical attention and rough handling by foremen.[65] Others went on strike when workers who said they were ill were imprisoned for desertion. Instead of relying on the consulate, the Hawaiian government finally set up a special board of inspection to investigate these complaints in August of

1885.[66] The government also issued a statement that forbad employers and overseers from physically abusing Japanese workers.

Resentment over work conditions and ill-treatment were the subjects of most complaints, but there were other reasons for worker dissatisfaction. One controversial issue concerned the salaries of the employees hired by the Bureau of Immigration, all of whom were Japanese. In 1886 seven doctors were hired at a salary of $108 a month, or more than seven times the wages of a plantation worker.[67] First-class interpreters and inspectors, also hired by the bureau, made $150 monthly, or ten times a worker's salary. These government employees facilitated the immigrants' arrival in Honolulu and worked to solve any problems that arose on the plantations. In particular, the chief inspector, at this time G. O. Nacayama, conducted inspection tours of plantations where there had been labor disturbances. Many of the workers resented the officials' high salaries because they were paying for them (see Table 6).

The Japanese workers also complained about another wage deduction. A portion of a worker's wages was withheld to cover any remuneration the sugar planter would be entitled to if the worker deserted; if he did not desert, that sum would be returned to the worker at the end of the contract period to pay for return passage to Japan.

The planters were afraid of workers deserting not only because of the shortage of labor it created on the plantation but because each planter stood to lose the money he had advanced to bring the worker to Hawaii. The Hawaiian government's fear was that hundreds, possibly thousands, of Japanese vagrants would remain in Hawaii after their contracts expired and become wards of the state. One idea that the sugar planters and the government discussed was a system in which a worker would have to show an official certificate of discharge before he would be allowed to work on other plantations, even after his first contract had expired.

But the solution for the planters and the government was to withhold workers' wages. In the beginning, 25 percent of the monthly wages was retained by the planters and sent to the Bureau of Immigration, together with a list of the workers.[68] This was turned over to the Japanese consul, who deposited the money in the Hawaiian government Postal Savings Bank and later with private banks. The withholding of workers' wages continued, although it was reduced to 15 percent in 1887.

In other words, these Japanese workers were not only paying the salaries of doctors, interpreters, and inspectors and contributing to a Japanese relief fund (see Table 6) but they also had one-fourth of their wages withheld for the length of their contracts.[69] Later this system allowed some of this money to be deposited into the Japanese government Postal Savings Bank, requiring only that at least $50 be kept in each account to pay for the return passage.[70]

The Japanese workers expressed dissatisfaction about all of these wage deductions by demonstrating, deserting, or going on strike. Both Japanese and Hawaiian officials set up a system to handle this problem.[71] Anyone who had a complaint had to first appeal in writing to the Bureau of Immigration. If he was dissatisfied with the bureau's investigation or decision, the worker could bring suit in local court. If that too failed, he could appeal to the Hawaiian supreme court. The last recourse was the Japanese consulate in Honolulu. This was a complicated system for the workers, and complaints seldom went through the entire process.

Like other immigrants entering a new society, a number of Japanese faced personal problems during their years in Hawaii. In 1891 Foreign Minister Aoki Shūzō complained to Irwin that he had heard there were "many cases of divorce, remarriage, adultery, prostitution . . . ."[72] He also mentioned that there were unmarried couples going to Hawaii under false pretences. Emigration guides (to be discussed in chapter 4) of this period warned Japanese workers about the dangers of gambling, alcohol, and prostitution. Nevertheless, because of the disproportionate sex ratio, these social problems emerged from time to time in the new immigrant community.

The year 1890 represented the midpoint of the ten-year government-sponsored immigration period for thousands of workers and their families in Hawaii. Officials there released 1890 census information three years later, and this formed the basis of a report written by James H. Blount, a special commissioner of the United States.[73] This report, dated 1 June 1893 and sent to the American secretary of state, offers a picture of the Japanese community in 1890.

The Hawaiian government claimed that 10,079 Japanese men and 2,281 women resided in the islands in 1890. Of this number, 2,964 of the men and 2,101 of the women were married. This left 7,115 men of whom 7,059 were still single, 50 widowers, and 6 divorced.[74] Of the 180 unmarried women, 148 were single, 29 were widows, and 3 had been divorced. This document also included an overview of the occupational situation of these Japanese. An overwhelming number—9,565 men and 1,404 women—had been employed as laborers. It also revealed a small number of men moved into secondary occupations. According to this survey, there were 42 mechanics, 36 farmers, 4 drivers or teamsters, 3 fishermen, and 2 mariners. There were also 27 merchants, 23 professionals and teachers, 20 clerks, and 115 in various other nonagricultural occupations. Of the women who did not work as laborers, only 14 held jobs.

After three years on the plantations the workers could sign another contract and stay in Hawaii, return to Japan with the money they had saved, or travel to the United States mainland to find better paying jobs. The Japanese consulate surveyed the choices made by those who traveled to Hawaii from 1885 until 1894, and the results are shown in Table 8.[75] One historian examined Hiroshima emigrants who arrived in Hawaii between 1885 and 1893.[76] Compared to others, Hiroshima immigrants tended to stay overseas rather than return to Japan as can be seen in the same table. The relatively high percentage of returnees (46 percent) among the government-sponsored immigrants was due to several factors, the most important being the dekasegi rōdō tradition. Working away from home in Japan was always seen as a temporary arrangement, although the actual period of separation might be quite long. Still at some point these workers expected to return home, hopefully with some money. Those who found some financial success in Hawaii often immigrated a second time after a stay in Japan. The less fortunate who could not save money or who had been dissatisfied in Hawaii were only too glad to return home.

TABLE 8

Japanese Workers after First Contract Period

Situation	*All Emigrants (1885–1894)*	*Hiroshima Emigrants (1885–1893)*
Settled in Hawaii	13,231 (44%)	6,895 (66%)
Returned to Japan	13,861 (46%)	2,629 (25%)
Deceased	2,034 (7%)	2,512 (24%)
Went to U.S. mainland	877 (3%)	368 (4%)

Sources: Report from the Consulate to the Foreign Ministry, 22 November 1902, Gaimushō, *NGB*, vol. 35, pp. 828–831; Yoshida, "Meiji shoki," pt. 1, pp. 296–297.

The End of Government-Sponsored Emigration

The labor convention continued until 1894, when government-sponsored emigration to Hawaii finally ended. For the Japanese workers, the end was 27 June 1897, when the contracts of the last group, the 1,190 men who went under the labor convention, expired.[77]

The Hawaiian government gradually became disenchanted with Irwin, who had overseen the Japanese end of this emigration system. It had numerous disagreements with him concerning the commission he was receiving for each emigrant, as well as Hawaii's reluctance to go along with Irwin and pay for the Japanese interpreters, inspectors, and doctors.[78] But these officials had other problems besides disagreements with Irwin. There was considerable worry that too many Japanese were entering the islands and thereby upsetting the delicate balance of races and ethnic groups.[79] The Hawaiian authorities hoped to discourage further Japanese immigration by no longer importing government-sponsored workers. At the same time, they began once again to think about replacing Japanese workers with Chinese workers.

Meanwhile, by 1894, the Japanese government was reconsidering its role as overseer of the emigration business, although it had to be pleased with the results of this first overseas venture. Through remittances, money carried back, and the money from the 25 percent wage deduction plan (in effect a forced savings system), a considerable amount of foreign capital had entered Japan. This was, of course, only a partial solution to the country's foreign exchange problem; but it was a welcome one. Emigration also served as a safety valve, though limited in scale, for the rural areas of southwestern Japan. Although initially the recruiting process seemed to involve a game of political favoritism, the villages in the areas selected for recruitment did benefit, as the significant economic returns show.

Japan's decision to turn the operation of emigration over to private companies was based on several considerations. During the early Meiji years, as part of its *shokusan kōgyō* (develop industry and promote enterprise) policy the government operated and established a number of new industrial enterprises seen as essential to the future of the nation.[80] After these became viable businesses, it withdrew and turned them over to the private sector. Thus the change from a government-sponsored emigration system to a private one was consistent with the political and economic policies of the time.

With a number of important international and domestic issues confronting Japan, the decision to streamline government operations and turn certain businesses over to private enterprise seemed logical and necessary. For example, during the Sino-Japanese War, the government's main concerns were conducting the war itself, the international negotiations at the end of the conflict, and the political and economic turmoil that would result in Japan. It was necessary, therefore, to ignore the transport of emigrants to Hawaii and allow the military to transport soldiers to China on ships that were used to carry emigrants to Hawaii. It was during this period that foreign shipping companies began handling the passenger traffic to Hawaii.

Also, the emigration business had grown more quickly than the Japanese government or anyone had anticipated. Workers going to Hawaii averaged 1,940 persons a year in the years 1885 to 1886, but that number rose to an average of 8,769 a year by the 1893–1894 period.[81] One of the reasons for this increase was that, despite the planters' reluctance to let more Japanese enter the islands, expansion of the sugar plantations depended on the availability of a large number of workers. This became particularly important after 1 April 1891, when Hawaiian sugar imports could once again enter the United States free of tariff.[82]

Another reason the Japanese government changed its thinking was the increasing pressure from other countries to send them Japanese workers. Only two years after the government-sponsored emigration had begun, Kanagawa prefecture officials reported an attempt to hire acrobats and performers to work in America. Again in 1887, employers in Australia who had been facing problems with Chinese workers appealed to Japan to allow its citizens to emigrate. Two years later, they sent a formal request to Foreign Minister Ōkuma for permission to recruit men to work on plantations in Queensland. There were also reports in 1888 of a Mexican colonization company inviting Japanese to work in an area the company claimed it had received as a land grant; they also predicted it could support up to three million people. In 1890 landowners in West Australia inquired about the possibility of hiring 100 Japanese workers and their families. From 1892 through 1894 Japan received similar inquiries from employers or government representatives in Peru, India, Hong Kong, New Caledonia, Canada, Australia, and Brazil.[83] They sought, in particular, Japanese to work as sugar cane plantation laborers, pearl shellers and divers, and miners.

The first indication of a possible change in government policy came in a letter from Hayashi Tadasu, the vice minister for foreign affairs. In

1891 Hayashi wrote to an Australian agent: "the Imperial Government will not only offer no objection to laborers going abroad *under proper agreements* [emphasis added], but will offer them every possible facility."[84] At the time the only "proper agreement" was of course with the Hawaiian government. Nevertheless, Japanese officials understood that there were a number of other countries who sought workers. They also realized that if emigration could succeed as well as it had in Hawaii, only on a wider scale, the entire country stood to gain from this expansion. The question was how to work out suitable and proper arrangements with foreign countries to insure that those going overseas would be protected from exploitation.

The solution, as far as the government was concerned, lay in the willingness of the private sector to take on the responsibility of handling wide-scale emigration. A number of Japanese businessmen made their desire to assume this responsibility known to officials. In fact, several attempts were made before 1894 to establish privately run emigration businesses.

From December of 1891 to April of 1894, at least five such companies were established. The first was Nippon Yoshisa (at times referred to as Kissa) imin gōshigaisha in 1891.[85] It had been encouraged in its efforts by Foreign Minister Enomoto Takeaki. The other companies, Yokohama imingaisha (later known as Yokohama kaigai shokumin gōshigaisha), Kaigai shokumin gōshigaisha, Meiji imingaisha, and Kobe tokō gōshigaisha, were all established in 1894.[86] Because there were no legal restrictions concerning such companies, they began to send small groups of workers to Australia, Fiji, Guadaloupe, and New Caledonia.[87] This occurrence not only offered a possible solution to the government's problems but also managed to put pressure on Japan's authorities to either extend the labor convention system to include other countries or to allow private companies to operate on a wider scale.

From the point of view of the Japanese government, the ideal form of emigration had been that of the 1885–1894 government-sponsored emigration: an orderly, closely regulated system with protection, even interference, from both governments involved. It felt that this form not only protected the emigrants but also maintained in international circles Japan's image as a modern nation. What the government did not want was disorganized and unregulated emigration. The result was the introduction of a set of rules that regulated this system and that came to be known as the Emigrant Protection Law.

CHAPTER 3

The Emigrant Protection Law

THE Japanese government divided control of private emigration from 1894 in three ways. It first drew up a strict set of regulations that gave itself absolute government control (national and local) over all aspects of the emigration process. This gave officials the authority to intervene in the activities of private companies or file legal charges against them when they violated the law. Secondly, within this legal structure, authorities allowed some individual initiative, particularly in the case of larger, more efficient companies. Finally, the central government generally relied on local authorities to enforce the provisions of these regulations, but there were times when it had to use its own authority, such as when it was confronted with serious national and international problems.

The Emigration Protection Ordinance of 1894

The government regulated overseas emigration from 1894 with a set of rules issued as Imperial Ordinance Number 42.[1] The original set of rules, known as *Imin hogokisoku* or the Emigrant Protection Ordinance, was proclaimed on 12 April 1894. Originally it consisted of nineteen articles and three supplementary regulations.[2] The ordinance became law on 29 April 1896 and took effect the following 1 June as *Imin hogohō*, the Emigrant Protection Law.

During the following years the law underwent several changes and new provisions were added to it in 1901, 1902, and 1907. The final version consisted of thirty-one articles and sixty regulations designed to aid the enforcement of the law.[3] In 1907 and again in 1909 separate sets of regulations concerning passports were issued.

In twenty-two short paragraphs the Emigrant Protection Ordinance of 1894 set up the general framework that would later become a much more complex—to some even complicated—set of regulations. *All* of the provisions of this ordinance were later incorporated into law in 1896 only in more detail. In other words, the relationship of the ordinance to the law was similar to that of guidelines to a text, because the law filled in gaps and provided additional details to the provisions contained in the original ordinance. It is important to remember that the ordinance was never meant to stand alone but to regulate the emigration process only until a law was passed by the national Diet. To avoid unnecessary repetition, the provisions of the ordinance will be examined on the basis of those contained in the law.

The Emigrant Protection Law of 1896

The basic provisions of the law for the protection of Japanese emigrants were divided into the following seven parts: Imin, Imin Toriatsukainin, Security, Emigrant Ships, Miscellaneous Provisions, Penal Provisions, and Supplementary Provisions. They defined what was legal in terms of overseas migration and pointed out how the government intended to regulate this process.

First the law defined who or what an emigrant was: "By the term 'Imin' in the present law are meant persons who emigrate for the *purpose of labor* [emphasis added] to foreign countries. . . ."[4] For this 1894–1908 period, those going to Hawaii went as agricultural workers to be employed on the sugar cane plantations. A later regulation added such occupations as fishing, mining, manufacturing, engineering (construction work), and transportation as alternative types of labor suitable for emigrants.[5]

The first chapter dealt with the question of authority, that is, the relationship between the government and the other participants in the emigration process. For example, a Japanese citizen was not allowed to go abroad without official permission. An emigrant seeking this approval could obtain it with the help of a private company; otherwise he had to provide the names of two guarantors, who were responsible for the worker if he became ill or was in distress overseas.[6] If the latter case, the worker would be brought back by the government, which had to be reimbursed either by the emigration company or by the guarantors.

Although it took only four articles to define the relationship between the emigrant and the government, it took fifteen articles to define the more complex one that existed between the emigration companies and the Japanese authorities. *Toriatsukainin,* a word used to refer to an individual agent, as well as to an incorporated company, was defined as "a person who . . . makes it his business to collect Imin or make arrangements for their emigration."[7] Here the law clearly describes this system as one based on private enterprise and undertaken by businessmen seeking profits.

Anyone who wanted to send a Japanese citizen abroad, individual or incorporated company, needed official permission to do so. If no one was sent during the six-month period after permission was granted, that permission was invalidated. Another restriction required that a company's members, partners, and shareholders had to be citizens and its main office had to be located in Japan. In addition, authorities retained the right to suspend company operations or to revoke the official approval to operate.[8]

The rest of the regulations on toriatsukainin dealt with their responsibilities to the emigrants. For example, their accountability did not end when the workers landed overseas. The law specified that if they were unable to return, the companies bore the financial responsibility to ship them back to Japan. The companies were accountable for this service for a ten-year period, even if their operations were suspended. They were also required to obtain permission from the foreign ministry to hire agents, one of whom had to be a resident in the area where workers were to be sent.[9]

One provision specified that government-approved labor contracts had to be signed by both the company and worker involved. As we will see later, one of the common complaints among emigrants was that companies and agents would demand "unofficial" commissions and illegal fees to facilitate processing. The result of these charges was that a provision stating that "the Imin Toriatsukainin shall not, under any pretext whatever, receive from the Imin money or articles other than his fees" was added to the law in 1901.[10]

The third part of the law dealt with the security deposit. During this period, the government asked each company for a security of at least 10,000 yen.[11] This was to be used to bring emigrants back to Japan if the company in question did not live up to its financial obligations as outlined in its contracts. The 1894 ordinance required that this money be placed in the hands of local authorities, but a revision of the ordinance (1901) stipulated it be deposited with the central government.[12]

A chapter that dealt with shipping companies was added to the law in 1907. As with the emigration companies, these companies and their ships were subject to strict regulations. It was also necessary for them to obtain official permission to transport emigrants, as well as to deposit a security. The government retained the right to designate ports of departure and ports of destination, and to oversee the amount of passage fare charged the emigrants.[13]

The articles of miscellaneous provisions were added to the law in 1900 and 1907. They extended government control to moneylending and boardinghouses, two particular areas of complaint.[14] Thereafter anyone who lent money to emigrants had to obtain official approval for the terms of the loan. Similarly boardinghouses with an emigrant clientele had their arrangements, maintenance, and rates subject to government scrutiny. This was also extended to those who made "arrangements relative to the embarkation of imin."[15] This applied to company agents who worked in the port cities and who saw to the final arrangements of the departure of those going abroad.

The law also included a chapter on penal provisions in which only one article dealt with the emigrants themselves. It stated that those who left Japan without permission or who submitted false statements would be subject to a small fine. The other provisions dealt with private companies and the penalties for illegal activities. The most severe penalty, major imprisonment, would be dealt to a company that "by means of false representations, collects Imin or makes arrangements for their emigration. . . ."[16]

Other provisions of this section dealt with fines for specific violations. These fines ranged from 10 yen to 10,000 yen. The scale of penalties for different violations reflected the government's concerns. For example, authorities were worried about the possibility of companies sending people abroad without permission, a practice which would lead to unregulated and unorganized travel. Thus a 10,000 yen fine was the maximum penalty for each such company violation while emigrants themselves were only subject to fines of between 5 and 50 yen. The penalties levied on commercial companies applied to their managing partner(s) or director(s), thus holding individuals responsible for company infractions.[17]

The main provisions of the Emigrant Protection Law emphasized government control over the essential parts of the emigration process —the labor contracts, the emigration companies, the security deposit, and the shipping companies. This law only set up the minimum guidelines participants in the emigration process were expected to observe. Thus in 1907 and in 1909, regulations in the form of additional articles were attached to the original law.

The Regulations for the Enforcement of the Law

These regulations appeared as sixty articles which were issued as Ordinance Number 70, "Detailed Regulations for the Enforcement of the Law for the Protection of Imin." They provided additional details to the original articles of the law. An example of this is Article 2 of the law, which stated that, "No imin shall, without the permission of the Administrative Authorities, emigrate to a foreign country." This left the question of how they should go about getting this approval. According to an article in the regulations, an application had to be submitted to the governor of the prefecture in which the emigrant lived.[18] This application gave his destination, purpose in leaving Japan, and planned length of stay abroad. It had to have the signature of a company agent or of two guarantors. Finally, if the emigrant had signed a labor contract, a copy of it had to accompany the application.

Likewise emigration companies were required to obtain government approval before starting their businesses, and this would come only after a detailed application was submitted to the proper authorities.[19] The application had to give, among other things, the official name of the company, its place of business, the amount of capital available, and the length of time it expected to operate. The company also had to list the places where emigrants were to be sent and the ways in which it would recruit them and how this process would take place. In addition, the personal histories of the partners and employees of this business venture, as well as information regarding the amount of property and stock held by each, had to accompany applications. After a business was established, the company had to report any changes that took place within its structure. For example, the company reported if it managed to start its business on time, whether there were any changes in staff personnel, or if branch offices were set up or closed.[20]

The government also placed restraints on the types of individuals who could work for these companies. Those not eligible included incompetent people, those who had their civil rights suspended, individuals who had been involved in a bankruptcy, and those who had spent time in prison. Employees who worked as recruiting agents sought approval from local authorities by submitting documents concerning their personal histories, proposed duties, and the amount of personal property each held. After gaining approval, agents carried government-issued permits as well as official certificates of approval while recruiting.[21]

The relationship between these companies and the emigrants was also governed by regulations. Companies were required to keep detailed registers that included information on emigrants' previous occupations, the locations of their homes in Japan, the names of their employers in Hawaii, the amount of their proposed wages, and so forth. Agents were also expected to keep a record of these workers' whereabouts overseas, particularly after they left the area to which they had originally migrated. In addition, advertisements and printed notices had to be approved by local authorities. The government also set up guidelines for contracts between a company and an individual. These had to clearly outline the term of the labor contract, the rate of commission charged by the agent, the method by which the company would provide passage fare, the wages to be earned, and the way in which workers in distress would be sent back to Japan. Other provisions pointed out that monthly reports had to be submitted to authorities about the number of emigrants leaving Japan, the number returning, the circumstances of those meeting with accidents, and any deaths that had occurred abroad.[22]

Included in these regulations were twelve provisions that pertained to the ships emigrants traveled on. Shipping company applications listed the trade name of the company, the name of the ship, its nationality, the ports of embarkation and destination, the approximate length of the voyage, the amount of capital in the company, and the estimated number of emigrants to be carried. The regulations also required that each ship have a "permit of conveyance" signed by Japanese authorities.[23]

Other provisions covered such topics as moneylending. People who lent money to those going overseas were ordered to reveal their rates of interest, the form of repayment, and a summary of the other contract terms before obtaining approval from local officials.[24]

According to the supplementary provisions, prefectural governors filled the roles of "local authorities"; emigrants from Tokyo, however, reported to the chief commissioner of police of that city. Similarly the term "Japanese authorities abroad" meant official government representatives, which included consuls general and their agents.[25]

The Rules of Procedure

Changes in the Emigrant Protection Law also took place in June of 1907 with the addition of the "Rules of Procedure Relative to the Detailed Regulations for the Enforcement of the Law for the Protection of Imin."[26] These rules, consisting of eleven articles, dealt with the relationship between local prefectural officials and the foreign ministry, and outlined the types of reports that had to be sent to the central government.

Prefectural authorities were responsible for compiling lists of local recruits and the amount of security deposits collected. They were also responsible for issuing permits to those who had received permission to leave Japan, as well as certificates to emigration companies that were allowed to operate in their particular prefecture. In addition, they had to put notices about emigration matters in the general information columns of the "Official Gazette."[27] This included news about new emigration companies, about those ending business operations, for example, and changes in the company and among its personnel.

The Consequences of the Law

The Emigrant Protection Law was thus divided into four parts: the ordinance of 1894, the law of 1896, the regulations of 1907 and 1909, and the rules of 1907. Together these parts established the legal framework under which overseas emigration after 1894 could continue, although under the management of private enterprise. As specific problems arose, officials quickly issued additional regulations.

There were a number of cases where overseas-bound Japanese were kept longer than necessary by boardinghouse owners. Boardinghouses catering to an emigrant clientele sprang up in the port cities from which workers left Japan and they of course made more money the longer their customers stayed in the port cities.[28] One person recounted:

> I waited in an emigrant house in Kobe, hoping to make some connection. But there were hardly any ships. Many youngsters like myself were waiting for boats headed for the United States. During that period I heard that Yokohama was an easier boarding place than Kobe, so I went to Yokohama and again lodged at an emigrant house. A worker at this emigrant house took me frequently for trachoma and hookworm examinations, but as for the most important thing—he wouldn't let me board. Presumably they were calculating to prolong my stay at the lodging houses day by day. I was kept there for three weeks. I spent all my travel money there and so I went back home. . . . [29]

There were other complaints about these houses concerning overcrowding, unsanitary conditions, and high prices.

In August of 1906 Kanagawa prefectural authorities issued a new set of guidelines which required that boardinghouse owners in Yokohama provide bright and airy rooms, limit occupancy in each room, provide adequate bedding, and post prices where they were clearly visible.[30] Lodging for those going overseas was also limited to a ten-day period, and authorities had to be notified about room rates and transportation fees. In addition, these houses were ordered to keep separate emigrant registers, which had to be shown to police officials within six hours after registration. Authorities also urged boardinghouse owners to form an association to pass along official regulations and suggestions.

Shipping companies and their passage fares were other areas of complaint, and this was one of the reasons these companies had to submit detailed applications before permission to transport emigrants was granted them. Regulations for these companies were so stringent the companies had to report the number of hours each ship would take to make their voyages within Japan, that is, from Nagasaki to Kobe and then to Yokohama.[31] In addition, bonds up to 30,000 yen had to be deposited with the foreign ministry by each company.[32] The government hoped that through these measures it could retain some control over the transporting of overseas workers and also establish a standard passage fare.

Authorities also tried to retain control over the emigration companies' recruiting methods and warned them about false advertising, which was a violation of the law. Other regulations covered newspaper advertisements and public notices put up in places such as bath houses and barber shops. [33]

At times officials took steps to investigate and remedy specific problems, which under the provisions of the Emigrant Protection Law they had the authority to do. In December of 1906, for example, officials searched, by order of the Yokohama district court, the offices of Tokio imin gōshigaisha. There had been a violation concerning licenses to travel abroad, and two employees were arrested and later dismissed. Also in 1906 Kanagawa authorities had reports that boardinghouses in Yokohama had violated regulations and were under police investigation.[34] In the same report, they warned that because some emigrants were being issued false passports, better supervision of emigration companies and shipping companies was needed.

Several companies had their licenses to operate suspended by government authorities because of illegal activities.[35] Kansai imin gōshigaisha, for instance, lost its license to send emigrants to Hawaii, as did Nankai imin gōshigaisha after it was accused of collecting "extra" commissions from its clients. In November of 1904 the governor of Wakayama prefecture complained about the questionable practices of Teikoku shokumin gōshigaisha (Imperial Emigration Company), and the governor of Niigata prefecture complained about Kobe tokō gōshigaisha.

The responsibility for enforcing these regulations was left to local authorities in the different prefectures. Officials in Kanagawa and Hyōgo, in particular, played major roles in overseeing the departure of emigrants from the port cities of Yokohama and Kobe. They had to submit regular reports as well as any news of irregularities or problems to the foreign ministry. The staffs of Japanese embassies and consulates abroad filled similar roles at the other end of the emigration process. In the case of Hawaii, this responsibility went to the staff of the consulate in Honolulu (see Appendix 8 for a list of the consuls general during this period).

The Emigrant Protection Law and its provisions can be viewed as the underpinning of a rigid and strict system. It reflected the government's stated policy of long standing to protect the interests of its overseas workers. Striving to achieve the status of a "modern nation," Japan was not about to let its citizens be mistreated or be viewed as coolies or slaves.

Nevertheless, as thousands of workers went abroad and as the system became more complex, efficient enforcement of the regulations suffered. Officials were able to file only nineteen charges against the emigration companies between 1895 and 1908.[36] Compared to the number of complaints filed, this was a very small number.

In 1894 the Japanese government set up a legal system of laws designed to regulate overseas migration, and it later filled in existing gaps as specific problems arose. Officials expected that this new system would be more than adequate to handle those going to Hawaii, and also to deal with expanded emigration to other countries.

This system met two major needs: first, a legal regulatory system was provided by the Emigrant Protection Law and additional regulations; and second, guidelines which private enterprise could follow to handle emigration that had been expanding over the past ten years were now available. Thus after 1894 private emigration companies handled a system that became quite complex, and a number of problems arose and some major changes took place. Yet this system succeeded in sending 125,000 Japanese to Hawaii and initiated emigration to other countries.

CHAPTER 4

Emigration Companies in Japan: The Stage and the Actors

IF the emigration company period between 1894 and 1908 had to be characterized in one word, it would be "complex."[1] The term "emigration companies" itself refers not to two or three but to at least fifty-one companies and emigration agents.[2] At least fifteen more were established but failed to send any workers abroad, and fourteen others were turned down by foreign ministry officials for various reasons.[3] Thus during this short fifteen-year period, at least eighty attempts to begin emigration businesses were made.

The complexity of this process was manifested in other ways. Small companies hired as few as five agents, but larger ones had as many as seventy-five. Similarly while some companies established only one branch office, others had up to fifty offices throughout the country. Agents operated out of these offices and recruited over 124,000 workers to go to Hawaii. Negotiations took place between individual Japanese companies and the owners of over fifty sugar plantations in Hawaii, each with different labor requirements.

The numbers themselves suggest how complex this system was and how difficult examining and analyzing overseas emigration over a fifteen-year period is. To look at this complex system in an orderly manner, I have divided it into two parts: the emigration process in Japan and the immigration process in Hawaii.

On each side of the Pacific Ocean there were five important participants, or "actors," who appeared on a historical stage.[4] The story of emigration is basically that of these actors and their relationships with each other. The Japanese who took part can be arranged on their stage in the manner shown in the diagram on the following page.

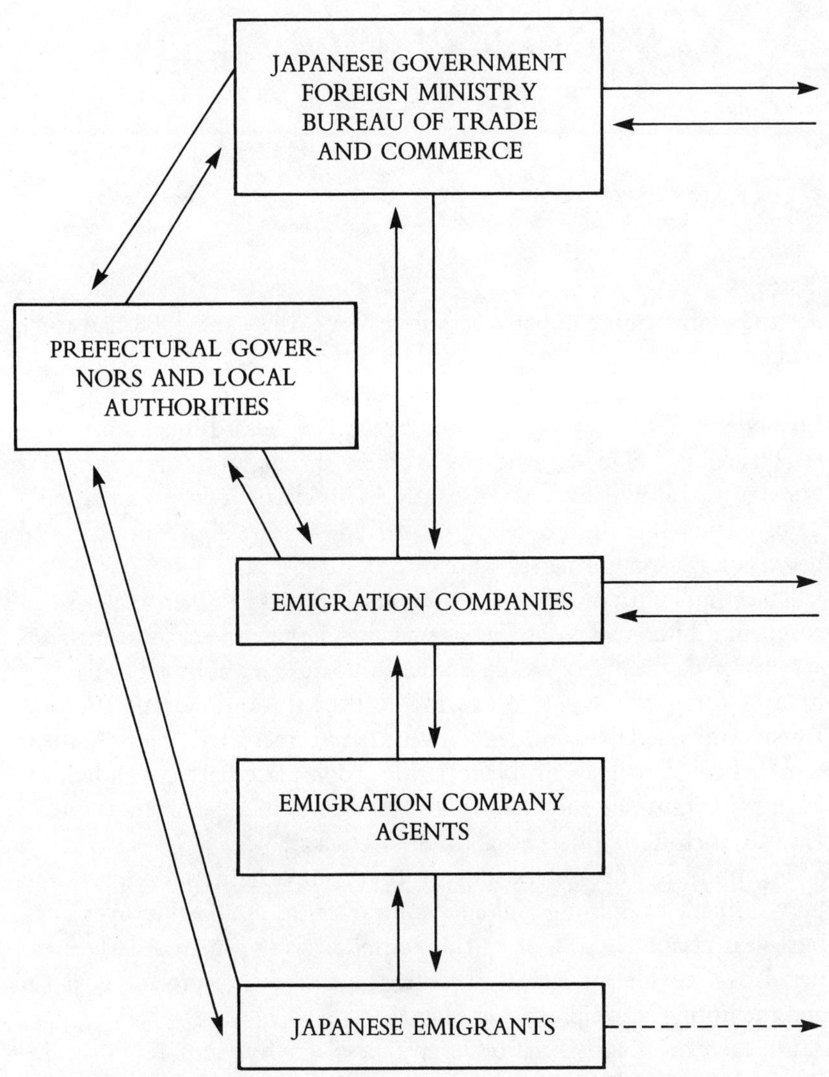
PACIFIC
OCEAN
JAPANESE GOVERNMENT
FOREIGN MINISTRY
BUREAU OF TRADE
AND COMMERCE
PREFECTURAL GOVER-
NORS AND LOCAL
AUTHORITIES
EMIGRATION COMPANIES
EMIGRATION COMPANY
AGENTS
JAPANESE EMIGRANTS

Each of these actors held a different status and specific role in the overall process, which was based on different levels of authority. For example, information from the foreign ministry concerning emigration matters was sent through prefectural offices, which passed it down through local authorities and company officials, who in turn made it available to potential emigrants. Emigrants' requests and applications took the opposite route and went up to the central government through local authorities and company agents. The bilateral and reciprocal relationships between the actors are indicated in the diagram by arrows. Since both the government and the companies developed trans-Pacific relationships with their counterparts in Hawaii, arrows reflecting this are shown on the right side of the diagram. The workers appear on both the Japan and the Hawaii stage as emigrants and immigrants, respectively. Their movement across the Pacific Ocean is indicated by the dotted arrow. The rest of this chapter will describe each actor, his role in this process, and his relationships with the other four actors.

The Japanese Government

The first actor on the Japan stage was the central government, which held the legal right to start or end overseas migration. It governed this process with laws, ordinances, regulations, and occasional intervention.

Within the government, the foreign minister and the officials of the ministry for foreign affairs were responsible for emigration. The ministry was divided into several parts, including the bureaus of political affairs, finance, and records. Government divisions responsible for specific geographic areas were not established until 1918. After 1885, emigration matters were dealt with by the Bureau of Trade and Commerce.[5]

In August of 1891, a special emigrant section was created within the bureau. The foreign ministry gave the following as the reason for its establishment: "In order to increase the popularity of Japanese overseas emigration, the government must first protect and encourage these [emigrants]."[6] All correspondence to the ministry dealing with this subject, whether from representatives of foreign governments, prefectural authorities, emigration companies, or individuals, first went to this bureau. They were then passed along to other appropriate bureaus within the ministry. Similarly outgoing correspondence that originated within the bureau was passed on the foreign minister or vice minister. All matters concerning emigrants residing abroad were handled by the ministry through representatives on its embassy and consulate staffs.[7]

One of the major tasks of the foreign ministry was to negotiate treaties that would allow Japanese emigrants to enter other countries. Whether these treaties were with the Hawaiian Kingdom, the United States, Canada, or various Latin American countries, officials of course sought the most favorable terms possible, but always with the understanding that the emigrants would be offered adequate protection.

The Emigrant Protection Law gave the government the right to restrict or even suspend overseas travel. At times the foreign ministry curbed emigration to Hawaii by limiting the number of workers each company could send abroad.[8] This caused serious problems for the sugar planters and the Hawaiian government. In 1891 a representative of the Hawaiian ministry of the interior went to Japan to discuss this problem.[9] Apparently workers had been complaining about the treatment they had received from overseers on the sugar plantations. Once news of this appeared in the Japanese newspapers, authorities temporarily halted travel to Hawaii. Later, in 1903, a representative of the United States government commented that "the Government of Japan closely supervises and regulates every detail of [Japanese] immigration. . . . It is stated that at times only a fixed quota of laborers is permitted to leave each province. . . ."[10]

The home ministry, from the beginning, oversaw and enforced regulations, governing emigration as outlined in the Ordinance of 1894. It helped draw up and issue rules that dealt with boardinghouses, shipping companies, and advertising. Letters of application for opening, closing, or moving company branch offices inside the country had to be sent to both the home ministry and the foreign ministry.[11]

The officials of the foreign ministry rewrote government policies on emigration, fitting them into the legal framework set up by law. Because these policies had to be modified as conditions in Hawaii and Japan changed, the job was all the more difficult. For example, sometimes the ministry had to hold down the number of people being sent abroad by rejecting applications of potential companies, as well as by imposing monthly quotas on emigrants after 1900.

The other important task foreign ministry and home ministry officials had was the protection of their citizens' rights at home and abroad. Within Japan this fell under the jurisdiction of the home ministry, but problems overseas were the responsibility of the foreign ministry. Thus ministry representatives overseas sent various reports on the Japanese community in their area detailing births, deaths, labor conditions, crimes committed, complaints filed, and so forth. Successful government supervision of the emigration system and protection of citizens' rights was vital to Japanese overseas workers and their families.

Prefectural Governors and Local Authorities

Although during the early years of emigration to Hawaii the central government was solely responsible for the welfare of its workers abroad, as the number of emigrants increased, prefectural authorities began to play a greater role in the emigration process. Applications to leave Japan were sent to the foreign ministry through them, as were emigration company applications, requests, and reports. During the 1894–1908 period, governors had to provide the following information about emigrants from their prefectures: the number of emigrants, their names, home addresses, passport numbers, status, occupations, and birth dates.[12] Other accounts to Tokyo included the number of those with labor contracts and the destination of each individual.[13] Most of this data was compiled monthly, but some reports had to be sent twice a year, in January and July.

Prefectural officials were also expected to keep track of emigrants even after they left Japan. They transmitted reports to the government about money being remitted to local banks, the number returning to their home prefectures, and so forth. If an individual failed to come back because of a death or a decision to remain abroad, these officials were expected to notify Tokyo.

In addition to these reports, prefectural officials drew up certificates and forms for emigrants to use. Thus the foreign ministry received forms that differed slightly from one another because they were from different prefectures. For instance, although all of the emigrant lists included the name and address of each Hawaii-bound worker, some gave the age of each person at the time of departure, while others offered no information about this at all. At times the overseas destination of each worker was given. Some lists also gave the status and occupation of each individual, and a few had the word for commoner, *heimin,* and the word for farmer, *nōmin,* already printed on them. Others gave the date the person received permission to leave Japan, the purpose for migrating (e.g., farming [*nōgyō*]), the date of departure, and the length of the contract period.[14]

The prefectural governors were also responsible for printing and distributing letter of guarantee forms, as well as applications everyone needed to obtain passports.[15] In addition, they issued letters of introduction for emigration company applicants based in their prefectures, a document which accompanied an application to begin a business.

Officials on the prefectural level could not both handle all of the paperwork and verify the information about emigrants requested by the foreign ministry and so they relied on the cooperation of local authorities. Thus news about laws and regulations from the central government passed from the prefectural office down to three lower levels of administration: county, city, and, in rural areas, town and village offices. Legal notices were posted in public places and showed what one had to do to become an emigration agent, how to fill in applications, what a letter of guarantee looked like, how to write a résumé, and so forth.[16] These notices generally followed guidelines specific to each prefecture and so they differed slightly from one another.

The local authorities also served other functions for those going abroad. For example, a notice dated 3 June 1896 issued by the Nagasaki prefectural office points out that to emigrate, an applicant must obtain from local officials a statement that verifies information about him or her.[17] As was mentioned in a previous context, individuals who left Japan without using emigration companies were required by law to furnish the names of two guarantors. Local authorities had to verify that these were men of good standing and that they had enough money to bring the person back if necessary.

The only people who did not use the services of prefectural authorities were the residents of the city of Tokyo, who were required to report to the chief commissioner of the Tokyo metropolitan police department.[18] The police department was part of the home ministry and submitted reports on emigrants from Tokyo to the officials of the foreign ministry.

These local officials did more for the overall emigration process than just handle reports and do paperwork. Local authorities in certain prefectures such as Hiroshima encouraged overseas work and helped popularize it by issuing their own notices. Undoubtedly this increased emigration from certain parts of Japan.

The Emigration Companies

Although the first official emigration company was not established until 1891, several individuals were already helping workers obtain passports and complete other paperwork they needed to travel overseas. These were operators of boardinghouses in Yokohama and Kobe. As "unofficial agents," they attracted would-be emigrants with claims that they had ties with shipping companies and so could promise low passage fare in addition to jobs in Hawaii.

With only five companies in existence before 1894, the announcement of the Emigrant Protection Ordinance led to a rapid increase in the number of such ventures.[19] Although the government attempted to oversee this growth in emigration businesses, record-keeping during the first four years of this period, 1894–1897, was haphazard.

Immediately after the passage of the ordinance, 1,329 emigrants were sent to Hawaii by two small firms, Itōhan *shōkai* (commercial firm) and Ogura (at times, Kokura) shōkai.[20] Although the former ended operations in late 1894, Ogura shōkai shipped an additional 768 workers in 1895. It was eventually taken over by Dainippon imin kabushikigaisha in 1896.[21] Kaigai tokō kabushikigaisha (Japanese Emigration Company of Hiroshima), a company organized in 1894, sent 1,036 workers to Hawaii in 1895, as did Kobe tokō gōshigaisha (Kobe Immigration Company) which shipped 542 emigrants.[22] The following year, 1896, saw both Nippon imin gōshigaisha (Japan Emigration Company) and Morioka Makoto (at times known as Shin) join the other three companies already in operation.

After 1898 relatively accurate statistics were compiled by the foreign ministry and issued in 1921 as a part of its *Ryoken kafusū oyobi imin tōkei* (Statistics on passports granted and emigrants). There are several estimates of the number of emigrants who went to Hawaii during the four years before 1898. In all probability, about 13,248 emigrants did so with the help of emigration companies during this period.[23] There is also evidence that a number went on their own during these years.[24] The emigration companies, their periods of operation, and the number of workers they sent abroad from 1891 to 1908 are listed in Table 9.[25]

As can be seen in this table, those companies that were established in the early years, 1894 to 1898, with the exception of Itōhan shōkai and Ogura shōkai, had better chances of surviving. Those that were formed later, 1900 to 1903, tended to dissolve after only a short period of operation. Most of the larger companies tended to be incorporated rather than partnerships or companies operated by individuals. This

TABLE 9
Japanese Emigration Companies, 1891–1908

Company	*Dates of Operation*	*Number of Emigrants Sent Abroad*
Morioka Makoto	1894–1921	18,313
Kaigai tokō kabushikigaisha	1894–1907	13,975
Tairiku shokumin gōshigaisha	1903–1908	13,133
Kumamoto imin gōshigaisha	1898–1907	12,020
Tōyō imin gōshigaisha	1897–1917	9,721
Nippon imin gōshigaisha	1896–1908	7,992
Tokio imin gōshigaisha	1896–1908	7,731
Nippon shokumin kabushikigaisha	1897–1906	6,985
Teikoku shokumin gōshigaisha	1898–1907	5,779
Kōsei imin kabushikigaisha	1897–1903	3,746
Ogura (Kokura) shōkai	1894–1896	3,431
San'yō imin gōshigaisha	1902–1908	3,174
Chūgoku imin gōshigaisha	1900–1908	3,120
Kobe tokō gōshigaisha	1894–1908	2,993
Hiroshima imin gōshigaisha	1901–1908	2,893
Meiji shokumin gōshigaisha	1906–1909	2,879
Bōchō imin gōshigaisha	1902–1909	2,807
Bansei imin gōshigaisha	1903–1908	2,655
Gōshigaisha sanmaru shōkai	1902–1908	2,628
Kōkoku shokumin kabushikigaisha	1904–1908	2,470
Morishima Hisao	1902–1907	2,369
Takemura Yoemon	1906–1914	2,216
Takaki (Takagi) Karoku	1902–1908	2,072
Kaneo Masatoshi	1902–1908	2,031
Sendai imin gōshigaisha	1902–1907	1,777
Omi Masataka	1902–1907	1,622
Nankai imin gōshigaisha	1902–1907	1,602
Kyushu imin kabushikigaisha	1897–1908	1,527
Kansai imin gōshigaisha	1903–1909	1,461
Suō imin gōshigaisha	1903–1908	1,374
Nippon Yoshisa imin gōshigaisha	1891–1908	920
Murayama Kojirō	1902–1907	918
Tōhoku imin gōshigaisha	1902–1903	885
Takada Heibē	1901–1903	856
Chūō imingaisha	1902–1903	609
Ōno Den'ei	1902–1905	586
Itōhan shōkai	1894	510
Chūgai shokumin gōshigaisha	1902–1903	406
Taiheiyō shokumingaisha	1902–1903	405

TABLE 9
(Continued)

Company	*Dates of Operation*	*Number of Emigrants Sent Abroad*
Mitsunaga Kyūta	1903–1904	350
Tosa imin kabushikigaisha	1903	302
Yamamoto Eiichirō	1899–1900	178
Tōyō shokumin gōmeigaisha	1899–1900	126
Murayama Yasutoshi (Yasuhisa)	1900	108
Kusakabe Shōichi	1900	61
Fukuda Seinosuke	1900–1902	57
Taniguchi Kaichi	1900	33
Meiji imin gōshigaisha	1908	21
Taiheiyō imin gōshigaisha	1900	2
Kaigai shokumin gōshigaisha	1894	?
Meiji imingaisha	1894	?

Sources: Kodama Masaaki, "Imingaisha no jittai," p. 482; Ishikawa, "Imingaisha," pp. 25–26; Gaimushō tsūshōkyoku, *Ryoken kafusū,* pp. 142–181; and other *JFMAD* files.

was also true of Morioka Makoto which became Morioka imin gōmeigaisha in 1912 and Morioka imin kabushikigaisha in 1918.[26]

Emigration to Hawaii during this period had three peaks as can be seen in Table 10. The increases in emigration were not related to the rise in the number of companies, because the latter occurred during the 1894 to 1908 years. In other words, events *outside* the sphere of the companies affected the number of Japanese going to Hawaii. In 1898 and 1899 the number of workers rose immediately after it was announced that Hawaii would become a territory of the United States. Sugar planters tried to sign up as many people as possible before 1900 because labor contracts would be invalidated by American law.[27]

The sharp drop in the number of emigrants in 1900 and 1901 was the unfortunate result of the Hawaiian government's attempt to halt a bubonic plague epidemic on 20 January 1900. A section of Honolulu was set afire and the flames quickly spread and destroyed a large part of the city where many Japanese and Chinese had been living. Because of this incident, Japanese officials suspended emigration to Hawaii from 20 January 1900 to August of the following year.[28] Thus another peak came in 1902 after the year-and-a-half suspension.

TABLE 10
Emigrants Going to Hawaii, 1894–1908

Year	*Number of Companies*	*Company Emigrants*	*Independent Emigrants*	*Total*
1894	2	1,329	?	4,036[a]
1895	3	2,416	?	2,445
1896	5	6,217	?	9,486
1897	10	3,286	?	5,913
1898	9	10,145	2,807	12,952
1899	12	19,532	3,441	22,973
1900	18	709	820	1,529
1901	12	3,061	t75	3,136
1902	29	14,022	468	14,490
1903	36	8,493	598	9,091
1904	30	8,911	532	9,443
1905	29	10,355	458	10,813
1906	30	24,887	865	25,752
1907	30	10,810	3,587	14,397
1908	23	450	3,005	3,455
Totals		124,623	16,656	149,911

Sources: Compiled from Gaimushō tsūshōkyoku, *Ryoken kafusū,* pp. 142–181; Kokusai kyōryoku jigyōdan, *Ijū tōkei,* pp. 66–67; and Gaimushō ryōji ijūbu, *Hyakunen,* pp. 42–43.
[a]This figure includes 1,491 government-sponsored emigrants.

The period after 1902 saw emigration restricted by the Japanese authorities. The final peak period was 1905 to 1907. Workers tried to enter the United States before additional restrictions would be placed on immigration, and indeed the Gentlemen's Agreement of 1908, which not only banned the movement of Japanese from Hawaii to the mainland United States but also persuaded Tokyo officials to stop issuing passports to "laborers" who wanted to work in America, was adopted.

As was noted earlier, in addition to the fifty-one companies that sent emigrants overseas, fifteen others obtained permission from the foreign ministry but failed before they sent anyone abroad. According to the Emigrant Protection Law, the problem was that "the permission to become an Imin Toriatsukainin shall be invalidated by failure to commence business not later than six months from the date at which such permission was granted."[29] It was difficult for a new company to set up operations and send workers overseas in less than six months because negotiations had to be carried out with plantation agents in Hawaii, boardinghouses in Yokohama, shipping companies, and local officials; agents had to be hired; and recruitment had to take place. Thus a number of companies and individuals had their permissions to operate revoked by the ministry because they failed to meet the six-month deadline (see Appendix 9).[30]

There were several individuals and small companies in operation about which little is known. They include Yokohama imin gōshigaisha, Senda Ichijūrō, Hiruma Kuninosuke, Morita Toshisaku, and Yamaguchi Yūya.[31] They at times worked as agents for other companies and also on their own trying to recruit emigrants.

A final group of individuals had their applications as emigration agents denied by the foreign ministry (see Appendix 10). They were turned down for various reasons, but most often it was because the ministry felt the particular individual or company did not have enough working capital. Also, officials discouraged a number of individuals from operating businesses even though they had previously worked for other emigration companies, because officials saw a sudden rise in the number of companies after 1900. Some individuals were turned down because they had histories of business failures; others, recognizing what was happening, withdrew their applications for "further study."

The results were that only four companies sent more than 10,000 emigrants between 1891 and 1910; twenty-six companies shipped between 1,000 and 10,000 workers; fourteen, between 100 and 1,000 others; seven probably shipped less than 100 each; and fifteen folded without sending anyone overseas. Fourteen companies never even got started. Clearly it was difficult for many of the companies to survive let alone make a profit in this business.

The history of the emigration business is filled with mergers, new business affiliations, and bankruptcies. Trying desperately to survive, companies changed their names, hired employees of competitors, and sought new capital.

In 1903 thirty-six companies were able to make a profit and survive. By 1909 only five companies were in existence.[32] Those that survived had gone through internal changes or had merged with other companies. Morioka Makoto, for instance, went from being a small independent company to an unlimited partnership to a joint-stock limited partnership, all in order to attract new capital. This particular company was also affiliated with Bansei seimei hokengaisha, an insurance company that offered policies to emigrants. Morioka himself also served as the head of Keihin ginkō, a bank that serviced an emigrant clientele.

The large Tairiku shokumin gōshigaisha (known in Hawaii as Trans-oceanic Migration Company) is an example of how several small companies could join forces to compete with their larger, more financially stable rivals. It had been established out of the remnants of six small companies: Tosa imin kabushikigaisha, Chūgai shokumin gōshigaisha, Taiheiyō shokumingaisha, Takada Heibē, Kōsei imin kabushikigaisha, and Tōhoku imin gōshigaisha.[33] The instigators of this move were the former employees of Chūō imingaisha who, after leaving the company, came back with enough capital to take over the operation from the original owners. By combining the assets and personnel of the seven small companies, they hoped to be competitive in the recruiting game and in obtaining lucrative labor contracts from overseas. The company prospered only for six years; nonetheless it stands as a reminder of the lengths people went to in order to survive in this competitive business.

Again, of the companies that had survived, five in particular played an important role in the history of the Japanese immigrants in Hawaii. These were Morioka Makoto (which operated overseas as Morioka Immigration Company), Japanese Emigration Company of Hiroshima, Kumamoto imin gōshigaisha (Kumamoto Emigration Company), Japan Emigration Company, and finally Tokio Immigration Company.[34] They were known among the Japanese in Hawaii as the "big five" emigration companies.[35]

Most of what we know now about the companies, the people who worked for them, and their role in the larger emigration process, comes from reports that private companies had to send to government officials and that were filed with the foreign ministry. From the information in these documents, it is possible to put together a picture of these companies and their activities.

The companies were first required to give their official names. As the Morioka Makoto example illustrates, a large number of them underwent internal changes, as well as merged with outside firms and consequently changed their names. In a number of cases, an individual would file the original application under his own name, but when the business prospered, incorporation papers had to be signed and the designation of the business changed. The original application of Kumamoto Emigration Company, for example, lists as its official name Koyama Yūtarō, the name of the head of the company. The change took place two years after the company started operations. Other cases include Takemura Yoemon, reorganized later as Takemura shokumin shōkan, and Tōyō imin gōshigaisha, which was previously known as Kumamoto imin kabushikigaisha. The situation was complicated by the fact that emigrants often used incorrect names in referring to certain companies. For example, Kaigai tokō kabushikigaisha was known to many people in Hawaii as Hiroshima imingaisha.[36]

In their applications, companies had to list the countries to which they wished to send workers. Although almost all included Hawaii on their lists, not all of them succeeded in shipping anyone there. However, the lists of emigrants and their destinations show that most of the larger companies did succeed. Of the twenty most successful companies (see Table 9), only Kōsei imin kabushikigaisha, Meiji shokumin gōshigaisha, and Kōkoku shokumin kabushikigaisha failed in this effort. Of the other companies that sent more than one thousand emigrants in the 1898–1910 period, only Takemura Yoemon and Suō imin gōshigaisha failed to send anyone to Hawaii, although they had intended to do so. In all, no more than twenty-six companies shipped workers to the islands.

One of the more interesting aspects of the emigration companies are the people who started these ventures. Applications which included personal histories of the individuals who asked for permission to operate and of investors show that a number of companies were started by local businessmen who lived in the same area.

Chūgoku imin gōshigaisha, which operated out of Hiroshima city, began with seven investors, all of whom were from Saeki county in that prefecture. Each of the seven contributed between 7,000 and 7,500 yen. San'yō imin gōshigaisha obtained financial backing from six Hiroshima businessmen. Meiji imin gōshigaisha was started by a group of seven men from Kumamoto prefecture. When Bōchō imin gōshigaisha was established in 1902, its investors all came from the Iwakuni area of Yamaguchi prefecture. They included a doctor, a tailor, a shipping company employee, a former insurance salesman, two merchants, and three local politicians. Similarly Tosa imin kabushikigaisha was organized by eight men—two pawnshop owners, a sake brewer, a money lender, two merchants, a medicine salesman, and a man who sold gun powder—all of whom lived in Kōchi prefecture. Twenty-two investors who put up the money to start Transoceanic Migration Company were mostly from eastern Japan. The largest amount invested in this case was 246,000 yen by Hinata Takeshi (also known as Terutake), who became the vice-president of the new company. Yokota Sennosuke, who became a director, invested 120,000 yen.[37] Another example is Bansei imin gōshigaisha, which, with the retirement of the company head, was taken over by the members of the Kumamoto branch office in 1906.[38] The branch office members invested money in the company, moved the head office from Hiroshima to Fukuoka, and ran the company entirely with Kumamoto personnel.

Some companies were set up by investors from different prefectures but were controlled by those from one area. Kōkoku shokumin kabushikigaisha had been organized by seven investors from Tokyo, four from Yamanashi prefecture, and one from Nagoya.[39] Later those from Yamanashi dropped out, and the company was run by the Tokyo members.

A larger than average number of those who started or invested in these companies were descendants of former warrior families *(shizoku).* Many others had a business background or had experience in local politics.[40] Six of the seven men who put money in the establishment of Meiji shokumin gōshigaisha were from shizoku families.[41] Katō Heishirō, a former politician who twice set up Nippon shokumin kabushikigaisha (also as Nippon Colonization Company), and Takeuchi Tadashi, the former newspaperman who founded Teikoku shokumin gōshigaisha were shizoku.[42] Others include Mizuno Ryū of Kōkoku shokumin kabushikigaisha, Ōno Den'ei of the company of the same name, Yotsumoto Manji of Tōyō shokumin gōmeigaisha (Oriental Colonization Company), and Fukuda Seisaburō (also as Seinosuke) of the company of the same name.[43] Kyushu imin kabushikigaisha was established in March of 1897 by members of the Kumamoto kokkentō, a small nationalistic group with their own views on overseas colonization.[44]

Ara Tokujirō, who started Tōhoku imin gōshigaisha in 1902, was a bureaucrat before he entered the emigration business, as was Ōno Den'ei. Asō Sakae (?) of San'yō imin gōshigaisha was one of several individuals who had served as a prefectural assembly member before he entered this field. Two of the original investors in the establishment of Tokio imin gōshigaisha, Kaiyama Daizetsu and Toyozuna (?) Kunizaburō, had previous political experience, Kaiyama on the village level and Toyozuna on the prefectural level.[45]

Yoshikawa Taijirō was the head of a large shipping company when he helped establish the first emigration company, Nippon Yoshisa imin gōshigaisha, in 1891. Morishima Hisao, who began the company bearing his name, had previously worked for another emigration company and for a bank. The head of Japanese Emigration Company of Hiroshima, Satō Iwao, was a banker before he started that company. A typical example of the type of individual who became involved in overseas emigration was Sakuma Teiichi, who helped organize Nippon Yoshisa imin gōshigaisha as well as Tōyō imin gōshigaisha.[46] He had a varied career as a printer, a cardboard box manufacturer, a book salesman, and a local politician.

Former elected officials or those with any political experience were particularly important to have on staff when a company was beginning operations.[47] These individuals could work within the network of the prefectural bureaucracy and also work with county, town, and village officials, and in this way make it easier and quicker to process the emigrants the company had signed up.

The money invested in emigration company ventures came from two sources. The first was the shizoku investors who had acquired their wealth during the Tokugawa period and represented traditional "old capital." The second source were businessmen and former politicians who had made their money after the Meiji Restoration and represented the "new capital," which was growing increasingly more important. These investors of course provided funds for other new business and industrial ventures. While neither group was able to dominate the other, ultimately the companies that sent the most emigrants abroad were those that relied on non-shizoku capital and that were started by non-shizoku businessmen.

In 1894, when Morioka Immigration Company was established, it had only 8,000 yen available for company expenses.[48] At that time, company officials estimated that 2,000 yen would be used to recruit about one thousand workers (they hoped to recover that amount later by collecting two yen from each person). Seven hundred yen was earmarked for setting up branch offices, with any remainder going toward running the business. One thousand yen was to be used to maintain the main office, 3,300 yen to keep a representative in Hawaii, and 1,000 yen for miscellaneous expenses.

Company applications had to include a list of the places where they intended to send emigrants. Some of the companies tried to concentrate on only one or two countries. Both Transoceanic Migration Company and Kumamoto Emigration Company expected to send workers to only Hawaii and Mexico.[49] Tōyō imin gōshigaisha was more ambitious and listed, in addition to Hawaii, New Caledonia, Peru, Brazil, Mexico, Australia, New Hebrides, and other Pacific islands.[50] Some mentioned the Philippines, Africa, Canada, the United States, Central America, Thailand, Russia, China, Korea, Cuba, the Malay peninsula, Argentina, and other South American countries. However, in general very few managed to send people to more than one or two places. Most were willing to follow the examples set by their predecessors and ship emigrants to countries already willing to accept Japanese workers, rather than explore new markets. The companies set up immediately after the passage of the Emigrant Protection Law generally favored Hawaii, the United States, and Canada. It was only after immigration restrictions were placed on Japanese entering these areas that some companies began to look elsewhere, particularly Latin America and the South Pacific region.

Emigration companies were forced to deposit a security of 10,000 yen with the government, but some deposited more than the minimum to prove their financial stability. For example, Japanese Emigration Company of Hiroshima deposited 40,000 yen in 1894.[51] Several others deposited between 13,000 and 30,000 yen each.

The Japanese government also required that companies reveal the amount of initial capital they had available. Officials worried that those lacking sufficient funds would not be able to operate properly until their businesses showed profits. Companies that were established in the early years had small amounts of capital, yet several somehow managed to survive. Morioka Immigration Company had assets of only 8,000 yen in 1894, but the company was worth 500,000 yen by 1902.[52] Other large companies started with capital ranging from 20,000 to 60,000 yen. When Transoceanic Migration Company was organized in 1903, investors put 1,000,000 yen into it, the largest amount on record.[53] However, a large amount of investment capital was no guarantee that a company would succeed and indeed despite its large amount of assets, this company managed to stay in operation for only six years. Of those ventures that failed to send emigrants during their first six months of operation, each had accumulated an average of more than 45,000 yen worth of assets but all to no avail.[54]

Records that were kept by these companies and sent to the foreign ministry show that small companies with only a few agents tended to recruit in only one or two prefectures. Taiheiyō imin gōshigaisha looked for workers only in Hiroshima before it joined Kusakabe

Shōichi in 1900. Even after the merger, the first of several moves to save the company, its recruiters went only to Wakayama. Others like Meiji imin gōshigaisha and Taniguchi Kaichi also concentrated on but one prefecture.[55] The most active companies often sent their agents to more than twenty prefectures, trying to get as many people signed up as possible.

Before 1894 there were a few recruiters who worked with officials to send workers to Hawaii. However, the emigration company, as an actor on this the Japanese stage, was the only one that was not present during the government-sponsored emigration period.

The Emigration Company Agents

In order to run their businesses and to recruit workers, emigration companies generally hired, on both a temporary and permanent basis, three types of employees: personnel to work in company offices, agents to represent them abroad, and recruiters to work in the rural areas of Japan.[56] The staffs of the main offices handled the paperwork for permits, passports, and official certificates the Japanese emigrants required; they dealt generally, then, with recruits who had already signed contracts. One method they used to attract people was the use of printed matter. For example, at times posters advertising travel to Hawaii appeared in public places. One such notice read, "Seeking several hundred workers to go to Hawaii! Those interested must apply by. . . ."[57] The second type—the agent—did not recruit but, as his company's representative in areas where it sent workers, was responsible for the welfare of these workers.

The recruiters were of two types. One type was mobile and would go from village to village to sign up workers. Often this type would be required to have previous experience with emigration matters or to have traveled abroad. The other type was already established in the village targeted for recruiting as a local official, perhaps an important landowner, or a village headman.[58] He would do, in other words, little active recruiting and instead work out of a branch office, which may have consisted of no more than a desk in a small room.

Branch offices gave a company an advantage over a competitor in the same area and so companies like San'yō imin gōshigaisha established eighteen local offices throughout southwestern Japan. Being a smaller organization, Kaneo Masatoshi could recruit in only five prefectures, while Nippon Colonization Company, based in Yokohama, had branches in twenty-eight different prefectures. In Hiroshima alone, the latter opened forty-nine offices. Suō imin gōshigaisha received government permission to set up thirty-one branches, while Transoceanic Migration Company had at least that many in Japan, in addition to ones in Mexico and the Philippines.[59]

These offices were placed in strategic areas, that is, areas that gave the agents the best chances for success. One example is Ehime prefecture, on the island of Shikoku. Ehime had not until then sent a large number of workers overseas, as compared to such places as Hiroshima, Yamaguchi, or Kumamoto. Nevertheless beginning in 1898 several private companies began recruiting there.[60] These included Transoceanic Migration Company, Japanese Emigration Company of Hiroshima, Takemura Yoemon, Kobe Immigration Company, and Kansai imin gōshigaisha (Kansai Immigration Company). Together they set up a total of thirteen branch offices in Ehime in the early 1900s. Three of them placed offices in the city of Matsuyama, Ehime's capital. Other branch offices tended to be situated in areas near the coast, as in the case of the three offices of Kansai Immigration Company which were located in areas along the western coast of the prefecture facing the island of Kyushu. The only branch office of Kobe Immigration Company was on the northern coast bordering the Inland Sea. Those of the other companies were located in similar areas along the coastline rather than inland, the reason for this being that many residents of these coastal areas had experience with sea travel and might therefore be persuaded to endure the long journey to Hawaii. Establishing offices in these select areas also reduced company costs and may have made recruiting easier for agents.

Those people who lived near the branch office signed up there. The recruiter would then send the appropriate papers to the prefectural authorities and to the company's main office. Occasionally this type of agent took short trips to villages near his office to sign up emigrants, but he always tried to remain within his own sphere of influence.

The agent was also available to perform a number of services for the workers after they left Japan. For example, he helped distribute to the appropriate families the remittances sent through the company from abroad.[61] He stayed in contact with workers' families if they were in his area and passed along relevant news to them. Fulfillment of these duties, as well as the initial recruitment, earned the agent commissions from the companies. Although they varied in amount, depending on where the workers were being sent and in what time period, commissions seemed to average about 1 to 2 yen per emigrant recruited. It was to a company's benefit to hire agents who had previously done this type of work or who had experience overseas. The personal histories of applicants hired by companies provide ample evidence that men experienced in this way were sought. For example, thirteen agents were hired by Oriental Colonization Company: the first had worked for Japan Emigration Company, one agent had lived in Chicago, another had gone to Australia as an emigrant, and still another had studied English in order to work as a company representative in California.[62] Because Transoceanic Migration Company was organized by members of six small companies, it found it easy to rehire former employees. Its first thirteen agents were experienced recruiters, with one having worked in Hawaii and another having been to the Philippines. On a smaller scale, Meiji imin gōshigaisha, which sent a total of twenty-one workers overseas, hired only two agents to recruit in Kumamoto prefecture.[63] One had worked for Murayama Kojirō; the other had recruited for Morishima Hisao.

While the smaller companies could not afford to hire more than four or five recruiters, others had enough money to employ a larger number. By having many recruiters, a company assured itself of being able to sign up more people—which meant additional commissions. This in turn meant the company could then afford to hire more agents. Imperial Emigration Company hired at least thirty-seven, and they operated out of a total of five branch offices.[64] Morioka Immigration Company employed seventy-three agents during its long history, and Transoceanic Migration Company had at least sixty-three agents on its payroll.[65]

These agents had varied backgrounds but the one interesting characteristic common to many of them was their shizoku status. Of the thirty-seven agents hired by Imperial Emigration Company, seventeen were shizoku. Kumamoto Emigration Company's first sixteen agents included five who claimed this status. Eleven out of the twenty-seven employed by Tōyō imin gōshigaisha between 15 April 1904 and 1 November 1907 were of shizoku status. Twenty-three of the seventy-three hired by Morioka Immigration Company were shizoku, while sixteen Transoceanic Migration Company agents claimed the same in their applications. Kobe Immigration Company hired twenty-six agents and eleven claimed to be of shizoku descent.[66] This was a very high percentage, much higher than what was true for the general population: emigrant lists reveal no more than one in perhaps two or three hundred persons claiming this status.

There were several reasons for the large number of shizoku among agents. Descendants of shizoku were viewed, even at this time, as "men of status," particularly in more conservative rural areas. This gave them an advantage in persuading farmers about the benefits of overseas emigration. Many shizoku of this period probably had more money than the average farmer, not to the extent that they could start a small business but enough so that most were not being forced for economic reasons to emigrate from Japan.[67]

Agents tended to move from one company to another, and a number of them worked for several at the same time. Some were stationed in foreign countries. The smaller companies, that is, those with limited capital, found sending an agent to represent them in Hawaii uneconomical and impractical. Were twenty-six agents necessary to look after the companies' business matters and interests in Hawaii? They chose to hire agents who were already in Honolulu, and several of them often shared the cost of maintaining a representative there. Tasaka Yōkichi, for instance, represented thirteen companies; Sawano Chūzō worked for twelve; and Sukie Ryōji was employed by ten.[68] Both Tasaka and Sawano were later prevented from working for others by the foreign ministry, which felt that both men were working for too many companies at the same time and therefore could not do an adequate job handling so many clients.The foreign ministry officials also turned down a number of agents, most often because they were already on record as being employed by other emigration companies. Gōshigaisha sanmaru shōkai had two of its ten applicants turned down. Taiheiyō shokumingaisha, Chūgai shokumin gōshigaisha, and Mitsunaga Kyūta all had one of their first eight applicants denied permission to work.[69]

In some areas of Japan over half the agents were employed by several companies. In Hiroshima prefecture, for example, Mugita Saizaburō served as a director for Japanese Emigration Company of Hiroshima while he also recruited for Chūgoku imin gōshigaisha, Kaneo Masatoshi, Omi Masataka, Bōchō imin gōshigaisha, and Transoceanic Migration Company.[70] Later, officials did not allow agents to work for more than five companies at a time.

There were several different recruitment methods used during this period. One type can be seen by following the activities of Kumamoto Emigration Company in Fukuoka prefecture in 1899.[71] Map 3 shows the recruiting route as described by emigrant lists for this company. Tadami and the other villages around the town of Fukushima were located in Yame county in the southern part of the prefecture.[72] Sixteen men, all from the village of Tadami, signed up. Next, sixteen residents of the village of Kamihirokawa, about 2.44 miles north of Tadami, agreed to contracts with the same company.[73] Lastly, Kasawara, 6.88 miles east of Tadami, had thirteen of its villagers on the lists. This method of recruitment could have been one of two types. If an agent went to these villages and signed up people himself, he would have been involved in active recruiting. Active recruiting involved going from house to house, village to village in rural areas.[74] This method of recruiting started years before the emigration companies were established; yet it was after 1894 that this method of signing up workers reached its peak.

If the agent was stationed at a branch office, possibly in the town of Fukushima, those wanting to go overseas went to sign up at his office. The map shows where each of the three villages were in relation to the town of Fukushima, as well as to the major roads in the district. Although the emigrants may have indeed come in groups to town, it is more likely that the agent made three short trips to the countryside. The agent probably signed up potential emigrants one village at a time and returned to Fukushima after each trip.

Village-to-village recruiting seems more probable when one looks at the patterns revealed in the same lists. In the same area in Fukuoka prefecture, an agent went from village to village seeking emigrants as can be seen in the map. He went first to the village of Nagamine to sign up three individuals. He then went along a major road passing through the town of Fukushima and turned east for almost 2.5 miles and registered eight more in Tadami. He then took a short trip north to the village of Kamihirokawa for eight workers, to Nakahirokawa for three more, and finally to Shimohirokawa for two others before he returned to Fukushima. All of the villages were within five miles of one another and could easily have been reached in a day.

A look at recruitment in Hiroshima prefecture in 1898 reveals other interesting case studies.[75] In particular, there was a group of emigrants who received permission to leave Japan on 10 December of that year and departed together on 17 December aboard the *Nippon Maru* from an area near the city of Hiroshima. As is shown in Map 4, the first fourteen members of this group came from the village of Niojima (at times referred to as Nihotō), about 2.5 miles southeast of Hiroshima

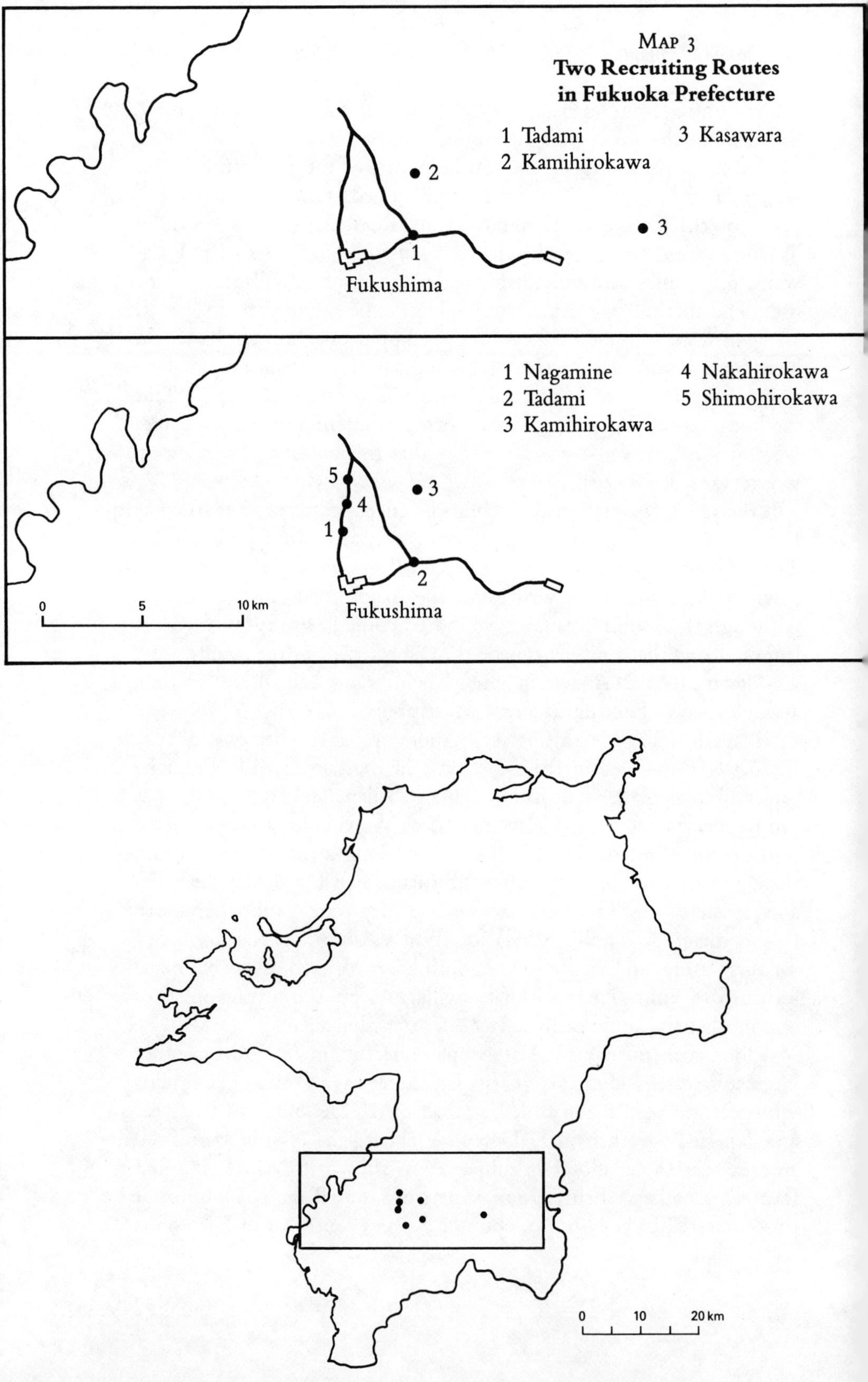

MAP 3

Two Recruiting Routes in Fukuoka Prefecture

1 Tadami
2 Kamihirokawa
3 Kasawara

Fukushima

1 Nagamine
2 Tadami
3 Kamihirokawa
4 Nakahirokawa
5 Shimohirokawa

0 5 10 km

Fukushima

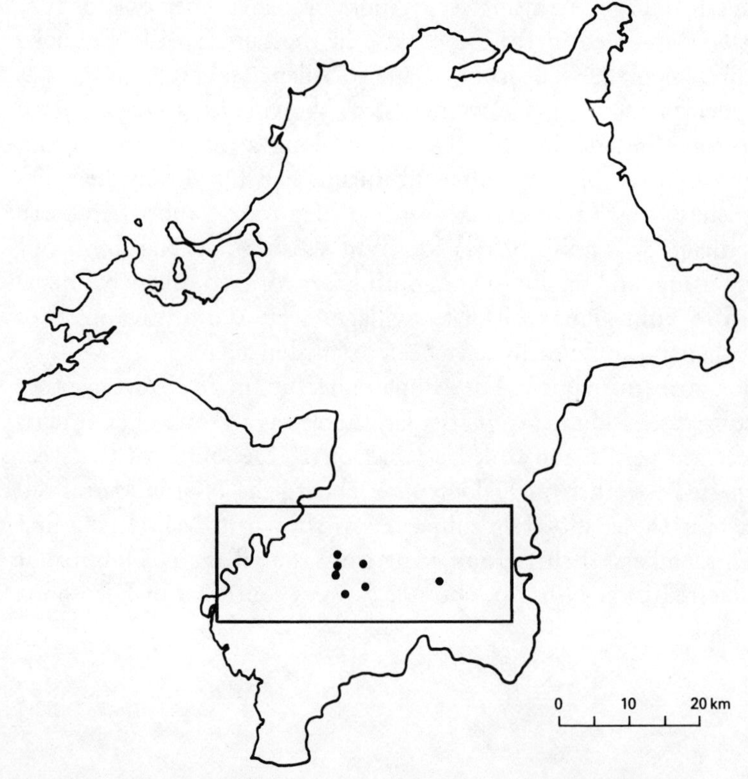

City. The next seven were residents of Yaga, just six miles north. Another emigrant signed up from the village of Fuchu, 1.2 miles east of Yaga. An agent probably recruited these men in their villages. There is a break in the list, where the names of individuals from an area west of Hiroshima City appear. The first three were from the village of Furuta, just west of Hiroshima and the fourth from Kouchi, some six miles further west. It is extremely unlikely that these emigrants went to the agent's office in Hiroshima and signed up in groups, first the group from east of the city and then the group from west of it. It is more reasonable to assume that recruiters went out into the countryside to seek them.

An agent's arrival in a village or town was usually preceded by advertising in the form of public notices.[76] To stimulate interest in emigration, details about the proposed labor contracts and the conditions in the country of settlement were included in these notices which were posted by people hired by the emigration company agent for that area. In 1895 the Hiroshima-based agent of Nippon Yoshisa imin gōshigaisha asked for 110 yen to hire people in 110 towns and villages to help recruit the first shipment of workers bound for Queensland sugar plantations in Australia. Agents conducted preliminary examinations of potential emigrants at temples, theaters, or other public gathering places in the area. In this specific case, those who were selected to go abroad were examined again in Hiroshima City by representatives of the Australian plantation company, the emigration company, and a doctor.

When recruitment took place at a branch office no more than two or three names of individuals from the same village would appear on the lists at a time. If represented on a map, the pattern would be like spokes of a wheel with the office in the center. This pattern would have no relation to the major roads in the area. Examples of this can be found in Kumamoto Emigration Company's activities in Wakayama prefecture in October of 1899.[77] In this case, individuals from three different counties in the prefecture—Kaiso, Arita, and Naka—were signed up. Workers from the same village signed up at different times indicating recruiting was not village to village. Another example was the 1899 recruiting effort made in the same prefecture by Imperial Emigration Company.[78]

There was a third method of recruitment which was a combination of village-to-village and branch-office recruiting. In this case, an agent

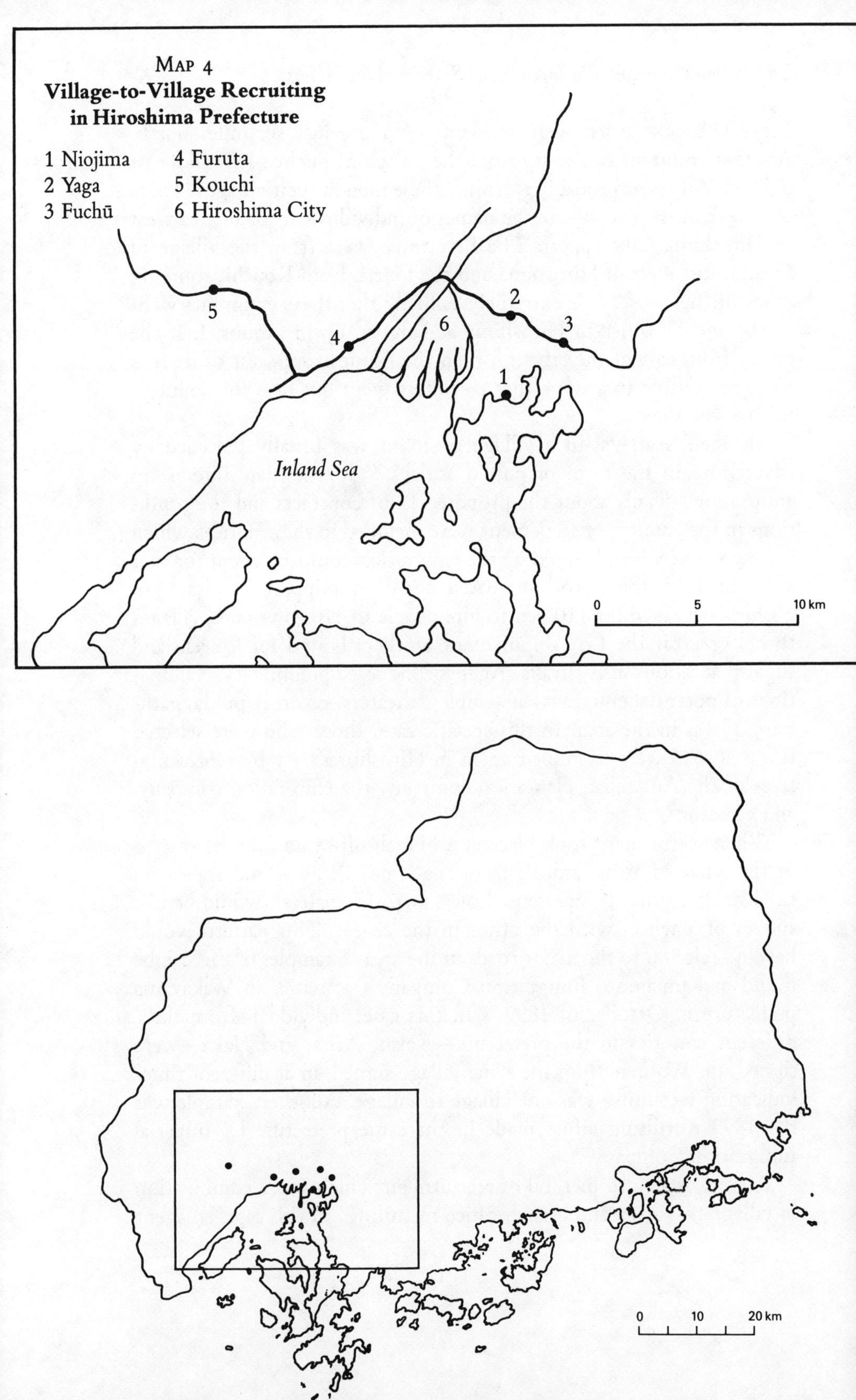
MAP 4
Village-to-Village Recruiting in Hiroshima Prefecture
1 Niojima
2 Yaga
3 Fuchū
4 Furuta
5 Kouchi
6 Hiroshima City
5
4
6
2
3
1
Inland Sea
0
5
10 km
0
10
20 km

operated out of an office and also made regular recruiting trips to villages in the immediate area. Emigrant lists indicate that this was the most popular method during this period.

There were thus three types of recruitment: village-to-village, branch-office, and a combination of both. The villages where recruiting took place can also be divided into three types. The first type was a village already known to the agent who recruited there because he was either from that particular region or heard from friends or relatives that potential emigrants were available there. The second type of village requested information about working overseas from emigration companies that had advertised in the villages. In this case, the company would send its closest available agent to the village. The third type was the "emigrant village," which had a history of sending residents overseas during an earlier period.[79]

In the end, the individuals who worked as company agents decided which villages to recruit in and which workers to sign up. Thus agents had influence over, among other things, which regions would be targeted for large-scale emigration. As an employee of Nippon Yoshisa gōshigaisha and Tōyō imin gōshigaisha, Doi Tsumoru, a village headman in Hiroshima prefecture, showed how important an agent's role was.[80] Because of his extraordinary efforts, 62 percent of the total number that left Hiroshima for Australia were from his home district of Kamo county. Of the thirty-one men from Kamo, all but three were from the western half of the county, the area in which Doi lived.

The Japanese Emigrants

The four actors described above had to persuade a large group of farmers, fishermen, and laborers to leave home to work in Hawaii. Despite the reality economic conditions in Japan painted, potential emigrants had to believe economic success was possible—but overseas.

Wages in Japan stayed fairly consistent throughout the years of major emigration to Hawaii.[81] Male agricultural day laborers who made 30 sen daily in 1900 earned 39 sen in 1908. Those who raised silk worms made 31 and 42 sen, for the respective years. Women doing day work in agriculture were paid 19 sen in 1900 and 23 sen eight years later.

Statistics on wages earned by silk mill workers during the 1897–

1908 period show that even these semi-skilled laborers earned much less than plantation workers in Hawaii, who made $15 a month.[82] Silk mill workers made on a national average 18.2 sen a day in 1897, or about 5.46 yen a month (at the time less than $3). By 1908 these workers made 24.5 sen a day, or about 7.35 yen a month.

A survey of wages for workers in Aki county of Hiroshima between 1886 and 1898, another peak period for emigration, also shows relatively little change over these thirteen years.[83] On the average, male farmers in this district earned 1.5 yen a month in 1886 and the same amount seven years later; at the beginning of the emigration company period (1894), they made only 1.8 yen a month. Sake brewery workers earning 15 sen a day in 1886 saw their daily wages rise to only 20 sen by 1893. While stonemasons, who made 22 sen a day in 1886, earned only 3 sen more seven years later, carpenters saw their wages drop from an average of 22 sen a day to 20 sen by 1893.

Day workers in Hiroshima prefecture who were making 36 sen daily in 1900 earned 48 sen in 1907.[84] While carpenters saw their wages increase 9 sen from 56 sen during this seven-year period, silk reeling operators (women) rose only 2 sen from 23 sen and metal workers saw their wages drop from 60 sen to 57 sen by 1907.

Wages were not the only indicator that the economic situation in the Japanese countryside had not changed significantly since the beginning of the government-sponsored period. In fact the amount of agricultural land under tenancy increased from 36.35 percent during the 1883–1884 years to 40 percent by 1892, and to 45.4 percent by 1903.[85]

Japanese learned about emigration from recruiting agents and through advertising campaigns, both of which played important roles in influencing them. They were also influenced by those who had traveled to Hawaii during the government-sponsored emigration period. Stories of success, of making enough money to buy land, raised the hopes of many tenant farmers. Nishimoto Otoichi related the following experience: "My birthplace in 1868 a village of only 60 houses—yet sent an average of two from each household to America, and those emigrants upon finding work sent back an average 100 yen per household. We, the youth of the village, thought: 'In America there must be trees which bear money.' "[86]

Okada Banzo wanted to go overseas and return with at least 500 yen because, as he wrote, "the amount people wanted to save was different . . . but in my home town in Tokushima prefecture, if a man had more than 500 yen it was enough to marry into a propertied family as an adopted son."[87] When 432 individuals from one region of the Wakayama prefecture were asked in a survey what attracted them to work overseas, 25 percent said, "seeing neighbors who emigrated, returning in affluent circumstances."[88] Nineteen percent mentioned the "prevailing tendency in the village to emigrate," and 11 percent were "exhorted by emigrants residing abroad and [those who returned]."

People were also influenced by emigration guidebooks to Hawaii and America published around the turn of the century.[89] For those thinking of going to Hawaii, several were available: Yōbi Tenkō's (?) *Hawai kikō,* Yamagishi Takashi's *Beikoku Hawai tokō mondō,* Mitsunaga Akira's *Konnichi no Hawai,* and Kimura Yoshigorō and Inoue Tatefumi's *Saikin seisaku Hawai tokō annai.*[90] Published guidebooks about America included sections on working conditions and wages in Hawaii. In particular, Katayama Sen's *To-Bei annai* was popular and was reissued in six editions.[91]

These guidebooks were designed to do two things: encourage more Japanese to go abroad and to simplify the emigration and immigration processes. Most of them were published between 1902 and 1904, when emigration was at its peak. A major theme in these books is that the opportunity to better oneself lies in jobs overseas. The guidebooks attempted to help simplify the immigration process by, for example, offering hints on how to handle interviews with foreign immigration officials and customs inspectors.[92] They offered suggestions about what types of clothes and goods emigrants needed going abroad and the amount of money emigrants should carry with them.[93] Most guidebooks also included simple English lessons.

Most of those who were sent to Hawaii by emigration companies were men. They made up over 84 percent of the total number who went (see Table 11).[94] The figure met the sugar planters' demand that women be kept at or below 25 percent of the total.[95] As is apparent in the table, there was a high percentage of men even after Japanese workers were released from their contracts in 1900.

Many of these emigrants were also young. Between 1898 and 1908, 74 percent of them were below the age of thirty.[96] The Japanese government and emigration companies encouraged those under the age of thirty to emigrate. In a labor proposition issued on 12 May 1898, Tokio Immigration Company announced its intention to provide Hawaii with laborers: "This company proposes to furnish a superior class of Japanese laborers, the same to be faithful farmers; each laborer to be insured by the Japanese Insurance Company before leaving Japan and shall be able-bodied and sound men, between the age[s] of 20 and 40 . . . .[97]

However, emigrant lists show that teenagers were allowed to work overseas as well. A random check of Yamaguchi prefecture workers sent by the Japan Emigration Company of Hiroshima in 1898 shows that twenty-seven of the sixty-one males were nineteen years old at the time of departure.[98] There is no evidence there was a regulation concerning a maximum age before 15 August 1896, when an age limit of fifty was placed on overseas workers.[99]

Most of these young men were farmers and members of the *heimin* (commoner) class like earlier emigrants. For example, all of the sixty-one men had farming backgrounds. The Hawaiian sugar planters wanted agricultural laborers, and announcements in Japan were clear on this point. A check of Niigata prefecture workers recruited in 1899 by Tokio Immigration Company shows that of the first 418, all

TABLE II

Number of Company Emigrants, by Sex, 1894–1908

Year	*Male Emigrants*	*Female Emigrants*	*Total*
1894	1,109	220	1,329
1895	1,972	374	2,346
1896	5,142	1,103	6,245
1897	?	?	3,286[a]
1898	8,293	1,852	10,145
1899	16,160	3,372	19,532
1900	537	172	709
1901	1,939	1,122	3,061
1902	9,444	4,578	14,022
1903	7,569	924	8,493
1904	8,219	692	8,911
1905	9,737	618	10,355
1906	23,698	1,189	24,887
1907	8,511	2,259	10,810
1908	278	172	450
Totals	102,608	18,647	124,541

Sources: Irie, *Hōjin hattenshi,* vol. 1, pp. 143–145 and Gaimushō tsūshōkyoku, *Ryoken kafusū,* pp. 142–181.

[a]Figures on the male-female ratio for 1897 are not available.

claimed heimin status and were farmers.[100] This company, as well as several others, assumed that the people they were seeking were non-shizoku workers and so had the word "heimin" printed on their lists in the space for status and "nōgyō" printed in the space for occupation and purpose of emigrating.

In a draft agreement it signed in 1899, Tōyō imin gōshigaisha promised its customers that those being sent were "bona fide agricultural laborers."[101] Similarly in a circular issued by the Hawaiian representative of Kumamoto Emigration Company, the following was included: "We will not only supply ABLE BODIED LABORERS but will endeavor to introduce a superior class of men and women, strictly Agricultural Laborers selected not from one, but from every available Agricultural District in Japan."[102]

Most of the company emigrants, like their government-sponsored predecessors, came from southwestern Japan. During the 1894–1908 period emigrants were primarily from Hiroshima, Yamaguchi, Kumamoto, and Fukuoka prefectures (see Table 12).

The 1885–1894 period played a part in insuring that these four prefectures would continue to dominate overall emigration. The fact that

TABLE 12

Percentage of Emigrants from Hiroshima, Yamaguchi, Fukuoka, and Kumamoto Prefectures, 1899–1908

Year	*Total Number of Emigrants from Japan*	*Number of Emigrants from Four Prefectures (Percent)*
1899	31,354	19,120 (61.0)
1900	16,758	6,263 (37.4)
1901	6,490	3,747 (57.7)
1902	15,919	13,089 (82.2)
1903	14,055	10,718 (76.3)
1904	14,663	9,199 (62.7)
1905	13,302	7,107 (53.4)
1906	36,124	16,502 (45.7)
1907	25,060	11,894 (47.5)
1908	10,447	4,890 (46.8)
Totals	184,172	102,529 (55.7)

Source: Kokusai kyōryoku jigyōdan, *Ijū tōkei,* pp. 68–69. From 1905 Okinawa becomes one of the four leading prefectures sending emigrants abroad.

workers from these four areas went in large numbers before 1894 meant this trend would continue after that because returning Japanese as well as letters received from abroad encouraged more people to emigrate. Also, newly established private companies, in order to sign up as many people as possible, concentrated on areas that were known as emigrant villages.[103] Evidence of this tendency can be found in prefectural reports for 1903 which showed that twenty companies were recruiting in Hiroshima, the same number in Yamaguchi, and seventeen in Kumamoto.[104] This meant more emigrants from these areas, which in turn led to further recruiting in the same areas.

There is also evidence that emigration was more difficult from certain prefectures than from others, which of course reduced the number leaving those particular areas. Tsuboi Kakichi from the island of Shikoku revealed that "Kagawa Prefecture limited passports to those who had clear purpose such as study abroad or business. Though prefectures such as Hiroshima, Okayama, and Wakayama issued passports without asking troublesome questions, our Kagawa Prefecture put more emphasis on domestic development rather than on emigration."[105]

Apparently this took place in several prefectures. Authorities probably had several reasons for imposing such a restriction. One reason might be that some areas in Japan, particularly in the north, were still being settled, and the opening of new agricultural land in these areas demanded more not fewer farmers. Some prefectures did not have a strong dekasegi rōdō tradition and had sent few workers overseas in the 1885–1894 period. Economic conditions in some areas may have been stable and less vulnerable to economic dislocation. Some prefectural officials may not have considered overseas migration as an appropriate solution to their specific economic problems. Although we can speculate further, it is certain nevertheless that prefectural policies and local officials had an important impact on the emigration process.

The government, as well as company agents, and guidebooks warned emigrants to carry enough money when they traveled to Hawaii. Adequate funds were needed for various expenses before the workers received their first monthly wages. Later, in Hawaii and the United States, immigration inspectors required that entering aliens (mostly Japanese) carry the equivalent of $50 to insure that they would not become wards of the state. To investigate this problem, Keihin Bank took a survey of workers leaving Japan between 8 August and 28 November of 1903.[106] Of the 1,023 who were carrying the suggested

100 yen (approximately $50), 273 carried their own money, while the remaining 750 had to borrow from a bank, an emigration company, or a moneylender. As we will see in chapter 7 this and other financial practices by the banks and the companies became the subjects of complaints by many people. There were, however, other means to finance someone going abroad. One emigrant remembered: "My father had put a mortgage on his property to get me the 200 yen I used when I sailed to Hawaii . . . the 200 yen had been my father's investment."[107]

Many of the characteristics of the government-sponsored workers can also be seen in the company emigrants. Almost all of those going overseas between 1894 and 1908 were young men with farming backgrounds. More than half came from the four emigrant prefectures of Hiroshima, Yamaguchi, Kumamoto, and Fukuoka. All who went abroad desired economic success to the extent that they borrowed money in order to get to Hawaii. Earlier workers, advertisements, guidebooks, and the recruiting practices of company agents played important roles in persuading young Japanese farmers to sign labor contracts and begin their long journeys to Hawaii.

CHAPTER 5

Emigration Companies and the Emigration Process in Japan

With all five actors in place, we can now examine how the emigration process actually functioned under private enterprise. There was such a variety of people involved in this field that it is difficult to say what motivated all of these "new entrepreneurs." Nevertheless it can be stated that their primary concern was to make a profit. For the companies, it was necessary to recruit as many people as possible, to get as large a commission from each one as legally permissible, to send them by the cheapest means available, and then get the maximum amount from the sugar planters in Hawaii. People involved with these companies could not have been expected to see the larger view of emigration and consider its long-range effects on Japanese rural society and on international relations. Nevertheless, their overriding concern to maximize profits led to practices which were criticized by the workers as well as by Japanese and Hawaiian authorities.

It also did not help that the period of privately sponsored emigration followed ten years of government-sponsored emigration, because comparisons were inevitable. This is not to say that there were no complaints by workers during the 1885–1894 period, but what complaints there were, were directed primarily at the sugar plantations and the treatment the workers received there. In contrast, there had been comparatively little discontent about the Japanese government's handling of overseas emigration. Authorities tried to send as many workers to Hawaii as was requested by their Hawaiian counterparts. They hoped that emigration would, to some extent, relieve some of the economic pressure on farmers in certain regions of their country. Their anticipated returns were therefore long-term. In comparison, the companies did not care how their management of this process affected the emigrants themselves and they expected only short-term returns.

A 1902 editorial from the *Osaka Asahi Shinbun* made clear what the result of this type of thinking was: "each emigration company takes advantage of the naivete of emigrants, charges unreasonably high commissions, robs emigrants of their savings and is only intent in its own self-centered profit making. . . ." A U.S. commissioner of labor commented on this same problem in 1905: "the association of companies is a virtual monopoly. . . . The result has been the growth of an evil, and something of a scandal, in the methods of controlling Japanese emigration to Hawaii."[1]

For companies that had received permission to operate, an early concern was finding agents to represent them. In small companies, work in the main office was done by the individuals who started them; they simply did not have the funds to hire many employees. Yet every company managed to employ men to recruit potential emigrants. The way this was done can give us some idea of how a company conducted its business.

The Oriental Colonization Company, which started operations in 1899, hired its first thirteen agents from the following prefectures: four from Hiroshima; one each from Kanagawa, Kagoshima, Kumamoto, Yamaguchi, Okayama, Shizuoka, Saga; and two from the city of Kobe in Hyōgo.[2] From this information one can conclude the following: the agent in Kanagawa and the two in Hyōgo staffed offices in the port cities of Yokohama and Kobe; those from Hiroshima, Kagoshima, Kumamoto, Yamaguchi, and Okayama were hired because many emigrants came from those prefectures; and the men from Shizuoka and Saga were engaged because both had experience overseas.

Another concern of companies just starting their businesses was finances. Mention has been made of the security that had to be deposited with foreign ministry officials. Although in the beginning 10,000 yen was required, after October 1901 this was raised to 30,000 yen.[3] Unless there were special circumstances, this amount covered the security deposit for the first 3,000 emigrants sent abroad. If more than that number were to be sent, the government required an additional deposit of 5 yen per person (later raised to 10 yen). Company capital was obtained in several different ways, with local financing being the most popular. In most cases, this initial funding was provided by groups of investors who contributed different amounts of money. For example, the ten original investors of Tōyō imin gōshigaisha contributed between 5,000 yen and 30,000 yen each when the company began operations.[4]

The Emigration Companies and the Sugar Planters

Financing and recruiting did not matter if the companies were unable to establish contact with sugar planters and obtain contracts. One of the methods the larger emigration companies used to accomplish this end was to issue labor propositions and publicize the terms for providing workers from Japan. The proposition from Morioka Immigration Company in 1896 included an offer to send "faithful farmers" between the ages of twenty and forty to work ten hours a day, twenty-six days a month for three years at the rates of $12.50 a month for a male worker and $7.50 for a female worker.[5] In return, the company asked the planters to cover expenses and the company's commission at $30 for each male and $25 for each female.

One article in the proposition issued by Morioka Immigration Company gave the sugar planters the right to withhold one or two dollars a month from worker's wages. This sum was a security against desertion and was returned at the end of the contract period if not used. The proposition also listed the holidays observed there, and pointed out that the workers would be exempt from personal taxes and under the protection of the laws of Hawaii. By issuing such plans, these companies made public the terms of the proposed labor contracts. In this way, they soon established standard wage and commission rates and work condition terms which other emigration companies had to offer in order to compete for workers and for plantation contracts.

In later years, the agents hired by the emigration companies and stationed in Hawaii played an important role in the company–plantation relationship. However, in the beginning, the larger companies relied on foreign agents to negotiate with the representatives of the sugar planters. For example, Morioka Immigration Company used J. A. Gilman to represent its interests in Hawaii.[6] Japanese Emigration Company of Hiroshima worked through H. Hackfeld and Company and Japan Emigration Company with G. E. Boardman. The owners of smaller companies tried to establish ties with the planters themselves.

Whether initiated by public labor propositions or private negotiations, contracts were drawn up between emigration companies and sugar planters. Imperial Emigration Company, represented by agent Hamano Y. (Hamano Yonetsuchi) in Honolulu, and the Treasurer of Palawai Development Association signed one such document on 23 May 1899.[7] In it the emigration company promised to send seventy-five workers within three months of the signing of the agreement. The plantation agreed to pay $30 for each worker to cover recruiting expenses, passage fare, and commission. Consequently the agents tried to use every means possible, legal or illegal, to reduce the expense of sending workers overseas since part of the $30 would be their commissions.

These agreements also outlined the terms of the labor contracts (in Hawaii only before 1900) and included sections designed to protect the interests of the sugar planters. For example, a provision was included in the contract for sugar planters who sought healthy workers: "Upon the arrival of such laborers in Honolulu, the Planter agrees to immediately cause them to be examined by a competent physician . . . for the purpose of determining whether they are able-bodied and fit to perform agricultural labor. . . ." Another provision discussed the possibility of workers discontinuing their services for reasons other than sickness or death. If such a person was absent for more than thirty days, the emigration company gave assurance that it would replace him with another worker free of charge. If this proved to be impossible, it promised to reimburse the planter the original $30.

Another provision dealt with the end of the three-year contract period when the sugar planter had the option of re-signing a worker if both parties were satisfied with the terms of the new agreement. In this event, the planter was required to pay an additional sum of $30 to the company. Thus second contracts enabled a company to collect a second commission, despite the fact that there were no longer any formal ties between it and the worker.

The emigration company had to place a deposit with a trust company in Honolulu to cover the initial expenses of the sugar planter.[8] Specifically, it was required to post a bond of $30 per worker up to a maximum of $10,000 with Messrs. Bishop and Company (established in 1858) of Honolulu within ninety days after the signing of the agreement. This money was used to compensate the sugar planters in the event that the terms of the contract were violated.

The Labor Contracts

Once basic agreement was reached between the emigration company and the sugar planter, recruiters were sent into the countryside with copies of the approved contracts (see Appendixes 3 and 4 for examples of these contracts). After June of 1900 immigrants entering Hawaii were not allowed to carry labor contracts, so the agreements they signed were for passage and help in departure matters only. All contracts were, of course, printed in Japanese; those of the larger companies included English translations. These were for the benefit of the inspectors in Hawaii who had to investigate the status of an immigrant, for the planters who had offered the original contracts, and for courts in Hawaii which settled disputes over contract provisions.

The contracts used by the emigration companies before 1900 generally followed the form used in the earlier period. They specified the wages to be paid, work conditions on the plantations, and the obligations of all parties concerned. Those issued by the different companies were generally similar, although there were changes over time as expenses and wages rose. For example, an 1896 contract of Laupahoehoe Sugar Company proposed $12 a month for the first two years of the contract and $13 for the last year.[9] Another offered by Ogura shōkai through G. E. Boardman quoted wages of $13.50 a month from the very beginning; later, these wages rose to $15 a month for men and $10 for women.[10]

The contracts also outlined the living conditions that awaited the Japanese immigrants. One contract promised "unfurnished lodgings, commodious enough to secure health and a reasonable degree of comfort, free of expense."[11] The sugar planters also guaranteed "fuel for cooking purposes, free of expense . . . as well as medicines and good medical attendance, free of cost."

The Shipping Companies

In addition to recruiting workers, company agents negotiated with shipping companies. Much attention was paid to them because passage fare to Hawaii was the largest expense. Although the emigration companies had the choice of using a number of Japanese and foreign lines, all had to be approved by the foreign ministry. Thus as was required of others who were part of this process, shipping companies had to submit applications to government officials before they could receive permission to operate.[12] In 1907 and 1908 the following applied to Japanese officials for permission to continue to transport emigrants to Hawaii: Pacific Mail and Steamship Company (USA); Occidental and Oriental Steamship Company (USA); Tōyō kisen kabushikigaisha; California and Oriental Steamship Company (USA); Nippon yūsen kabushikigaisha (also known as Japan Mail Steamship Line); Ocean Steamship Company, Ltd. (England); Shiyarujuru Reyuni kisen kabushikigaisha (also known as Chargeurs Réyuni) (France); and Boston Steamship Company and Boston Tow Boat Company (USA).[13]

The applications submitted by the shipping companies were quite detailed. From these documents we know that the foreign ministry required a security of 30,000 yen ($15,000) from each company, and most had enough capital to post these bonds. For example, Occidental and Oriental Steamship Company reported assets of $300,000; Nippon yūsen kabushikigaisha, assets of 22,000,000 yen ($11,000,000); and Tōyō kisen kabushikigaisha, capital worth of 6,500,000 yen ($3,250,000).[14]

During the 1885 to 1894 period, all of the ships carrying workers to Hawaii were Japanese, with the exception of the *City of Tokio,* which was used for two shipments.[15] However, during the 1894–1908 period, the transport of the emigrants was done largely by foreigners, particularly Pacific Mail and Steamship Company and Occidental and Oriental Steamship Company. Most of the larger Japanese ships had been pressed into service during the Sino-Japanese War (1894–1895). Thus between 1894 and 1900, foreign ships transported emigrants to Hawaii 122 of the 170 times this was done.[16] During the 1904–1905 Russo-Japanese War, the Japanese ships were once again needed to transport soldiers to the continent.

A number of the larger shipping companies had agents in Japan to handle business negotiations, and it was through them that arrangements for transporting emigrants took place. However, the great expense of stationing an agent in each port city inspired shipping companies to form a joint agency as the emigration companies had done for agents in foreign countries. By 1903 an agency was set up to serve Pacific Mail and Steamship Company, Occidental and Oriental Steamship Company, and Tōyō kisen kabushikigaisha.[17] B. C. Howard represented its interests in Yokohama, W. W. Campbell in Kobe, Messrs. Hollie, Ringer and Company in Nagasaki, and H. Hackfeld and Company in Honolulu. With this joint agency, these three companies were unrivaled in the shipping of emigrants to Hawaii.

Passengers left from Nagasaki and Kobe and sailed to Yokohama where final arrangements for leaving the country were made. In 1907 the fare from Nagasaki to Honolulu was 60 yen; from Kobe, 55 yen; and from Yokohama, 50 yen.[18] At that time, it took about twenty-eight hours to travel from Nagasaki to Kobe and then about twenty-four hours to reach Yokohama.[19] The voyage from Yokohama to Honolulu took from ten to fourteen days.

The ships were of varying sizes and carried up to 1,500 emigrant passengers on a single voyage. From April of 1894 until the end of 1907, ships carrying workers made a total of 426 trips to Honolulu.[20] A typical example of the ships that carried a large number of Japanese during these years was the S.S. *Siberia,* owned by Pacific Mail and Steamship Company. Built in Virginia in 1903, it was a four-deck ship 555.1 feet long and 63.2 feet wide with net tonnage of 5,655.[21] From May of 1903 until the end of 1907 this ship carried emigrants to Hawaii twenty-two times.

Emigrants complained about illegal practices and collusion between shipping companies and emigration companies. A statement from the *Honolulu Republican* which was reprinted in an article in the 17 October 1901 issue of the *Japan Times* read in part, "The Pacific steamers' regulation not to ship a laborer to Hawaii who does not possess 90 yen supplies an excellent pretext to extort money from such laborers." One American official commented that, "Agents of the steamship companies and emigration companies do not occupy offices together. They are, nevertheless, very closely connected through the brokers and hotel-keepers, and it is hard to draw a line of separation of interests."[22]

There are other examples of unsavory financial dealings between emigration companies and shipping companies.[23] In 1906 it was rumored that emigrants could only be sent to Hawaii by one shipping line, a charge that government authorities quickly denied. At times those in Hawaii complained about some shipping agents who charged different fares for the same passage. A victim of this kind of practice, Tamesa Uhachi related: "I left Kobe via the *Ryojun maru* the 4th of October, 1899 . . . to my great surprise, even in the same third class cabin area the fees were different. I only paid 30 yen, but some paid 90, and some said they had paid as much as 180."[24]

In later years two companies, Morioka Immigration Company in 1908 and Takemura Yoemon in 1910, attempted to send workers to Latin America on their own ships.[25] This would have allowed them to control the entire process from recruiting to shipping the emigrants.

The Boardinghouses

Emigration companies had to house their workers, who waited in port cities for several days until their ships were ready to leave. Most companies used specific boardinghouses for their clients, and this also became an area of complaint. One Japanese testified to American government officials: "We have sworn affidavits of laborers that the [emigration] companies have made [the emigrants] pay . . . big hotel bills at hotels connected with the companies while the men were waiting at the port."[26] One emigrant's experience was testimony that the houses had questionable ties with the doctors and inspectors stationed in the port cities: "When I took my physical examination at the emigrant house in Kobe, the doctor said I had trachoma. Therefore, I had twelve eye operations. Looking back on it now, I suspect that the operations, instead of curing me, made it worse. I was afraid that the doctor, shaking hands with the operators of the lodging houses, was deliberately delaying me, whereupon I went to Nagasaki, took the examination and passed it at once."[27]

As a result, government regulations on boardinghouses were designed to create better living conditions.[28] In response to complaints about people being crowded into small dark rooms for days at a time, officials set standards for the rooms. To hold down costs for boarders the government put a limit on their stay in these houses, required that rates be approved by local authorities and clearly posted.

Even with these regulations, home ministry officials found evidence of illegal practices. For example, although the government had divided boardinghouses into two classes with rates appropriate for each class, officials found cases where company agents had put emigrants in second-class houses but charged them first-class rates. (First-class houses were 50 sen per night and second-class houses 15 sen.) Obviously, emigration companies, through their agents, negotiated with certain boardinghouses and made illegal agreements with them.

Free Emigrants

During the early part of the emigration company years, most of the Hawaii-bound Japanese signed labor contracts. They went abroad with the understanding that they had to work for three years in order to pay back their various financial obligations to the sugar planters, the emigration companies, and, in some cases, banks. For everyone involved it was a workable system—if the terms of the contracts guaranteed a three-year period of stability. A number of individuals wanted to work in Hawaii without signing labor contracts, however. From their point of view, going there without any obligations and finding jobs either on or off the plantations gave them a better chance of achieving financial success. Others who went free from labor contracts were nonworking wives, children, and relatives; they had been "called" to Hawaii by workers already there. Since they were not under any of the constraints of a labor agreement, all were "free emigrants."[29]

Still, many of them used emigration companies to make travel arrangements to Hawaii and other departure matters; others borrowed money from a company or a bank. From the standpoint of the companies, it was more profitable to send contract workers abroad and receive commissions from the sugar planters, but if others wanted to go overseas and were willing to pay commissions for the paperwork and passage arrangements, the companies did not turn away a chance to make a small profit. In 1903 companies such as Chūgoku imin gōshigaisha, Ōno Den'ei, and Tōhoku imin gōshigaisha were charging each individual, male or female, 20 yen if over the age of fifteen and 10 yen if between the ages of twelve and fifteen.[30]

These emigration companies remained an important part of the free emigrants' lives. Almost all of them knew nothing about the procedure for leaving the country, a process which took about two months, and so many faced an assortment of problems in their attempts to go abroad. For example, passports in the early years were issued only to prefectures that had a *kaikōjō* (open port, in this case a treaty port). Thus even as late as 1900 it was not possible for residents of certain areas of Wakayama prefecture to obtain passports from local officials, and they had to travel to neighboring Hyōgo to obtain them.[31] Potential emigrants relied on company agents not only to arrange loans but also to obtain passports, visas, deposit certificates, and official permits allowing them to leave. In return, the agents collected commissions of 10 to 20 yen, in addition to the passage fare to Honolulu, from each individual.[32] During the 1894–1900 period, 2,948 workers, or a little less than 7 percent of those sent by the companies to Hawaii, were free of labor contracts.[33]

Japanese officials restricted free emigrants from traveling to Hawaii after 1 August 1901.[34] Thereafter those who were allowed to leave the country without labor contracts were either sent for by family members or were previous emigrants returning to Hawaii. The latter were restricted to sixty per ship, also, each company agent could send no more than twenty-five free emigrants per ship.

One reason the companies sent free emigrants to Hawaii was they had already been sending them to the United States and Canada. Because contract laborers were not allowed in America after restrictions were placed on Chinese immigration in 1885, only free workers went to that country. However, this was on a very limited scale, and a foreign ministry source lists only six such attempts before 1900.[35] In July of 1894 Yokohama imin gōshigaisha sent five industrial workers, all without labor contracts, to America. Beginning in the same year, Kobe Immigration Company sent thirty-three farmers over a period of four years. Japan Emigration Company sent fifty-three free emigrants between January and March of 1898. At about the same time, Morioka Immigration Company, Kōsei imin kabushikigaisha, and Japanese Emigration Company of Hiroshima each sent a small number of farmers to the U.S. mainland. Although these were some of the largest companies, all six managed to send only 165 free emigrants. The same source reported that the companies sent 5,648 workers to Canada, most of them free.

Because companies sent only a small number of emigrants directly to North America, only a few agents were stationed there.[36] (The names of some of them, the areas in which they worked, and the companies they represented are listed in Appendix 11.) These agents worked mostly with former company emigrants resident on the west coast who had come from Hawaii.

The companies had no choice but to send free emigrants to Hawaii after it became a territory of the United States in 1898. United States federal law prohibited the immigration of laborers carrying work contracts, but because American laws did not apply to the islands until after June of 1900 emigrants from Japan could legally enter Hawaii before that date but not after. We will see later that this change played an important part in reducing the emigration companies' profits and helped bring about an end to their activities in Hawaii.

Independent Emigrants

A number of people managed to travel to Hawaii without using the emigration companies or their agents. They did not sign any contracts and made their own arrangements for passports, visas, and ship passage. As did the free emigrants, they sought work by themselves once they arrived in Hawaii. Many of them had family members or friends waiting there, and arrangements for lodging and jobs had already been taken care of through these informal networks. At times emigration companies tried to prevent them from leaving Japan. One incident of this involved a group of Okinawa prefecture workers who tried to go to Hawaii in 1903. They were temporarily prevented from leaving Yokohama by agents of an organization that represented the interests of some emigration companies.[37] The number of people who traveled to Hawaii but who did not use companies or their agents can be seen in Table 10. After 1908 all those going to Hawaii did so without labor contracts and without the help of companies, and thus they were all independent emigrants.

Expenses and the Banks

For those going abroad, whether they were company, free, or independent emigrants, a major problem was finances. Although different sources provide different estimates for the amount of money a worker needed to travel to Hawaii, generally speaking, 90 to 95 yen was used for passage fare. One estimate, prepared by Kōkoku shokumin kabushikigaisha in January 1906, gives a breakdown of expenses based on the company's experience with free emigrants. The breakdown, shown in Table 13, did not include transportation costs within Japan. Travel by train from Hiroshima to Yokohama cost 6.3 yen at this time.[38] The estimate in Table 13 also does not include the 100 yen to be carried as *misegane* (show money). This misegane system was used on the U.S. mainland from 1891 but not in the Hawaiian islands until 1894. The interest on a 100-yen loan was anywhere from 3.5 to 12.5 yen.

Hawai Nichi Nichi Shinbun points out in a 1905 editorial that with passage fare and the 100 yen misegane, emigrants were paying more than 232 yen (about $114). According to one survey conducted by Kobe Immigration Company of forty-five individuals going to Hawaii, they carried between 17 and 75 yen, with the majority holding between 50 and 75 yen each.[39] This was of course during the period when misegane was not necessary for Japanese holding labor contracts and when passage was paid for by the sugar planters.

Even after emigrants received permission to leave Japan, they had to have a minimum of 30 yen in addition to passage fare and misegane.

TABLE 13
Emigrants' Expenses as Determined by One Emigration Company

Expenses	*Amount (Yen)*
Official commission [for the Company]	20.00
Passport charge	.50
Lodging in Yokohama	2.00
Lunch on day of departure and departure costs	.58
Fumigation fee in Yokohama	1.50
Passage fare [to Hawaii]	61.00
Registration fee at the Honolulu consulate	.50
Interest and service charge for Keihin Bank loan	5.00
Total	91.08

Source: Attachment to a letter from Kōkoku shokumin kabushikigaisha to the Foreign Ministry, 5 March 1906, *JFMAD 3.8.2.196.*

Few were able to pay their own expenses without loans from emigration companies, banks, or moneylenders. Some were fortunate enough to be able to borrow money from relatives or friends. Sōga Yasutarō, who eventually became an influential newspaperman in Hawaii, was able to go to Hawaii only because he could borrow 100 yen from a friend. Another emigrant spoke about how he managed travel to Hawaii: "For the cost . . . to come to Hawaii our land was placed under a mortgage. And we borrowed some money, about $100, from the moneylender. After we came to Hawaii we sent money back. If we didn't pay it back, our land would have been taken away."[40]

Hawaii-bound emigrants used a number of Japanese banks to help finance their passage abroad. These included Yokohama Specie Bank, Keihin Bank, Sumitomo ginkō, Kansai ginkō, and Hongō ginkō. The one that caused the most problems was Keihin Bank.[41]

It was officially known as Kabushikigaisha Keihin chokinginkō and unofficially as the "emigrant bank" because it was started by Morioka Immigration Company, Japanese Emigration Company of Hiroshima, and Kumamoto Emigration Company.[42] Morioka Makoto was the head of this bank. A number of other bank officials were at the same time working for emigration companies.[43]

With capital of 100,000 yen Keihin Bank established its main office in the Nihonbashi area of Tokyo in 1898. It set up two branch offices in other areas of that city, as well as one in Yokohama and one in

Honolulu. The three companies that organized the bank guaranteed its initial success by requiring their agents to use it when they arranged loans for workers going overseas. One of the complaints emigrants had was the high rate of interest this bank charged on a 100-yen misegane loan.[44] They received the money or a certificate in Yokohama and after a twelve-day trip to Hawaii, were required to repay 112.5 yen to the bank.

Many people were upset by the fact that Keihin Bank issued certificates printed only in English, which made it difficult for them to read and understand the various provisions. Also, several individuals from Wakayama prefecture who had forgotten to ask for the return of the promissory notes after they had repaid their loans including the high interest said the bank demanded payment again.[45] Loans required the signatures of two guarantors and at times bank representatives would approach them in Japan and demand payment of what was falsely claimed to be unpaid loans. The impression most people had of Keihin Bank is reflected in the following account of one emigrant: "My mother took me back to Japan when I was three years old so I must have been five or six years old at the time. I remember my mother crying when the [warrant of] attachment came from Keihin Bank. I don't remember what it meant at the time or how it eventually turned out. The memory I still have, however, is that of being afraid merely at hearing the words 'Keihin Bank.' "[46]

At times Japanese failed the medical examinations at the port of Honolulu or deserted the plantations before their contracts expired. For the emigration companies either case meant a financial loss since they were required to compensate their clients—in the first case shipping companies and in the second, the sugar planters—for their inconvenience. To guarantee compliance with the terms of the labor contracts, they forced the workers to deposit between 90 and 100 yen with Keihin Bank.[47] In return, these individuals received a note guaranteeing that this money was on deposit. If the worker fulfilled the terms of his contract, the money would be returned to him after three years; if he did not, he was transported back to Japan and the money was paid to the party that was due compensation.

Such a system guaranteed the emigration companies against financial loss, and also made a large amount of interest-free money available to Keihin Bank for three years. At the end of the three-year period, the bank gave the worker a choice. He could either receive the money back in small monthly payments, which meant that the bulk of the money would still be used by the bank, or he could receive it in a lump sum. The problem with the latter was, according to bank officials, that since the money had originally been deposited at the bank's main office in Tokyo, the money could only be withdrawn by the worker himself and only from that office in Tokyo!

Even for those who borrowed money from Keihin Bank and managed to repay the loan, life in Hawaii was difficult because of this financial obligation. An emigrant from Hiroshima wrote: "It was 1903 when I arrived at Honolulu with my two comrades. . . . I had borrowed 100 yen from Keihin Bank, which organization was also running an immigration company. . . . Due to the heavy labor and lack of rest I got pleurisy. . . . Since I owed 100 yen to the bank, I could not afford to rest. . . . I worked hard, and in two years I was able to pay back the 100 yen. I often wished I was back in Japan instead of enduring this hardship in Hawaii."[48] The practices mentioned above gave Keihin Bank its deserved reputation in the Japanese immigrant community as a corrupt institution.

Conscription

One of the problems that faced young Japanese men who wished to go abroad was their obligation to the national conscription service. Japan's modern conscription law was promulgated on 10 January 1873 and underwent changes in 1879, 1883, 1889, and 1906.[49] When overseas travel began, emigrants, like students studying abroad, had an exemption which delayed their entry into the military.[50] According to the changes of 1889, enrollment in this system could be postponed until those eligible reached the age of twenty-six.[51] Later this was extended so that men returning to Japan under the age of thirty-two could be enrolled upon arrival, and those above that age would be made members of the militia service.[52] Thus those going abroad and registering with consular authorities could not be conscripted after they reached the age of thirty-two.

There were a number of problems with this system, and the government issued in 1908 new rules that prevented men from going abroad just to evade their military obligations.[53] The rules affected emigrants between the ages of seventeen and twenty-eight who had to obtain certificates from their local conscription offices before they could leave the country. There is no evidence that these offices withheld permits from those wanting to emigrate, but the new rules enabled officials to control the number of men going abroad in the event of a military emergency. Despite these rules, a number of individuals became emigrants because of the threat of conscription. Higa Toden remembered his reason for leaving Japan: "I was still in Okinawa when the Russo-Japanese War [1904–1905] began. My parents were afraid that I would be drafted if I stayed in Okinawa. So that is why my parents asked me to go to Hawaii."[54]

Departure from Japan

After all arrangements had been made for leaving Japan, emigrants traveled to Yokohama (in later years, to Kobe and Nagasaki) to await passage to Hawaii. While staying in boardinghouses, they were kept under quarantine for a period of five days, during which time they underwent medical examinations for trachoma, hookworm, and syphilis.[55] Some of those who supposedly passed the exams in Yokohama failed them during the quarantine period in Honolulu. This caused problems for both governments, the emigration companies, the shipping companies, the sugar planters, as well as for the afflicted individuals. At times the complaints about the reliability of these examinations came from the shipping companies. In 1903 Pacific Mail and Steamship Company, Occidental and Oriental Steamship Company, and Tōyō kisen kabushikigaisha asked the foreign ministry to have emigrants board the ships only at Yokohama; they claimed that there were better disinfecting facilities, as well as a competent ship surgeon in residence there.[56]

In addition to the medical clearance, emigrants had to go through certain official procedures before being allowed to leave the country. Although the government insisted that emigration company representatives be present at the docks when the ships left, there were occasional problems with the departure, cases of falsified passports, and poor living conditions on departing ships.[57] A number of suggestions for changes in the supervising of the departure arrangements came to the foreign ministry from Kanagawa prefectural authorities.

With these procedures completed, the emigrants anxiously waited for their ships to take them to Hawaii. After a ten- to fourteen-day voyage, they would no longer be dekasegi workers leaving Japan but immigrants waiting to land in Honolulu.

CHAPTER 6

Emigration Companies in Hawaii: The Stage and the Actors

THE history of the emigration companies has been covered in previous chapters, but this story does not end with the workers leaving Yokohama because the overseas experiences of the Japanese were continually being influenced by the emigration process that enabled them to leave Japan. Thus company emigrants who went to Hawaii had experiences that were unlike those of free emigrants or of independent emigrants; and these became a part of their lives. Furthermore the response of the Japanese community in Hawaii to the practices of the emigration companies was as much a part of their history as were the organizational and recruiting activities in Japan. The experiences of the immigrants in Hawaii point out the successes and the failures of not only the companies but also of the private emigration system as a whole.

Like the emigration process in Japan, the immigration process in Hawaii revolved around the activities of five central actors. These actors can be arranged in the manner shown in the diagram on the following page.

The Hawaiian stage had several levels of authority which reflect the status and role of each actor. However, unlike their Japanese counterparts, the actors on this stage were involved in a more complex network of relationships. In Japan the emigrants were in direct contact with only the agents of the emigration companies and with local authorities. In Hawaii the immigrants dealt directly with the other four actors—the officials of the Hawaiian government, the sugar planters, the Japanese consulate in Honolulu, and the agents of the emigration companies.

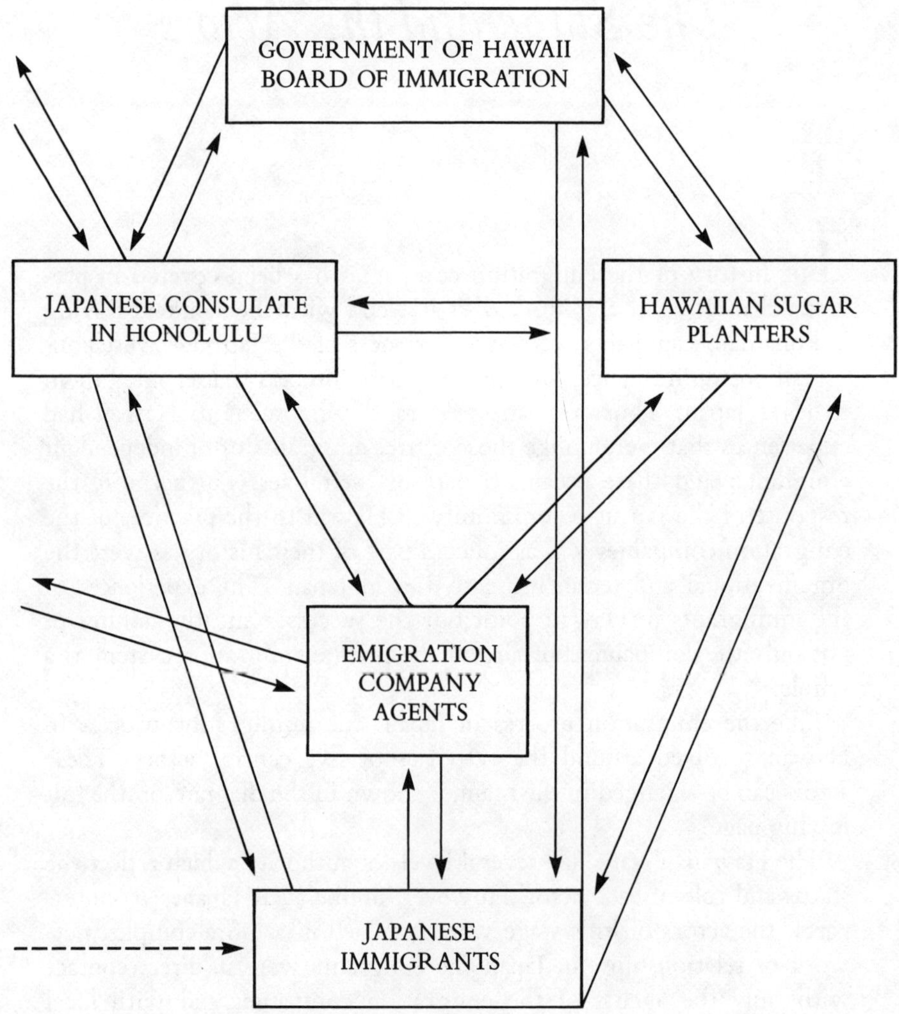
PACIFIC
OCEAN
GOVERNMENT OF HAWAII
BOARD OF IMMIGRATION
JAPANESE CONSULATE
IN HONOLULU
HAWAIIAN SUGAR
PLANTERS
EMIGRATION
COMPANY
AGENTS
JAPANESE
IMMIGRANTS

The Hawaiian Government

Although the structure of the Japanese government basically did not change after 1868, Hawaii underwent two major transformations during the period in which Japanese workers arrived in the islands. Government-sponsored immigrants landed when it was still a monarchy and known as the Hawaiian Kingdom. Then in 1893 a number of American residents staged a bloodless coup d'etat and established the Hawaiian Republic. It was under this government that emigration companies began to send workers to the islands. Five years later in 1898, the republic became an American territory and consequently was governed by U.S. federal law beginning in June of 1900. The change in government in 1893 did not affect immigration because the sugar planters sought workers before and after the establishment of the Hawaiian Republic. The change in 1898 had more of an impact and eventually it brought about the end to Japanese immigration.

There was a difference in the way in which Hawaii and Japan officials approached the problem of the Japanese entering Hawaii, regardless of the changes which took place in the islands. The Japanese foreign ministry viewed emigration as its responsibility because it was an issue of international relations. The Hawaiian officials naturally viewed it as a domestic concern since, after the initial agreements were made, further involvement with immigrants took place on their native soil; thus it put the responsibility for immigration matters in the hands of the Ministry of the Interior while Hawaii was a kingdom and the Department of the Interior when it became a republic. The specific agency set up to handle these matters was known as the Bureau of Immigration (Hawaiian Kingdom) and later the Board of Immigration (Hawaiian Republic).

For the emigration companies, the Board of Immigration was a vital part of the emigration process. All requests for foreign workers, Japanese or others, had to receive the permission of the board. It was this agency that held the right to restrict the number of immigrants entering the Hawaiian islands.

The board and its predecessor were responsible not only for immigrants in Hawaii but also for seeking external sources of labor. Government officials of both the kingdom and the republic realized that large numbers of foreign workers were needed on the sugar plantations and to support the economy. From the beginning, authorities had been working with representatives of the sugar planters to find this labor. The first private group that sought workers, the Royal Hawaiian Agricultural Society, was organized in 1850.[1] In 1864 the Planters' Society was formed to recruit men for the sugar plantations. The Planters' Labor and Supply Company was established in 1882, and became the Hawaiian Sugar Planters' Association in 1895.[2] The HSPA became the principal agent for recruiting foreign workers and also represented the sugar planters in negotiations with the government and various labor groups.

The original Bureau of Immigration was created by legislative act on 30 December 1864 and underwent some changes in 1868. Thereafter, the minister of the interior and five individuals, all appointed by the king, made up the bureau. This act proclaimed that the members "shall have entire charge and control of all matters relating to immigration and immigrants; shall superintend the execution of all laws relating there to. . . ."[3]

In its earliest days, the bureau was involved with importing workers from China, Portugal, Austria, Norway, Germany, and a number of Pacific islands.[4] With the beginning of government-sponsored emigration in 1885, the bureau began to concentrate on Japanese immigrants and devised ways of increasing their numbers.

This did not mean that the Hawaiian authorities ignored the recruiting of workers from other countries, however. In May of 1895 an attempt by H. Hackfeld and Company to import workers recruited by Japanese Emigration Company of Hiroshima was postponed by the board until, in its words, "the result of the movement to introduce Chinese laborers is known."[5]

The board itself was aware of the large number of Japanese entering Hawaii and tried to encourage the sugar planters to hire individuals of other racial and ethnic groups. A letter sent by the board to H. Hackfeld and Company on 9 August 1895 read in part: "your application for 545 Japanese laborers was approved on the following conditions, viz: That you agree to accept from the government in Honolulu a number of Portuguese laborers equal to twenty per cent of the total number of Japanese. . . ." In a later note, this was raised to 30 percent. In 1896 the original requirement was revised to read, "a number of Portuguese or other European laborers. . . ." Later that year, the board again amended its statement to include workers from America in addition to Europeans.[6]

In his letter of 23 May 1899 to the sugar planters, the president of the board, J. A. King, summarized the board's policy regarding immigration: "The government . . . considers the importance of keeping the introduction of Asiatic labor immigrants down to the absolute requirements. . . ."[7]

The board regulated the number of immigrants entering Hawaii by requiring the sugar planters to have government permission to import workers. The plantations submitted applications which outlined their labor needs and the contract terms reached with emigration companies. No one was given special status so that the rules that applied, for example, in 1897 to Henry Waterhouse, who wanted to import only 18 workers, also applied to W. G. Irwin and Company, which sought 425.[8]

Another duty of the board was to promote the hiring of Japanese workers, and they did this from the early days. In a circular sent in February of 1885 the president of the bureau introduced the new workers to the sugar planters as being "all tenant farmers. . . . If they like Hawaii and find themselves well treated, their intention is to remain here with their families . . . they will work many hours beyond the contract time, without extra compensation. . . ."[9] Although these statements were exaggerations, this circular shows the effort the Hawaiian government made to persuade the planters to hire Japanese.

The board hired Japanese to fill two important jobs. Men who were able to speak English were hired as interpreters and inspectors. They helped with immigration procedures at the port of Honolulu and when necessary investigated crimes or incidents of abuse on the plantations. An example of the latter was an incident that took place at the Pioneer Mill Company in 1896. Reports had reached the board that the manager of the plantation had struck one of the Japanese workers. After the board had studied this incident by sending one of its inspectors to the plantation, it sternly warned the manager against such behavior. Several Japanese men worked for the Hawaiian government beginning in the mid 1880s. For example, G. O. Nacayama, who had been the chief Japanese inspector during the government-sponsored emigration period, held the same job during the first two years of the emigration company period. After 10 July 1895 his duties were turned over to Igarashi Naomasa. Nacayama later became a managing director of Tōyō imin gōshigaisha.[10]

The roles of inspectors and interpreters were clearly defined, as can be seen in a letter received by Okkotsu Kanezō at the time of his appointment: "Your duties will be to obey . . . the Minister of the Interior, and to interpret between the Planters and Japanese Laborers and you may be detailed to remain in the sugar fields. You will also act as Interpreter in the Hawaiian courts."[11] In the same letter Okkotsu was prohibited from accepting any presents or fees from either the sugar planters or the immigrants and also barred from corresponding with any newspaper. At first inspectors and interpreters were divided into three wage levels, with monthly wages of $150, $60, and $33, respectively.[12] Later, these amounts were raised so that by 1895 some were being paid as much as $200 a month.[13] (See Appendix 12 for a partial list of inspectors and interpreters.)

The Board of Immigration also hired Japanese to serve as doctors. During the quarantine periods in both Yokohama and Honolulu, they helped in the inspection procedures. Health examinations were mandatory for immigrants for two reasons. The authorities in Honolulu worried that disease-carrying individuals would enter the islands. They were particularly concerned about trachoma, a common eye disease in Japan at the time. Although emigrants were examined in Yokohama by board-appointed doctors, Hawaiian officials insisted on having them examined again before they left the immigration depot located in the Kakaako district of Honolulu.[14] In one instance in 1892, two Japanese workers with smallpox landed in Hawaii. In the uproar that ensued the board of health demanded that the doctor in Japan in charge of inspecting the ship be fired.[15] The other reason examinations were made mandatory was that the sugar planters wanted healthy workers who could survive the three years in the fields. The health examinations helped weed out the obviously ill or weak individuals who could become burdens to their employers.

Doctors were also needed in the plantation camps to supply medical care for workers and their families. At times the doctors, too, were the subject of immigrants' complaints. There was some basis for this dissatisfaction, as can be seen in the case involving Mōri Iga, a doctor who while earning $150 a month had not treated a patient during the year he was employed by the board.[16] In addition, he had joined Morioka Immigration Company and was also suspected of having "suspicious ties" with the consulate.

The functions of the Board of Immigration ended after June of 1900. After that date, foreigners coming into the islands became the responsibility of the U.S. federal government. This did not mean that the Hawaiian territorial government ceased to have any interest in immigration affairs. It continued to seek foreign workers and the board itself was reinstituted by the territorial legislature in April of 1905 to stimulate non-Asian immigration.[17] At times its policies were at odds with those of the federal government. Later, representatives from Honolulu urged U.S. congressional committees to change federal laws covering foreign immigration. The Hawaiian government's role during the 1885–1900 period was important when it, along with the sugar planters, increased the number of Japanese entering the islands in order to guarantee economic stability.

The Hawaiian Sugar Planters

The second important actor on this stage was the sugar planter for without labor contracts, there would have been far fewer immigrants entering Hawaii. A small number of Japanese went to Hawaii without labor agreements; but for the large majority, a contract to work on a sugar plantation became one of the essential items they carried with them overseas.

Although the plantations had started as one-family operations, by this time they were the pillars of the economy.[18] The saying in Hawaii "cane is king" was uttered not only by those in the economic sphere but by those in the political sphere as well. A U.S. commissioner of labor once commented: "As sugar is the dominant economic interest of the islands, it is consequently the dominant political interest."[19] What was essential for the sugar planters was regarded as necessary for Hawaii.

The plantations were divided among a number of companies, but five large enterprises eventually came to dominate the sugar business.[20] These were Alexander and Baldwin, Ltd., C. Brewer and Company, Ltd., Castle and Cooke, Ltd., Theo. H. Davies and Company, Ltd., and H. Hackfeld and Company, Ltd.[21] They operated the largest sugar plantations, which supported their other economic ventures. They have dominated the islands economy so long that even today they are known there as the Big Five. Smaller plantations owned by individuals or companies tried unsuccessfully to compete with them.[22] The Big Five held huge tracts of land when agricultural land was limited and thus were able to outlast smaller plantations for which there was no possibility of expanding operations.

Since the time Japanese workers were first imported legally in 1885,

TABLE 14
Sugar Produced in Hawaii, 1886–1908

Year	*Sugar in tons*	*Year*	*Sugar in Tons*
1886	108,112	1898	229,414
1887	106,362	1899	282,807
1888	117,944	1900	289,544
1889	121,083	1901	360,088
1890	129,899	1902	355,611
1891	137,492	1903	437,911
1892	131,308	1904	367,475
1893	165,411	1905	426,428
1894	153,342	1906	429,213
1895	149,627	1907	440,017
1896	221,828	1908	521,123
1897	251,126		

Sources: Compiled from Watanabe, *Hawai rekishi,* pp. 279–280; Commissioner of Labor, *Third Report,* p. 90; and Commissioner of Labor, *Fourth Report,* pp. 18–19.

the sugar planters prospered as the area of land under cultivation and the yield of sugar increased. Between 1885 and 1894 the amount of sugar produced rose as can be seen in Table 14. This continued during the years of company emigrants (1894–1908). Although some workers returned to Japan after their contracts expired, enough remained on the plantations.

As the planters were well aware, the increase in exports and rising profits were made possible by the growing work force available to them. They also realized that the Japanese immigrants made up an increasingly larger percentage of this labor force, as is apparent in Table 15.

The planters saw that Japan provided a large and cheap labor force on a steady basis, and this was the key to further expansion of the sugar cane fields. However, as has been mentioned earlier, this did not mean that they gave up attempts to find workers from other countries; Japanese workers were simply the easiest and cheapest means of manning the plantations.

The planters began to face problems when it became obvious that the Japanese were becoming the largest ethnic group in Hawaiian society. The inability of the sugar planters to attract large groups of white European workers who would be willing to accept wages the Japanese

TABLE 15
Japanese Working on Sugar Plantations, 1882–1915

Year	*Total Number of Workers*	*Number of Japanese Workers*	*Percentage of Japanese*
1882	10,243	15	—
1886	14,459	1,949	13.5
1888	15,578	3,299	21.2
1890	17,895	7,560	42.4
1892	20,536	13,009	63.3
1894	21,294	13,884	65.2
1895	20,120	11,584	57.6
1896	23,780	12,893	54.2
1897	24,653	12,068	49.0
1898	28,579	16,786	58.7
1899	35,987	25,644	71.3
1901	39,587	27,537	69.6
1902	42,242	31,029	73.5
1904	45,860	32,331	70.5
1905	44,951	28,030	62.4
1906	42,150	26,255	62.3
1907	42,122	28,035	66.6
1908	45,603	31,774	69.7
1909	44,486	31,280	70.3
1910	43,095	28,351	65.8
1911	44,797	28,327	63.2
1912	45,214	27,066	59.9
1913	46,159	25,297	54.8
1914	45,629	24,080	52.8
1915	44,904	24,046	53.5

Sources: Watanabe, *Hawai rekishi,* pp. 403–404 for the 1882–1890 years. Commissioner of Labor, *Second Report, 1902,* p. 761. Commissioner of Labor, *Fifth Report,* p. 18.

did was one of the main reasons that by 1910 only one in every thirteen residents in Hawaii was white. This trend was the principal reason the government insisted that 20 to 30 percent of the imported workers come from Europe or America. A U.S. commissioner of labor warned in 1906 that the plantation working force was overwhelmingly Asian and that a secondary population had come into Hawaii and had begun to enter almost all fields of industry.[23]

The planters preferred to hire Hawaiians or white workers, but they had little choice except to use Japanese. They faced the dilemma that confronted many "colonizers" in other parts of the world. They could insure economic success by importing nonwhite workers, or they could guarantee their own political domination of Hawaii by keeping out immigrants of color. It was impossible to do both. In the end the planters continued to import workers from Japan because, as an American government official pointed out in 1905, "In spite of the large Asiatic population, there is frequently a very real and keenly felt shortage of labor on the sugar plantations."[24]

In sum the planters chose to place the economic welfare of their plantations ahead of all other considerations. Attention was drawn away from the inevitability of a predominantly nonwhite population and of the possibility of expanded franchise. The focus became only maximizing profits and this led to the callous treatment of white as well as nonwhite workers on the plantations. We will see in chapter 7 that wage scales were based on each worker's racial or ethnic background. However, this did not mean that whites earned higher wages or necessarily received better treatment than others. On 14 August 1885 the *Daily Bulletin* (Honolulu) reprinted an article from the *Sydney Town and Country Journal.* Part of this article, written by a white Australian who had emigrated to the Hawaiian sugar fields along with nineteen other friends, reads as follows:

> Under anything like favorable conditions two years of a man's lifetime is a comparatively short period, but if he wishes to see how time can apparently lengthen itself out, let him ship for that period on . . . a [Hawaiian] sugar plantation. . . . The terms were for 24 months of 26 working days, 10 hours a day, the pay 15 dollars . . . a month with house, room and food. . . . There was nothing very captivating about the terms of the contract, but as times were very bad . . . there was no difficulty whatever about getting the necessary number [of people willing to leave Australia]. The agent who hired us could give no information whatever beyond what was set down in the contract papers. We had a short stay in Honolulu (part of two days), and were kept to the run by our escorts . . . who were held responsible for our safe delivery on board the steamer to convey us to the island of Kauai, where the plantation is situated. . . . [W]e found our future residence was not quite finished, we were to camp in the small houses for the time being. . . . The quality of the food soon became a cause for complaint; grumbling became a daily occurrence. The first victim who was made an example of was . . . a painter, who had been put to bullock driving.

> He was a well brought up, intelligent young fellow, to whom bullock driving was something new. He fell sick out in the cane-field, and had actually the audacity to [return] . . . without reporting himself to the manager or sub manager, both gentlemen happening to be absent at the time. He was summoned before a native magistrate and without having explained to him very clearly what he was summoned for, was fined. I believe he told them that the whole thing was a farce, and that he did not know what it was all about.
>
> On one occasion the meat being semirotten, a sample of it was taken to the manager's office. He had to hold his nose, but still made a laughing matter of it and gave no encouragement for us to hope for an improvement. The grand smash up then came, and twenty six of [us] . . . refused to work. . . . When brought before the authorities, four out of the twenty six paid their fine. The other twenty two went to prison. Eleven having been before the magistrate on previous occasions on civil charges, got forty days, the remaining eleven twenty days.[25]

The Japanese Consulate in Honolulu

During the period of emigration company activity, nine different men served as head of the Japanese consulate in Honolulu. Some served their term as consuls general, while others as deputy consuls general or official representatives (see Appendix 8). The most well known was Saitō Miki who spent more than eight years (three terms) in Hawaii. Despite the changes in command, policy remained unchanged over the years. This policy and the duties of the consulate can be divided into five parts.

First, the consulate carried out its government's policy on emigration. It monitored efforts by the Hawaiian officials to find workers from other countries because it realized that each one recruited in the Azores, the Philippines, or Puerto Rico meant one less from Japan. The consulate reported to the foreign ministry what these workers were earning and how large that non-Japanese work force had become.[26] It also sent back articles from Honolulu newspapers (complete with written comments) about immigration matters. The consular staff was particularly attentive to the efforts of the Hawaiian government to reinstate the immigration of Chinese workers. One such attempt, which eventually failed, occurred in 1896 when authorities tried to set a limit on Japanese immigrants so that the ratio among the plantation workers would be two Chinese for every Japanese.[27]

Second, the consulate served as the official channel by which messages were transmitted between the two governments. Therefore requests for workers were sent through the consulate to the foreign ministry which was responsible for controlling the number of emigrants leaving Japan.[28] These requests were made by letter and occasionally by telegram.

The third task of the consul and his staff was to serve as the official guardian for the Japanese living in Hawaii. This responsibility often placed the consulate between the discontent of the workers and the rigid stances taken by the emigration companies and the sugar planters. For example, in 1899 Saitō wrote to the emigration companies: "I feel bound to report all these facts to my government . . . but before doing this I deem it proper to make known to your companies the foregoing facts, with the hope that your suggestions to the agents and managers may prevent governmental interference. . . ."[29] Saitō was reporting on his inspection trip to plantations; this after receiving many complaints and pleas.

The consulate was fairly cooperative about investigating plantation living conditions and financial matters because it felt that solving specific, minor complaints was a method of preventing serious problems from emerging. However, during labor disputes, it was much more reluctant to take the side of the workers. In almost all of the cases when workers left their jobs, the consulate urged them to return. This was consistent with the Japanese government policy for overseas workers. They had to be protected when it came to cases of physical abuse, unsafe conditions, and blatant discrimination. These were the main issues of contention over the years between the consulate and the Hawaiian government. In return, Japanese officials expected workers to fulfill the terms of their contracts and not to resort to desertion or labor strikes. The Japanese consulate's position on the latter was demonstrated when the first major Japanese strike occurred in 1909, as a U.S. commissioner of labor reported: "The Japanese government representatives in Honolulu gave no support or encouragement to the strikers."[30]

Fourth, although it had no legal authority in Hawaii, the consulate was expected to keep track of the thousands of Japanese workers and their families after they arrived in the islands. For instance, the members of the staff were often asked by the foreign ministry to investigate the whereabouts of individuals in Hawaii.[31] As an example, family members left in Japan would stop receiving letters from someone in

Hawaii and would send a request through the foreign ministry to the Honolulu consulate. In one instance, an emigrant had left Niigata prefecture and during the ten years he was away, no money was received at home. After three years of no communication, his mother requested an investigation. In another case, a Hiroshima family reported missing a relative who went to Hawaii in 1899 or 1900. He had sent for two of his sons but the family did not receive further letters or money. The family asked for information. Families in Japan occasionally included with their letters pictures of the emigrants presumed to be missing.[32]

The consulate also reported on the number of immigrants who died in Hawaii. At times the staff in Honolulu was asked to undertake special investigations of the deaths of certain individuals. In one case a village headman in Chiba prefecture wanted a complete report on the death of one of his villagers.[33] A returning emigrant had brought news of the death, but the family wanted more details about the matter.

When an immigrant died from an accident, the consulate was often asked to provide additional details because of inheritance problems. There were questions about wages owed to the dead worker and the different financial agreements he may have had with an emigration company, a sugar planter, or a bank. In such cases, a plantation would send a notice of death to the consulate along with the balance of wages due the person in question. The foreign ministry in turn passed this through prefectural authorities to the family of the deceased. When a problem of inheritance or a request for an investigation was initiated in Japan, the procedure was reversed. In 1902, to take an average year, consular officials in Honolulu investigated the deaths of thirty-seven individuals.[34]

At times the consulate was called upon by foreign companies and banks to determine the whereabouts of workers who had returned to Japan.[35] In these cases, individuals were alleged to have left the country without paying their bills. Thus a number of stores and institutions would ask the consulate to conduct investigations in Japan and to reconcile debts.

The consulate also sent the foreign ministry information on crimes committed by Japanese in Hawaii, immigrants' complaints, the types of illnesses afflicting them, and the various organizations being formed in that community.[36] Government officials were interested in the movement of the immigrants after they finished their initial contracts. Would they stay and work on the plantations, or would they return to Japan?

Fifth, the consulate was also responsible for submitting reports on various events and trends that occurred in the Japanese community. These included reports on the number of men and women arriving in Hawaii, the number returning to Japan yearly, and reports on births.[37] The last included the name of the father, his official residence in Japan, the sex of the child, his or her position in the family, and the date of the birth. These reports were compiled daily in Honolulu and sent to the foreign ministry on a monthly and yearly basis.[38] This process continued through to the early 1920s.

Other reports included information on the number of Japanese under contract as compared to those who had already finished their three years of work, the number that had deserted their jobs, the number and types of labor disputes, and so forth. Consular authorities also reported the amounts of money immigrants had on deposit in Hawaiian and Japanese banks. Apparently the latter retained close ties with the consulate because information reached the foreign ministry about the amount of money immigrants were sending back to their families.[39] These reports were still being transmitted to Japan in the early 1930s.

The Japanese government requested information on its citizens in Hawaii and received it in the form of articles, editorials, and at times advertisements from the English and Japanese language newspapers. These were accompanied by a translation, when necessary, and by consular officials' comments.

The consul general was expected to be able to negotiate with Hawaiian officials, make on-site inspections of plantation camps, and mediate labor disputes. In addition, as the leading representative of the Japanese community, he took part in activities involving the larger Hawaiian community. In the Japanese community, he headed charity drives and welcomed political and military visitors coming from Japan.

The immigrants going to Hawaii had their first contact with overseas Japanese officials when they signed the consulate register upon arriving in Honolulu. The relationship ended when they returned to Japan. The consulate represented their closest tie to the country they left behind.

Emigration Company Agents in Hawaii

Agents were hired to staff emigration company offices in Honolulu and played an important role in the Japanese community there. Their main job was negotiating with the sugar planters on the number of workers they needed at a particular time. For example, if a plantation wanted an additional 200 workers within six months, it contacted an agent who would send the request to the head office in Japan. When the immigrants arrived at the port of Honolulu, they were met by the agent and a representative of the plantation.

A number of men held the post of agent in Hawaii during this period. (The names of forty agents are included in Appendix 13.) Some of them represented only one company at a time while others, like Tasaka, Sawano, and Sukie, served more than ten each.[40]

One thing these agents had in common was a tie with political groups in Japan. A number of them had been or became politicians; others had ties with the anti-government, "popular rights" political party *Jiyūtō*. For example, Hinata Takeshi had been a member of the lower house of the Japanese Diet, as had Yamaguchi Yūya.[41] Watanabe Kanjūrō later became a Tokyo city official, as did Inoue Keijirō. Koizumi Sakutarō maintained close ties with the political scene in Japan. Hirayama Katsukuma, Inoue, Hinata, Watanabe, and Yamaguchi had been active with the popular rights movement before they went overseas. Hirayama was related to Hoshi Tōru, the Jiyūtō leader and later a foreign ministry official who had ties with Keihin Bank. It has been claimed that these Jiyūtō sympathizers sent money from Hawaii to their political party in Japan.

At times company agents were asked to mediate disputes between workers and the sugar planters, but they were not always very effective. A Hawaiian government representative reported in 1900 about labor strikes: "Two Japanese Commissioners from the Immigration companies have labored among their countrymen at Lahaina, Olowalu, Kihei, Sprecklesville and beyond, but seem to have no influence whatever."[42]

Although these men helped the emigration companies on a short-term basis, in the long run they did more to damage the already tarnished image of these companies. A number of agents gained notoriety in the Japanese community for their questionable practices and disreputable behavior. Immigrants charged that they frequented geisha houses and expensive bars and also kept mistresses in large mansions in Honolulu.[43] Other complaints included charges that agents were giving presents worth up to $1,000 to sugar planters so they could obtain large orders of workers.[44]

Since these agents represented emigration companies in Hawaii, they had to answer to complaints directed at the companies. Japanese immigrants claimed that they were paying them too large a commission to go abroad, that different fares were charged ship passengers, and that the company agents were receiving illegal rebates from shipping companies and the planters. In May of 1894, for example, eighteen emigrants from Hiroshima sent overseas by Yokohama imin gōshigaisha registered complaints with the foreign ministry. In March of 1905, another complaint was filed with Kanagawa prefectural officials by an individual from Shimane prefecture who claimed that he was overcharged by an emigration company. Sasaki Gonroku pointed out that when he went to Hawaii in 1906 "the companies charged 75 yen as commission. From time to time they sent disreputable women, calling them immigrants, and petty gangsters went abroad to seek their fortunes. Unreasonable companies charged double the fee from ignorant victims."[45]

Although legally their sources of income were limited by the Emigrant Protection Law, emigration companies managed to find other ways of accumulating money. As a result, their reputation was almost as bad in Japan as in Hawaii. As the *Japan Times* reported on 29 September 1901: "Several of our metropolitan contemporaries charge the emigrant companies which supply contract laborers to Hawaii as being guilty of extortion, or even worse, at the expense of the ignorant laborers."[46]

In response to such complaints, the Japanese government took legal steps; from 1895 through 1908, it filed nineteen charges against the companies and their agents.[47] These were directed against some of the largest firms in the business, including Japanese Emigration Company of Hiroshima, Kobe Immigration Company, Morioka Immigration Company, Kumamoto Emigration Company, and Transoceanic Migration Company. During this period ten others were charged with various crimes, such as sending workers abroad illegally, keeping false emigrant registers, and violating recruitment advertising regulations. Individual agents were accused of receiving excessive interest on loans, falsifying health examination reports, and selling ship passage tickets for above the normal cost.

Complaints about the behavior of these companies came not only from workers in Hawaii. In a report on emigrants going to Mexico, Secretary to the Japanese Ambassador to the United States Hanihara Masano asked in 1908, "Who is guilty of putting our harmless emigrants into such a miserable situation?"[48] Hanihara pointed out that Oriental Emigration Company and others were recruiting workers for coal mines and agriculture and promising them a chance to enter the United States to get better paying jobs. He also mentioned that the agents showed no concern for the workers once they landed in Mexico.

When faced with this type of problem, immigrants in Hawaii and other countries could petition directly to the Japanese government. In 1909 one group did so:

> We are emigrants who were handled through Meiji Emigration Company and went to a foreign country many miles away. We left our parents, wives, and children in Japan and worked every day, saving money out of our wages so that we could send it back to Japan. It is a successful man who can do this among others who are sick or merely lazy. This money was as precious as if it came out of our blood. However, since the end of last year we realized that Meiji Emigration Company had not been sending the money back as we had asked. When we went to talk to the branch office manager, he told us to deal with the accountant, but when we went to speak to him, he told us only the manager knew about this matter. Since both men refused to answer us, we went to plead at the [Japanese] consulate, but they told us this was a matter which did not concern them. These people have embezzled the money which was like our blood. Please do something to help us.[49]

The Japanese Immigrants

The Japanese workers arriving in Hawaii during this period expected a difficult life on the plantations but nevertheless hoped to succeed there. They wanted to send money home during their stay overseas and eventually return to their villages with enough earnings to buy land or farm tools. They did not go abroad seeking religious freedom like the Puritans of New England, nor were they fleeing political and social persecution like the Jews from Europe. Perhaps more than any other group, these Japanese went abroad as living extensions of their country. They were not outcasts of society like the English prisoners who settled the Australian continent. Rather, they were a group of low-income, mostly tenant farmers who were willing to sacrifice three years overseas in order to benefit their families economically. Few of them intended to stay in Hawaii for longer than the contract period, always considering themselves Japanese nationals. Hawaii was merely a temporary perch for these birds of passage.

Although "lodgings commodious enough to secure health and a reasonable degree of comfort" were promised by written contract, the actual conditions on most plantations were much more severe. After an inspection tour of the plantations in 1899 the Japanese consul reported on the inadequacy of the camps:

> The camps for the Japanese laborers on some of the plantations are very unsatisfactory. At one camp six families are forced to stay in a single house of 12 X 30 feet without any partitions, and there is no cookhouse furnished to them, they being obligated to cook in their rooms. At other plantations several hundred persons of both sexes are also mixed up and kept in one large square house without any partition in it. Their sleeping bunks are long shelves of rough wooden boards, consisting of four stories. These shelves run in a row about thirty-five or forty feet long. Six or eight rows of these shelves constitute the sleeping apartments of several hundred workers in a single room. Each bottom shelf in every room is given to one married couple, the other three upper shelves being given to single men. The laborers who have been obligated to live in such houses for the long time of three years. . . .[50]

The consul went on to cite one example in which married couples and single men lived in the same building at one camp. Because a baby's crying kept the others awake, the mother and her child were forced to spend the nights in the sugar cane fields. These living conditions were one of the major areas of workers' complaints.

Despite these conditions and the smaller number of women, the population of Japanese in Hawaii increased every year. From only 116 in 1884, before the start of the government-sponsored emigration period, it rose to 12,360 in 1890, 22,329 in 1896, and to 56,230 by 1900.[51] Ten years later, the number had reached 79,674 out of a total population of 191,909. The Japanese community was still predominantly male and relatively young. In 1900 6,165 Japanese males were below the age of twenty-one and 18,595 were older than that.[52] At the same time, there were only 1,345 females over twenty-one and 3,915 under that age. The increasing number of immigrant workers arriving every year and the rise in births after 1900 (see Table 16) led to the growth of the Japanese population in Hawaii. By 1916 it had risen to 96,749 and by the following year to over 100,000.[53]

Although the Japanese immigrants arriving in Hawaii have been characterized as poor and uneducated, this characterization may be based on unfair comparisons. According to American government sta-

TABLE 16
Japanese Births in Hawaii, 1898–1910

Year	*Number of Births*	*Year*	*Number of Births*
1898	415	1905	2,263
1899	458	1906	2,247
1900	573	1907	2,353
1901	1,134	1908	2,904
1902	1,605	1909	3,090
1903	3,437	1910	3,713
1904	2,490		
		Total	26,682

Source: Attachment to a report from the Consulate to the Foreign Ministry, 8 June 1929, *JFMAD J.1.1.0 J/X1-U3.*

tistics released in 1903, while the average incoming immigrant carried $16.16 each, Japanese entering the country since 1898 held about $47.07 upon arrival, or about three times more than the national average.[54] During 1902 only English, French, and Scottish immigrants entered the country with more money than the Japanese. The same report showed that there were very few illiterates among the incoming Japanese. Only 1.2 percent over the age of fourteen were unable to read while the average of all entering groups was 28.2 percent. Only Scandinavian, Scottish, and Finnish immigrants had a higher literacy rate than the Japanese.

This high rate of literacy of these Japanese workers is not surprising in view of their educational background. The percentage of school-aged children in Japan attending school in the 1882–1897 period was relatively high, as can be seen in Table 17.[55]

Despite his assets, educational and monetary, it was difficult for the average worker to survive on his wages and still send money back to his family. A store clerk reported in 1906 that an average Japanese family of four spent about $12 a month for expenses, including food. He also described the average unmarried laborer's monthly budget: "One-half bag rice, $2.50; one-half bag flour, $.80; kerosene, $.25; washing, $3.50; meats and vegetables bought outside the store, about $2.70. . . ."[56]

The situation had not changed much by the end of the emigration company period. In an article that appeared in *Nippu Jiji* on 4 December 1908, a sugar plantation worker from Honomu on the island of

TABLE 17
Percentage of Japanese Children in School, 1882–1897

Year	*Boys*	*Girls*	*Year*	*Boys*	*Girls*
1882	64.7	31.0	1890	65.7	31.1
1883	67.2	33.6	1891	71.7	32.2
1884	67.0	33.3	1892	71.7	36.5
1885	65.8	32.1	1893	74.8	40.6
1886	62.0	29.0	1894	77.1	44.1
1887	60.3	28.3	1895	76.7	43.9
1888	63.0	30.2	1896	79.0	47.5
1889	64.3	30.5	1897	80.7	50.9

Source: Sekai kyōikushi kenkyūkai (ed.), *Sekai kyōikushi taikei,* vol. 34, p. 261.

Hawaii wrote about his expenses and wages.[57] For the past eight years this bachelor had averaged twenty-one working days a month, which gave him an average monthly income of $14.60. The breakdown of his monthly budget of $12.33 is shown in Table 18. After paying his expenses this worker was left with an average of $2.27 a month.

Although Japanese wives were few in number, they were an important part of surviving in Hawaii. Their role in the immigration process should be recognized and acknowledged. Many of these women labored in the fields or held jobs in the sugar mills; others operated small stores and bakeries on plantation property. And some of them cooked and did the laundry for unmarried workers. One woman described this experience as follows:

> I did the laundry by hand. I took the clothes to the bathhouse to wash, using a washtub. . . . On the first day I tried to wash off only dirt, so I soaked the clothes in soap and water. The next morning after all the men left, I put the laundry in two empty five-gallon oil cans. And I used three steel train rails to make a fireplace to boil the laundry. . . . And as for ironing it was charcoal iron. We put two pieces of charcoal and adjusted the heat until it got warm. . . . I got up at 3:30 A.M. I had washed the rice the night before and put it in a large container. It was cooked by firewood which was set up in place beforehand. . . . People ate breakfast on Saturday and Sunday too. I prepared it, and on Sunday I also washed and starched the bags they carried lunch in. . . . I got paid one dollar a month per person. I did cooking, washing, everything. I only got one dollar. That is all.[58]

TABLE 18
Average Monthly Expenses for One Plantation Worker, 1900–1908

Expenses	*Amount*
Board	$ 7.00
Laundry	.75
Tobacco, paper, and matches	1.00
Bath	.25
Raincoat and raincoat oil	.70
Oil	.15
Contributions	.25
Shoes and socks	.60
Stamps and stationery	.30
Send off money, etc.	.25
Hat	.08
Haircuts	.25
Working clothes	.75
Total	$12.33

Source: Attachment to an open letter to W. O. Smith, Secretary of the HSPA, January 1909, attached to a letter from the Consulate to the Foreign Ministry, 21 February 1909, *JFMAD 3.7.2.3,* vol. 1.

A survey taken for the first *Report of the Commissioner of Labor on Hawaii* released in 1902 revealed how vital these wives had been to the immigrant families.[59] Of the sixty Japanese families studied only three reported a deficit at the end of the year (1900). In two of these cases the wives did not work, and in the third she earned only $20 that year. Of the twenty families headed by Japanese fieldhands, all the wives contributed to the family income. In eighteen of them, their financial contributions made the difference between having something left at the end of the year and going into debt. Most of them came from a farming background where women worked alongside their husbands in the fields. Their financial contributions to the immigrant families in Hawaii were of utmost importance for the entire community.

It is also necessary to remember that the establishment of overseas communities like that in Hawaii helped the Japanese economy by creating markets for export commodities. Before emigration to Hawaii began, no Japanese products were shipped there. However, the

TABLE 19
Japanese Exports to Hawaii, 1895–1908

Year	*Exports*	*Year*	*Exports*
1895	$ 207,125	1902	$ 909,113
1896	276,125	1903	970,519
1897	292,318	1904	1,205,055
1898	354,324	1905	962,651
1899	673,410	1906	1,247,470
1900	647,395	1907	1,557,411
1901	915,355	1908	1,874,670
		Total	$12,092,941

Sources: Fujii, *Dainippon,* pt. two, p. 6; Watanabe, *Hawai rekishi,* p. 441.

market for these exports grew, particularly during the latter half of the emigration company period when immigrants began settling down. Table 19 shows this growth.[60]

The 1902 report cited above gives us a picture of the Japanese community in Hawaii midway through the emigration company period. In 1900, 45,017 Japanese men and 11,213 women lived in Hawaii.[61] The ratio of males to females in that population was slowly changing with the emergence of a second generation. By 1900, 2,491 males and 2,390 females had been born in this community.

Although by this time a few immigrants gradually began to move off the plantations to seek jobs in the larger Hawaiian community, most were still working for the sugar planters. According to the 1902 survey, Japanese made up more than 69 percent of those engaged in "agricultural pursuits."[62] They constituted 30 percent of those in "domestic and personal services," 27 percent in "manufacturing and mechanical pursuits," 22 percent in "trade and transportation," and only .5 percent in "professional services."

In 1900, 15,997 Japanese fieldhands were employed on thirty-eight sugar plantations.[63] On the average they worked ten hours a day, six days a week, and earned about 75¢ daily, or about $4.50 weekly. The average Japanese worker was described by Hawaiian authorities in the following way: "He has a wide-awake, well washed look, his trousers are stuck in a pair of canvas leggings, and the women have covered their hair with cloths or handkerchiefs to keep out the field dust."[64]

CHAPTER 7

Emigration Companies in Hawaii: The Immigration Process

THE immigration process in Hawaii began with the arrival of the Japanese workers at the port of Honolulu, where they were put under quarantine and underwent a series of medical examinations. These examinations by inspectors and doctors were not superficial, nor were they set up to annoy the would-be immigrants. Confined to an isolated chain of islands in the middle of the Pacific Ocean, Hawaii's native population had been decimated when diseases introduced into the islands by outsiders caused a series of epidemics. The medical examinations at the port were meant to protect Hawaiian residents and thus a number of individuals who did not pass them were refused entrance and forced to return home. Japanese workers had been sent back even in the days of government-sponsored immigration.[1]

Later, in January of 1902, one group was not permitted to land—the fault, the local Japanese language press said, of the emigration companies for not sending workers in better health.[2] In another case, sixty-five of the immigrants who arrived in Honolulu on the *Hong Kong Maru* on 19 January 1903 were sent back because they were afflicted with trachoma.[3] Unfortunately for the Japanese, these were not isolated examples. Three hundred and forty-five individuals were refused entrance in 1903, eighty-four in 1904, and seventy-five during the first six months of 1905.[4] Although trachoma was the most common reason for sending Japanese back, others were hookworm, small pox, syphilis, and physical deformities. The last was of particular concern for the sugar planters because they were promised healthy, strong workers who could survive the three years on the plantations. Some of the incoming Japanese were kept in quarantine for long periods, but most were held for about eighteen days and then released.[5] They were detained in a crowded building known to the local Japanese community as *sennin goya* or "the hut for a thousand people."[6]

Another reason some Japanese workers were prevented from landing was they did not have enough money with them. In the early days of immigration to Hawaii, there had been no requirements about how much each person had to have when he landed; in fact, a lack of funds was assurance to some planters that the workers would not desert and instead would provide a stable labor force. With the emergence of the emigration companies and the increasing number of Japanese immigrants, particularly free immigrants, the Hawaiian government insisted that these individuals without labor contracts possess a certain amount of "show money" (misegane) which would guard against their becoming wards of the state. Inspectors required a minimum of $50 carried in hand or a bank certificate showing the worker's assets to be worth more than 100 yen.

On 1 March 1894 the legislature of the Republic passed "An Act Relating to the Landing of Aliens in the Hawaiian Islands," which made it unlawful for aliens to enter the country who did not have a "means of support which . . . may be shown by the bona fide possession of not less than fifty dollars in money or a bona fide written contract of employment with a reliable and responsible resident of the Hawaiian Islands."[7] This regulation applied to all workers, to women who did not accompany their husbands or who had no relatives residing in Hawaii, and to children over the age of ten. Authorities used this regulation to restrict the number of immigrants arriving in the islands, a method of control that had already been used by American authorities to limit the number of Japanese entering the U.S. mainland.

Until 1900 a majority of the Japanese immigrants carried contracts and did not need this $50, but after contract labor was prohibited, free immigrants had to meet this rule. Most of those entering the United States carried the required amount of money, which often was borrowed from banks, emigration companies, moneylenders, or relatives. Other workers acquired their money during previous stays abroad and used some of this for their misegane on later trips to America.[8]

At times, the Japanese failed to satisfy this financial requirement and the results were predictable. In March of 1897, 183 of the 665 passengers of the *Shinshū Maru* were refused landing in Honolulu for not having sufficient funds.[9] All of the workers had been recruited by

Kobe Immigration Company, and when the ship was refused landing permission, two agents of the company were placed under arrest. Although this emigration company and the ship captain used a Hawaiian law firm to represent them, in the end only 75 passengers were found eligible to remain. Thus Kobe Immigration Company suffered a loss of 60,000 yen.[10] Later, the ship owners, the emigration company, and the individuals who were denied entry in this and three other similar cases were partially reimbursed by the Hawaiian government.[11]

One problem Japanese immigrants faced concerning the $50 misegane was the Hawaiian government's reluctance at times to accept bank certificates in lieu of cash. In March of 1895 seventy-one passengers holding these certificates were refused permission to land in Honolulu.[12] Collector of Customs J. B. Castle wrote to Ogura shōkai, which tried to bring in these workers: "I must refuse to allow the 71 to land, and will add, so far as drafts [drawn to the Yokohama Specie Bank] are concerned, that I do not consider any promise to pay money, is, in the words of the law, 'money.' "[13]

During the period between 1 January 1903 and 30 June 1905, 503 Japanese were detained and refused entrance at the port of Honolulu.[14] The majority, 430, were accused of carrying a "dangerous contagious disease," while 43 were deemed potential public charges. Twenty-eight others were found to be in violation of labor contract laws and two individuals were accused of illegally importing women into Hawaii.

When immigrants arrived in Honolulu, they were met by representatives of the Board of Immigration, the emigration companies, and the sugar planters. The board was represented by inspectors, interpreters, and doctors. Agents of the emigration companies verified that the correct number of workers had arrived, and they grouped them by plantation. Agents of the planters confirmed the count, checked the condition of the workers, and escorted them to their destinations. However, before leaving Honolulu, all Japanese entering Hawaii had to register with their consulate upon arrival. The register *(nyūkoku chōbo)* listed the name of the immigrant, the date of his arrival, and his plantation destination.[15]

Immigrant workers bound for plantations on the island of Oahu found the process that followed the examinations and registration to be simple. Accompanied by a plantation agent, they left Honolulu by wagon or on foot. Those bound for the outer islands traveled by ship, and there was often a short wait in Honolulu where they stayed in Japanese boardinghouses.

These boardinghouses provided workers with more than a place to stay. Often they functioned as labor agents for those Japanese coming to Hawaii without labor contracts and arranged for ship passage and contacted consular officials. They also served as agents for different emigration companies.[16] All of this was done on a commission basis and was an important source of income for these houses. The men who ran them had been among the first government-sponsored immigrants to move off the plantations and start businesses in Honolulu.

We will see later in this chapter that these boardinghouses were also important when Japanese workers in Hawaii were being recruited to work on the United States mainland. The major boardinghouses in Honolulu and their owners during this period included those listed in Appendix 14. Other individuals active in this business and also members of the Japanese Boarding House Association included Imanaka Ichitarō, Iikawa Momozō, Hirano Sōichi, Mamiya Shichizō, Izuno Jintarō, and Watanabe Munegorō.[17] A number of small boardinghouses operated on the outer islands. In 1899 the boardinghouses in Honolulu charged 40¢ a night for lodging and 15¢ per meal.

Life on the Plantations

The problems that Japanese immigrants faced on the sugar plantations between 1894 and 1908 involved living conditions, relationships with overseers and managers, and wages. In spite of the expanded area of land under cultivation and the increase in sugar production, the sugar planters worried about desertion, which threatened the stability of the plantation labor system.

The living conditions that awaited the immigrants who had just arrived have been described in the previous chapter. One person who visited a number of plantations was surprised that there weren't more sick workers due to the unsanitary conditions in the labor camps. Of the barracks, he wrote: "Rather than places for humans to live in, it would be more appropriate to call them shacks for pigs."[18] Consul General Saitō's public circular in 1899 revealed the extent to which Japanese were being crowded into what was certainly inadequate housing. Shigeta Ko, who arrived in Hawaii in 1903, wrote the following about his own living conditions: "Fifty of us, both bachelors and married couples, lived together in a humble shed—a long ten foot wide hallway made of wattle and lined along the sides with a slightly raised floor covered with a grass rug and two tatami mats to be shared among us. We also shared the same bathing facilities; while I was washing myself the wives of others stepped over me matter-of-factly as if I were a dog or cat in their path. I remember the cold drops from the ends of their hair falling on my back."[19] Yoshitake Taro described life on the plantation this way: "We lived in a bunkhouse, sleeping on blankets, spread over hay, on tiers of bunks like silkworms."[20]

Constant complaints by workers and pressure from the Japanese consulate convinced most planters that adequate housing and improved sanitary measures were necessary to maintain a stable labor force in the fields; consequently living conditions on the plantations slowly improved over the years. In particular, after 1900 the sugar planters upgraded living conditions as they searched for new inducements to keep workers released from their labor contracts on the plantations.

Some of the workers complained about the food served in the barracks. Most, however, had the attitude of Komoto Nobuji, who wrote: "I ate at the Japanese boarding house [on the plantation] . . . and there wasn't any reaction or pleasure."[21] This was partly because the workers themselves decided how much they would spend on food. Their main concern had always been to save as much money as possible regardless of the nutritional value of their meals. Eventually Hawaiian officials became worried about the diet of the Japanese. In a letter to Chief Inspector G. O. Nacayama, the president of the Bureau of Immigration wrote him to instruct the physician and interpreter at Spreckelsville "to do their best toward inducing the laborers to eat more nourishing food including meat, and to desist from using the pickled preparations, the conditions of the climate here are such that their use appears often, if not invariably, to be attended by injurious and frequently fatal results."[22]

In 1894 when the emigration companies began to send workers to Hawaii, the plantations found themselves already dominated in numbers by Japanese who had come as government-sponsored immigrants. At the end of that year, the labor situation on the plantations was as is shown in Table 20. The number of Japanese continued to increase, and in 1910, 65 percent of the 44,048 workers on the plantations were Japanese.[23]

For the most part, the different racial and ethnic groups lived in separate sections of the plantation camps, although at times this was not always possible on the smaller plantations. There are several possible

TABLE 20
Plantation Workers, by Nationality or Place of Origin, 1894

Nationality (Origin)	*Number*	*Nationality (Origin)*	*Number*
Hawaiian	1,515	Americans	119
Portuguese	2,187	British	138
Japanese	12,631	Germans	160
Chinese	2,613	Others	160
South Sea Islanders	178		
		Total	19,701

Source: Enclosure, February 1896 (?), *AH Bureau Letters* (1893–1897), p. 171.

reasons for this informal type of segregation. From the planters' point of view, this practice lessened language communication problems for the new workers, reduced the chances of intergroup conflict and of intergroup organizing in labor disputes.[24] Although there may have been some antagonism between the Japanese and the other groups on the plantations (typically over wage scales), there is no evidence that any of the labor disputes in which they took part were aimed at any specific racial or ethnic group. On the other hand, one strike that occurred in Waipahu in July of 1904, involved 1,800 Japanese workers who demanded that a countryman who had been appointed overseer be fired.[25] A closer examination of these labor disputes will take place later in this chapter, but in essence, Japanese labor agitation was directed against those in authority on the plantations and not against those working alongside them.

The sugar planters themselves had little, if any, personal contact with the workers, Japanese or others. One U.S. government official described this employer-employee relationship as being semifeudal. He went on to point out that workers lived in isolated village communities and were "accustomed to [regarding] the plantation manager as an earthly Providence whose paternal business it is to supply them with certain utilities . . . with or without their advice and consent."[26]

Overseers and foremen, known as *lunas*, supervised the workers in the sugar cane fields. During the period of government-sponsored immigration, plantations hired few Japanese as overseers. Although the situation slowly began to change, even in 1905 the Japanese, 62.8

TABLE 21
Average Monthly Wages of Overseers and Managers, 1905

Ethnic Group (Number)	*Monthly Wages*
Caucasian (339)	$84.36
Hawaiian and Part-Hawaiian (116)	44.24
Portuguese (273)	42.19
Chinese (24)	31.90
Japanese (125)	31.33

Source: Commissioner of Labor, *Fourth Report,* p. 26.

percent of the labor force, made up only 14.3 percent of the overseers and earned the least amount, as can be seen in Table 21.

The overseers were important because many labor disputes began with charges by workers about ill-treatment and violence at the hands of these men. In addition to several incidents which became *causes célèbres* in the Japanese community, many other cases went unreported. Nevertheless the Japanese consulate tried to investigate a number of them which they knew about. For example, a consular staff member reported to the foreign ministry about an incident in 1894 in which a foreman on a plantation in Koloa used physical force in dealing with some workers.[27] One person's experience with overseers was as follows: "Even if one were sick, he could not stay in his bunk without a doctor's certificate. If one was discovered in camp, in bed without this certificate, the Portuguese foreman came with a long whip and drove him out."[28] Even government officials acknowledged that acts of physical violence occurred from time to time. A U.S. commissioner of labor reported in 1903 that although physical ill-treatment of workers was illegal, it still took place on the plantations. He also pointed out the concern the Hawaiian and Japanese governments had about this problem: "In 1885 the Bureau of Immigration issued a circular to the effect that thereafter beating and similar ill-treatment of laborers would not be permitted. . . . The Japanese Government promptly intervened upon complaint of unwarranted severity toward its own citizens."[29]

At times authorities would investigate a case but never solve it. An example of this is a bizarre incident in which an overseer, accused of violence against Japanese, was found unconscious in the field with marks on his back.[30] Although the manager of the plantation felt that the overseer had been flogged by angry workers in a retaliatory act, this was never proven and the case was never solved.

Japanese also complained about pay scales, which often were based on one's racial or ethnic background. The sugar planters used this pay scale system for many years.[31] The different wages angered the Japanese, who saw it as a clear case of discrimination. They argued that "if a laborer comes from Japan, and he performs [the] same quantity of work of [the] same quality within the same period of time as those who hail from [the] opposite side of the world, what good reason is there to discriminate one as against the other?"[32]

A number of Japanese fled the plantations before their contracts were over. Some did so because of poor living conditions, others because of low wages, and finally some because of ill-treatment by overseers. Many were attracted to the nonplantation jobs in Hawaii or to the possibility of working on the U.S. mainland. Planters began to worry because desertions led to a scarcity of labor, as well as to instability on the plantations. They were particularly concerned about how soon after being hired Japanese workers abandoned their jobs. Table 22 offers such information about fifteen Kumamoto workers who fled the plantations during the first six months of 1898.[33]

Some Japanese workers barely had time to settle down on the plantations before they left (numbers 8, 9, and 15 in the table). Was a month or two of work in the sugar cane fields enough to disillusion some people? Or did they merely obtain contracts with the emigration companies and the sugar planters so they could leave Japan? The workers tended to desert in small groups made up apparently of friends with whom they had traveled to Hawaii (numbers 1 and 2; numbers 5, 6, and 7; numbers 8 and 9). Some deserted with their wives (numbers 3 and 4 and 10 and 11). During the first six months of 1898, a total of 140 men and 19 women deserted; in the latter half of the same year, 207 workers, 26 wives, and 1 child left the plantations illegally.[34]

The number of desertions each plantation had seemed to correspond with the quality of living conditions and the treatment of workers there. When Consul General Saitō made an inspection tour in 1899, he pointed out that several had acceptable living conditions for the Japanese. He argued: "There is no reason why the other plantations should not furnish laborers with comfortable quarters; as it is admitted

TABLE 22
Dates of Arrival and of Desertion for Fifteen Workers

Worker Number	*Date of Arrival*	*Date of Desertion*
1	24 April 1897	17 May 1898
2	24 April 1897	17 May 1898
3	15 October 1897	17 May 1898
4[a]	15 October 1897	17 May 1898
5	12 January 1898	3 July 1898
6	12 January 1898	3 July 1898
7	12 January 1898	3 July 1898
8	16 January 1898	17 March 1898
9	16 January 1898	17 March 1898
10	24 February 1898	26 June 1898
11[b]	24 February 1898	26 June 1898
12	24 February 1898	13 July 1898
13	24 February 1898	18 July 1898
14	12 April 1898	3 May 1898

Source: Report from the Consulate to the Foreign Ministry, 9 January 1899, *JFMAD 3.8.2.143,* vol. 1.

[a]Worker number 4 was the wife of worker number 3.

[b]Worker number 11 was the wife of worker number 10.

that the laborers are the principal sources of their prosperity, and as human beings these laborers should have fit places in which to live.''[35]

Some of the plantations had more than their share of desertions and Hawaiian officials wanted them to locate those who left and find some solution for the problem, rather than order more workers from Japan; they felt more workers meant only more deserters. When one plantation tried to import replacements, government authorities ordered that the number of Japanese being shipped to Hawaii would ''not . . . include any for Paauhau plantation because 140 laborers have deserted from that plantation since January 1st last and no efforts have been made by the officers of the plantation to recover them.''[36]

Desertion was a serious problem for the sugar planters and the emigration companies because of the amount of money involved. Contracts required that the emigration companies either replace workers who had deserted or reimburse the planters. But in any case, the plantations were left temporarily short of workers. Some companies tried to circumvent this situation by requiring that the immigrants be bonded. Kumamoto Emigration Company advertised in its labor proposition: "this company has the assurance of the Japanese Government that it will be allowed to exact a bond from the laborer before his departure . . . that he will not desert from his Employers during the term he has been contracted for."[37] Requiring the workers themselves to post bonds partially cleared up the problem of desertion, but as we will see later labor disturbances could not be solved so simply.

Immigrants and their Finances

At the time the Japanese workers signed contracts with the emigration companies and with the sugar planters, their financial arrangements were not complicated. Their agreements promised them wages of between $12.50 and $15.00 for twenty-six days of work. Various fees and charges for passports and visas were paid through company agents. Those who had borrowed money to travel abroad had to worry about repaying their loans. The arrangements became more complex once companies began to require that each worker be bonded to guarantee against desertion. Some forced each person to deposit 5 yen before leaving Japan, and if the contract was not fulfilled, the money would not be returned.[38] In some cases, would-be emigrants had to show proof of financial security by placing a sum in trust in Japan—40 yen for a male worker and 30 yen for a female.[39] Proof of this deposit was handed over to the company in return for a certificate of deposit. It held this money until the end of the contract period. Later most companies dropped this bond system and instead asked the sugar planters to withhold one or two dollars from workers' monthly wages as security against desertion; otherwise, the amount was returned to the worker in a lump sum after three years.

Authorities also wanted each worker to be responsible for their return passage. For the worker who was still uncertain whether he would return to Japan after his contract expired, Hawaiian authorities wanted a guarantee that if a return was foreseen, the worker would at least have passage fare home. Thus most plantation employees had $2.50 withheld from their wages each month after signing the following type of certificate:[40]

Honolulu, Territory of
Hawaii __________ 1902

Messrs ____________________
Gentlemen:

I, the undersigned ____________________ do hereby request and authorize you to deduct from my monthly wages at the end of each and every month, the sum of two dollars and fifty cents ($2.50) until further notice, the same to be remitted to the Kei Hin Bank, Ltd. of Tokio, Japan, through its Agency at Honolulu, in my name and account.

Despite the low wages, the high interest on loans, and the various deductions, most of the Japanese workers managed to save some money over the period of their contracts. In 1897 Japanese Emigration Company of Hiroshima reported to the consulate on the financial condition of those it had sent to Hawaii.[41] In November of that year, the company claimed that the 2,541 workers it had under contract had savings of $37,377, or an average of almost $15 each.

Because Japanese residents in Hawaii felt that the practices of Keihin Bank were unfair and illegal, they went to other banks, notably Yokohama Specie Bank (Yokohama shōkin ginkō), to conduct their financial transactions. For example, during the period between 1 June and 31 December of 1901, 927 immigrant workers had $84,502 on deposit in Keihin Bank.[42] During the same period, 23,930 depositers held $1,274,703 in Yokohama Specie Bank. Figures on the amount of savings held in banks do not reflect the total amount workers managed to save. In most cases, they sent whatever money was left at the end of the month back to Japan.

Sending money *(sōkin)* to families left behind was part of the established tradition of dekasegi rōdō. This sōkin system had been a characteristic of the immigrant community in Hawaii from its very beginning. One historian has estimated that Japanese immigrants sent back an average of 2 million yen a year in the 1885–1893 period, 3 million yen yearly in the 1894–1899 period, 4 million yen a year between 1900 and 1907, and 5 million yen annually until 1934.[43] Thus between 1885 and 1934 about 200 million yen was remitted to Japan. If correct, this sum was equivalent to about 77 percent of the total amount Japan received from *all* of its exports in 1902.[44] One foreign ministry source

TABLE 23
Money Sent to Japan from Hawaii, 1907

Method of Sending Money	*Amount*
Yokohama Specie Bank	
a. Remittances	$ 882,834.32
b. Bank drafts	328,581.75
c. Deposited in Main Branch	1,224,856.69
Total	$2,456,272.76
Money sent through foreign banks	$ 318,450.72
Money sent through postal savings money drafts	$ 913,865.12

Sources: Gaimushō tsūshōkyoku, *Enkaku,* pp. 157–158; and a report attached to a letter from the Consulate to the Foreign Ministry, 6 February 1908, *JFMAD 3.8.2.152.*

estimated that about 28 million dollars was remitted by Japanese workers in Hawaii between 1892 and 1909.[45]

Immigrants sent this money through banks, the postal service, and several emigration companies. The breakdown of how this was sent back in 1907 from Hawaii can be seen in Table 23.

Returning emigrants also carried with them money they had accumulated while overseas. One method of estimating this amount is to look at the bank drafts sold to workers in Hawaii. Since money remitted to Japan did not require the purchase of bank drafts, we can assume that these were sold to those who were hesitant to have large sums of money on their persons. Besides the $328,581 worth of drafts sold by Yokohama Specie Bank in 1907 (see table), this bank reported sales of drafts worth $398,484 in 1906 and $751,508 in 1908.[46]

In 1901 the consulate reported the total amount all Japanese residents in Hawaii (including the former government-sponsored immigrants) remitted during the first half of the emigration company period (see Table 24). The amount of money sent back in 1897 was 61 percent of the amount Japan received from its export of cotton products in that year.[47] It was about what the nation received from its exports of kelp and vegetable wax. In the latter half of the emigration company period, workers and their families sent remittances to their

TABLE 24
Money Sent to Japan, 1894–1908

Year	*Amount*	*Year*	*Amount*
1894	$ 532,162.79	1902	2,582,727.96
1895	484,618.61	1903	3,011,009.04
1896	660,949.56	1904	2,906,037.97
1897	776,527.23	1905	3,644,085.00
1898	841,637.42	1906	3,460,702.44
1899	1,380,704.61	1907	3,688,588.86
1900	1,846,024.25	1908	4,449,079.88
1901	2,462,932.32		
		Total	$32,727,787.94

Sources: Doi, *Hawai,* p. 173; reports from the Consulate to the Foreign Ministry, *JFMAD 3.8.3.152:* 14 November 1901; 6 February 1908; and 25 March 1909.

homes in Japan of an amount that was more than 26 percent of the value of all of the nation's exports in 1897.[48]

Hiroshima, Yamaguchi, and Kumamoto annually received the largest sums from Hawaiian residents because a large number of the remittors were from these areas and not necessarily because each individual from these areas sent more money than residents of other areas. At one point during the latter half of 1901, 203 immigrants from Yamaguchi sent $7,393.50, or an average of $36.42 per person.[49] Former Hiroshima residents sent a larger amount—$8,787.80—because they numbered 242 individuals.

Plantation workers were not the only ones remitting money to Japan; so were some individuals engaged in business in Hawaii. This was indicated by the fact that in 1901 forty-three men, formerly of Tokyo, sent back $51,907, by far the largest amount that year. This meant that each of them remitted an average of $1,207 during a six-month period, something plantation workers were not likely to be able to do. Although the average amount sent on a national basis at this time was $91, Japanese who were not from Tokyo were each sending about $37.

This money represented an important source of foreign capital for the rural areas of Japan. What were the economic consequences for those who remained behind in the villages? Did they benefit from sending relatives overseas to Hawaii?

During both the government-sponsored emigration period and the emigration company period, Hiroshima prefecture sent the most people to Hawaii. A survey taken at the end of 1891 shows that 6,528 Hiroshima immigrants lived in Hawaii.[50] Of this number, 52.7 percent remitted money to families during that year. If we do not count the 1,936 individuals who went during 1891 and who probably did not yet have any money to send, the percentage rises to 74.9. These workers sent back 270,732 yen, or about 54.3 percent of the proposed prefectural budget for that year. The same study shows that 35 percent of this money was used to buy land or tools, 26.9 percent was placed in savings accounts, and the remaining 38.1 percent was used to repay loans and manage other financial matters.

In 1898, 4,736 former Hiroshima residents working in Hawaii sent 305,062 yen to their homes.[51] This, together with 134,834 yen brought back by 654 former emigrants, made up a total of 439,896 yen. This meant that each worker remitting money sent more than 64 yen and those returning carried an average of more than 206 yen. The families used this money in several ways as can be seen in Table 25. During the following year, 7,854 immigrants remitted to their households in the same prefecture a total of 572,145 yen, or an average of 73 yen per person. An additional 769 returned, each carrying about 240 yen, making the total amount carried back 184,993 yen. This money, 757,138 yen, was generally used in the way it was in the previous year (see table).

In 1904, the $305,394 (610,788 yen) sent back to Hiroshima repre-

TABLE 25

Money Sent and Carried Back to Hiroshima, 1898 and 1899

(In yen)

How Remittances Were Used	*1898*	*1899*
Savings	152,983	254,128
Repaying loans	122,394	237,846
Buying land and tools	79,576	119,330
Miscellaneous	84,943	145,834
Totals	439,896	757,138

Source: Report attached to a 12 January 1902 letter from Hiroshima prefectural officials to the Foreign Ministry, *JFMAD 3.8.2.152.*

sented 53.8 percent of that prefecture's budget for the year, or 117 percent of the combined expenditures for public works and education.[52] A survey shows 39.13 percent of this money was saved, 24.12 percent bought land or tools, 20.99 percent paid off loans, and the final 15.67 percent was used for other purposes.[53]

All of this new wealth slowly began to change parts of this prefecture. In 1910 the local governor told returning emigrants: "About fifteen years ago, Niojima village was a lonely place, but now everywhere I can see grand houses surrounded by walls of white mortar. This is all the result of overseas emigration."[54]

Individuals from the village of Miho in Shizuoka prefecture sent back about 12,000 yen annually between 1906 and 1913.[55] This was used to build an irrigation system and start a greenhouse industry in the village. In Wakayama prefecture, remittances were used to build an elementary school.[56]

In Ōshima island, off the coast of Yamaguchi prefecture, island residents faced problems of overpopulation and a scarcity of farm land before overseas emigration began. It was so poor that people labeled the island *Imokuijima,* meaning that people there were only able to eat sweet potatoes.[57] Later, after money had been sent back by former Ōshima residents in Hawaii, it became known as *Ōgonjima,* or island of gold.

The Emigration Companies, the Bank, and the Consulate

In Hawaii the emigration companies, Keihin Bank, and the consulate played crucial roles in the lives of the Japanese. These roles included not merely performing the usual functions of such institutions. Eventually they played an involuntary but vital role in the development of political consciousness in that community. This in turn inevitably led to the start of organized political and labor movements in Hawaii. In the beginning, like the sugar planters in the area of labor relations, these three institutions had a large advantage over the Japanese workers in terms of capital, political support, and prestige. Yet during the early years of the twentieth century, these immigrant laborers created the basis for two political movements, one directed against the emigration companies, Keihin Bank, and the consulate, and the other against the sugar planters.

Keihin Bank, the object of much criticism by immigrants, was one of several Japanese financial institutions in Hawaii during this period.

The first, Yokohama Specie Bank (currently Bank of Tokyo), opened a branch office in Honolulu on 8 August 1892.[58] Keihin Bank was not set up in Hawaii until 1898. Perhaps Yokohama Specie Bank's early establishment gave it an advantage over its competitors in accumulating deposits from the immigrants. Although it obtained only $236 of deposits in 1892, this bank held deposits of $230,598 in 1901 and $383,170 by 1910. Others established in Hawaii included Japanese Bank (June of 1909), Pacific Bank (1913), and a branch of Sumitomo Bank (1916).

Keihin Bank, as one historian has written, "was set up to squeeze the sweat and blood out of immigrants. . . ."[59] Organized by three emigration companies specifically to service an immigrant clientele, the bank officers and major stockholders were all affiliated with these companies.[60] This bank was accused of charging high rates of interest, collecting more than once on loans, forcing emigrants to buy bonds that guaranteed their good health, and of outright fraud. Immigrants were also angered by the fact that while they paid 12.5 percent interest on money borrowed from Keihin Bank, it only paid 4 percent on deposit certificates.[61]

Keihin Bank acted as an agent for Bansei Insurance Company and sold to departing workers policies that promised to reimburse the sugar planter if the workers were not healthy enough on arrival to fulfill their contracts. It made huge profits from these policies because it insured individuals who had passed medical examinations in Yokohama and thus who were already in good health when they reached Honolulu.[62]

Accounts of its activities appeared regularly in newspapers in Hawaii and Japan. In one article it was revealed that Keihin Bank officers refused to believe that one of its depositers had died and would not release the money in his account which was needed to pay for funeral expenses.[63] Eventually the friends of the deceased brought the corpse to the bank and forced the officers to release the money.

The bank was also investigated by authorities in both Japan and Hawaii. An article in *Hawai Shinpō* in 1905 pointed out that Japanese officials were investigating a case of fraud involving bank officials and that it was likely that some would be punished.[64] The first head of the Hawaiian branch of Keihin Bank, Ishizuka Chūhei, and his successor, Shiota Okuzō, had ties with the Jiyūtō political party.[65] People in Hawaii saw them as followers of Hoshi Tōru, who visited Hawaii several times during this period while he was posted in Washington D.C. Others who worked at Keihin Bank included Murakami Taizō,

Ōtsuka Shizuo, Komabayashi Hiroshi, Hayashi Kenkichirō, Hinata Takeshi, and Ueno Tōnosuke.[66] Bank officials, particularly those living with Hoshi in Honolulu, were criticized by the larger Japanese community for their lavish lifestyle.

Most of the complaints directed against the emigration companies and their agents concerned financial matters, but some involved the behavior of agents stationed in Hawaii. These agents were seen by the immigrant community as exploitive and their behavior, objectionable. Their behavior was such that geisha houses in Honolulu became known as the "emigration companies' villas."[67] The agents lived in large mansions and walked about in fashionable clothes and sported canes, flaunting their wealth. A U.S. commissioner of labor in 1906 described these emigration companies as being "an evil, and something of a scandal. . . ."[68]

In the early days of immigration, many Japanese workers felt grateful that an official representative of their government had been posted in Honolulu. The consul general was seen as the leader of the growing community. During both the Waipahu strike of 1904 and the Lahaina strike of 1905, he headed mediation teams that helped settle disputes. However, consular staff officials, who rotated back to Japan every one or two years, tended to look at the immigrants as their charges. Their relationship, as one historian characterized it, resembled that between "a Japanese lord and his retainer. . . ."[69] A number of workers complained about the activities of the consular staff, particularly its restrictive supervision of the Japanese community in Hawaii and the alleged "secret" relationship it had with several emigration companies.[70]

The event that shifted the community's attitude toward the consulate from one of support to widespread criticism occurred in 1903. In that year, a drive to consolidate the various Japanese community and business groups into one major organization that could speak for the immigrants in Hawaii took place. On 30 November the *Chūō Nipponjinkai,* also known as the Central Japanese League, established itself at a community-wide meeting.[71] With 25,000 members contributing 60¢ each, it was able to propose a budget for 1904 of $14,147.[72] This organization, headed by Consul General Saitō, promised to lower the number of labor disturbances on the plantations, to halt worker migration to the mainland United States, and to improve the educational situation for Japanese children born in Hawaii.[73]

The immigrant community watched the activities of the Central Japanese League for almost two years before it responded to it by accusing the organization of being friendly toward Keihin Bank and several emigration companies. They pointed out that representatives of the bank and of the companies served as directors of the League.[74] Furthermore they claimed that the number of labor disturbances had increased during the two years the League was in operation, and that the League had sided with the planters in the 1904 Waipahu strike.

In 1905 the Japanese community took action and formed the *Kakushin Dōshikai,* also known as the Japanese Reform Association. By taking this step, the workers and their families declared their opposition to the practices of the emigration companies, Keihin Bank, the consulate, and the Central Japanese League. In a petition to the Japanese government on 2 June, the Reform Association demanded that Saitō be transferred, that certain practices of the emigration companies be curtailed, and that questionable activities of Keihin Bank be stopped.[75]

In response to the first demand, the Japanese government recalled Saitō for "consultations" in December of 1905. When he returned to his post in Honolulu he had a reported "better attitude" toward the immigrant workers. At the same time, the foreign ministry began to restrict the activities of emigration company agents and as a result some of them, including Japanese Emigration Company of Hiroshima and Kumamoto Emigration Company, recalled their employees stationed in Hawaii.[76] In August of 1905 Japanese officials forbad Keihin Bank to hold immigrants' contracts.[77] They also invalidated all outstanding agreements between the bank and immigrant depositers.[78] By spring of 1906 most of the company agents and bank officials had left Hawaii. Finally the foreign ministry prevented Keihin Bank from continuing operations after 6 October 1907.[79] The Reform Association itself disbanded on 9 September 1906 and announced:

> The Reform Association, formed on May of last year to extricate the 70,000 Japanese from the clutches of the Keihin Bank and the immigration companies, has fulfilled its mission. . . . Legal protection afforded . . . by the Japanese Foreign Ministry's new immigration policy did not extend coverage to [those] in Hawaii, which led to the highhanded acts of the immigration companies and the wily activities of the Keihin Bank. The Reform Association, therefore requested the Japanese government to take certain action. Action has been taken by our government and our job has been accomplished. . . . We 70,000 strong can easily unite again if the need arises. This is to declare that the dissolution of the Reform Association does not mean the demise of its fighters.[80]

The success of the Reform Association represented a major turning point for the Japanese community in Hawaii. It had demanded specific changes and secured them primarily by identifying the Japanese workers' exploiters. They directed action not against an unidentifiable government bureaucracy or a particularly large group of people but specific individuals. The Japanese community saw this as a simple matter: the continued presence of agents and bank officials in Hawaii meant failure and forcing them to leave was a victory.

A number of Hawaii-based Japanese language newspapers also played an important part in this confrontation. In particular, *Shin Nippon, Hawai Shinpō,* and *Hawai Nichi Nichi Shinbun* led the criticism against the alleged exploiters. Several newspapers in Japan also helped when they charged the emigration companies of illegal practices and brought this to the attention of the Japanese government.

It also helped that the foreign ministry was responsive to the immigrants' complaints. It is doubtful whether the Hawaiian government would have responded in the same way if some of its companies or banks were accused of illegal or unethical practices in a foreign country. In all of the disputes between the sugar planters and the workers, Japanese or others, it supported the stand taken by the planters. The Japanese government, on the other hand, responded in this instance in an active and positive way to help its citizens overseas.

The last reason for the success of this movement was the ability of the Japanese workers to present a united front against those they perceived to be their enemies. Not only were they able to gain the support of the Japanese newspapers in Honolulu but they convinced many of the initial supporters, including directors of the Central Japanese League, to join the new Reform Association. Although fifty-eight delegates had founded the League in 1903, only twenty-three attended the second meeting in 1904.[81]

Through the Reform Association Japanese workers in Hawaii were able to confront a specific political problem and attempt to reach a solution. It is ironic that the contribution of the emigration companies to the political development of the Japanese community was that they stimulated criticism and political organizing against them. The formation of the Reform Association was, at the time, the most important political act undertaken by this immigrant group. The success of the Reform Association gave the workers a sense of their own power and began a trend of nationalistic organizing to confront problems facing the community. Undoubtedly this played an essential role in awakening the political and social consciousness of the Japanese community and in leading to the sugar plantation strike of 1909.

Labor Problems and Strikes

The second important political movement of the Japanese community in Hawaii sought to find solutions for the numerous complaints the plantation workers had, including poor living conditions, low wages, and ill-treatment by overseers. Early on, a worker would confront these problems alone; he simply fled during the night and sought better conditions elsewhere. However, it was not realistic to assume that thousands of workers would be able to flee the sugar cane fields and, like the early deserters, manage to find better jobs elsewhere. The solution lay in correcting whatever was wrong on the plantations with the intention of continuing to work there. Although deserters created serious problems for the planters, the latter had only to replace these workers. As the years passed, the Japanese workers abandoned this solution and started to demand changes on the plantations, using the threat of a strike as leverage. The increase in labor disturbances and strikes around the turn of the century indicated the beginning of this tendency to institute reforms in the system rather than to escape from it. This reflected a remarkable change in the thinking of the immigrants, a modification of goals that one American government official commented on: "With their families here, [Japanese workers'] expenses become higher and they demand higher wages, or they seek more independent positions than those of common field laborers, leasing if possible a tract of land."[82]

One method of analyzing this change in the thinking and behavior of the Japanese workers is to examine the labor strikes, the causes behind them, their duration, and their results. In 1900 and 1901 Japanese sugar cane workers participated in nineteen work stoppages, including one in which Chinese workers also took part.[83] None of these were ordered by any labor organization, nor did any involve more than one plantation. The longest lasted eight workdays and the shortest a single day, with the average lasting four or five days. Some of the disputes centered around one demand, while others involved several. The demands can be divided into five areas of concern: overseers, wage increases, living conditions, working conditions, and lastly financial or contractual matters.

In four of the strikes, workers demanded the discharge of specific overseers. Five listed wage increases as the criterion for settlement. The only time living conditions was the issue was when those residing on Lahaina Plantation asked for an increase in the camp water supply. However, poor working conditions did cause a number of disturbances. Two groups of men demanded the employment of Japanese as overseers, while two others asked for the reinstatement of discharged laborers. One walkout occurred because workers were dissatisfied with their work hours; in another instance the issue was holidays. One group of fieldhands protested against the "task system" in which each person was paid according to the amount of work he had done rather than given a regular salary.

In three cases Japanese workers objected to having part of their wages withheld. Other plantations were struck because workers wanted contracts canceled, uniform wages, and payment for injuries suffered while on the job. Only in five of these nineteen cases were the demands completely or partially met by the planters; the others ended in failure, and disappointed Japanese had to return to their jobs.

A similar survey taken of the twelve strikes that occurred between 1903 and 1905 shows some changes in the nature of these walkouts.[84] As in the earlier years, they lasted anywhere from one to eight days, but on the average about three-and-a-half days. In general there were two issues behind these walkouts. In six of the labor disturbances the workers asked for the discharge of their overseers, and in five of these cases the plantations gave in and fired the overseers. However, in the five instances in which the Japanese asked for increases in wages, only two strikes were partially successful. The sugar planters found firing one or two overseers (if that alone placated the workers) preferable to raising wages—which meant financial loss. The sugar planters stood firm in resisting changes in this area. In such cases, there may also have been some pressure exerted by neighboring planters to keep wages uniform because it benefited them. Three of the five strikes in 1905 were ordered by Japanese labor organizations—another sign of changing times.

During the 1900–1909 period Japanese workers' demands for higher wages increased, and they were no longer satisfied with the firing of a few overseers. Still the sugar planters refused to change the existing wage scale. Furthermore, because they realized that labor unions would inevitably lead to prolonged strikes that could involve more than one plantation, they expressed complete opposition to organized labor. The planters were supported by the Japanese government and consular officials. During the 1909 strike, Consul General Ueno Sen'ichi wrote to Foreign Minister Komura Jutarō that while the cost of living had gone up for the workers, the planters had spent a great deal of money to benefit their employees. He concluded: "it is obviously inequitable to pay all men the same wages."[85]

Nevertheless, supported by their community and a group of crusading newspapermen, more than 7,000 Japanese workers walked off their jobs on *all* of Oahu's plantations in May of 1909. It was, at the time, the most important labor event in Hawaiian history. It was the beginning of a trend of labor organizing and political activity not only by the Japanese but also by other ethnic groups in Hawaii.

Activity After the End of the Contracts

Beginning in 1897 the first Japanese workers sent to Hawaii by the emigration companies faced the end of their contract periods. They and others who had joined them by the thousands during the following three years all had the same options government-sponsored immigrants had.

Between 14 June 1900 and the middle of 1904 over 23,000 workers opted to leave and return to Japan.[86] From 1905 through the first half of 1910 almost 25,000 others, including more than 6,000 children, began their long journeys home. Generally two types of people returned during this period. The first managed to save a considerable amount of money and went back as examples of what could be achieved by working overseas. The second type consisted of those who for various reasons had not been able to save very much. These people would have been grateful that money had been deducted from their wages so that return passage to Japan was guaranteed. Migration had been a failure to them and when they landed in Yokohama, they carried only memories of three years of hard work in Hawaii.

After their initial contracts had expired or were outlawed by federal law in 1900, some immigrants chose to work as "free laborers" for any sugar planter who would hire them. As can be seen in Table 15, the number of Japanese on the plantations remained relatively stable even after 1900. However, the same table shows that their numbers, as compared to the total population of plantation workers, had declined. By 1924 only 15,339 Japanese, or 34 percent of the plantation labor force, remained in the sugar cane fields in Hawaii.[87]

Another option open to Japanese immigrants during the early years of the twentieth century was to leave Hawaii for the mainland United States through the port cities of San Francisco and Seattle. Just as Japanese had been encouraged by letters from earlier emigrants to go to Hawaii, Japanese workers in Hawaii were told success lay in the west coast of the United States and Canada. There were even reports of individuals arriving in Hawaii in 1904 and wanting to leave for California after working only two days.[88]

According to federal statistics, between 1 January 1902 and 31 December 1905, 20,266 Japanese left Hawaii for the U.S. mainland.[89] In 1906, 13,578 others departed from Honolulu for Seattle and San Francisco.[90] After Japan's acceptance of the Gentlemen's Agreement, the number of its citizens going from Hawaii to the mainland fell to 755 in 1908 and 1,106 in 1909. Futhermore as travel to the east became more restricted, the only Japanese leaving Hawaii were on board ships going west. Between 1911 and 1915 only 215 individuals left Hawaii for the continental United States, while 15,737 returned to Japan.[91] Japanese went to the U.S. mainland in large numbers between 1900 and 1907 because of the promise of wages higher than those paid in Hawaii. The following are translations from two newspaper advertisements calling for workers to leave Hawaii:

> Recruiting Laborers to America
>
> For the [Southern Pacific Railroad] Company, 800 men; for Alaska, 200 men. Advance $20 for passage to San Francisco. Applications for Alaska close 28th instant. Egi Kyujiro, Prop. Shiranui Hotel, S.F. Apply to the below mentioned hotels in Honolulu. . . .
>
> Great Recruiting to America
>
> Through an arrangement with Yasuzawa of San Francisco, we are able to recruit laborers to the mainland, and offer them work. The laborers will be subjected to no delay upon arriving in San Francisco, but can get work immediately through Yasuzawa. Employment offered in picking strawberries and tomatoes, planting beets, mining, and domestic service.[92]

Another company seeking 600 workers in the Seattle-Tacoma area guaranteed wages of $1.25 to $1.35 per day for railroad work and similar wages for jobs in salmon canneries.[93] It was rumored that Japanese were employed on railroads or in fruit orchards, earning a dollar a day or almost twice as much as Hawaiian plantation workers.

The U.S. commissioner of labor in 1906 wrote that there were two reasons for this movement. He pointed out that while the economic incentive was foremost in the minds of these Japanese, "the conditions of labor are freer in the Pacific States than on the large plantations of Hawaii where the traditions of penal contract days have not disappeared."[94]

Three groups were involved in recruiting Japanese for mainland jobs. The first were boardinghouse owners mainly from the San Francisco area; they stood to gain from large numbers of workers passing through their city. One observer noted: "The Japanese Boarding House Keepers Association of San Francisco have incorporated and one of their chief aims will be to bring Japanese from Hawaii to San Francisco."[95]

The boardinghouses and hotels served as or worked with labor agents. They signed up workers for jobs in railroads, the lumber and fish industries, and agriculture. These men of course received commissions from the American companies for their recruiting efforts. The *San Francisco Chronicle* reported in a 15 June 1902 article that the labor agent "is in a position to furnish employment for hundreds of Japanese and, as the demand is very great, he has entered into the ring of boarding-house and hotelkeepers to import coolies from Honolulu."[96] It went on to mention that seven of the largest Japanese boardinghouses in the city were providing this service. Not only did these houses advertise in Hawaiian newspapers but they also sent agents out to do active recruiting. The San Francisco owners and agents who led this drive included the individuals (hotel name) listed in Appendix 15.[97]

The San Francisco group succeeded in enlisting the cooperation of their counterparts in Honolulu, the Japanese Boarding House Owners Association (see Appendix 14).[98] The boardinghouses in Honolulu made most of their money from travelers coming in or going out of port and so as the number of incoming immigrants decreased in 1900 and 1901 (see Table 10) competition for new clients among boardinghouses and hotels increased. Yamashiro Matsutarō, who established the boardinghouses Yamashiroya and Geishūya in Honolulu, claimed that he helped a group of twenty-one workers travel to the U.S. mainland in July of 1901, the first of such attempts.[99] The Honolulu boardinghouse owners realized that Japanese workers going to the west coast would be forced to stay at the houses while waiting for the departing ships. They not only collected money from these workers for arranging their ship passage but also commissions from their San Francisco counterparts for their recruiting efforts.

These two groups received help from several shipping companies that wanted to carry these workers to San Francisco and Seattle. There is evidence that at least one shipping company offered special "bulk rates" for large groups and free passage for agents who escorted groups of more than forty.[100] Shipping companies also paid for the newspaper advertisements that displayed their offers to carry Japanese workers to the U.S. mainland at special low rates.[101]

Several groups were opposed to allowing laborers to migrate to the U.S. mainland: the Hawaiian sugar planters who were losing workers, the U.S. government, which had been trying to hold down the number of Japanese arriving on the west coast, and Tokyo officials, who had become aware of the growing anti-Japanese movement in the United States. The sugar planters tried to keep their workers on the plantations in Hawaii with financial incentives. From 1 May 1905 wages were raised, and the planters asked the consular staff to issue public notices to this effect.[102] In a letter to the consul, the president of the HSPA wrote: "it is hoped that the increase of wages now proposed will have the effect of satisfying them with their work and surroundings so that they will remain in the islands."[103]

The planters also turned to Hawaiian government authorities for help. Realizing that the migration of workers might endanger a fragile economy, on 21 April 1905 the territorial legislature passed "An Act in Relation to the Licensing of Emigrant Agents." This act defined an emigrant agent as being a person who is "engaged in hiring laborers in the Territory of Hawaii . . . to go beyond the limits of the Territory of Hawaii for the purpose of being employed."[104] This law did not prohibit recruitment of workers in Hawaii; it merely forced recruiters to acquire business licenses—and to pay an annual fee of $500. Those who were convicted of operating without proper license were subject to fines of between $500 and $1,000 for *each* violation.

The emigration companies, meanwhile, began to recruit in areas they had previously ignored (particularly in the Okinawan islands) so they could replace the workers going to the U.S. mainland from Hawaii. They hoped that these untapped sources of labor would provide enough men to satisfy the sugar planters and the Hawaiian government. Those from Okinawa proved to be good workers, as they tended to stay on the sugar plantations and form communities in Hawaii. From only 45 emigrants in 1903, the number of workers from that prefecture rose to 1,233 in 1905, 4,467 the next year, and 2,525 in 1907.[105] It was estimated that by the end of the Meiji period (1911) more than 10,000 Okinawans were living in Hawaii.[106]

The U.S. government dealt with migration primarily through legal measures. A Presidential Order on 19 March 1907 prevented those who had left Japan with passports for Mexico, Canada, and Hawaii from entering the United States mainland. This of course caused many problems for those in Hawaii who wanted to work there. Tamashiro Baishiro had saved enough money for passage fare and in 1907 made arrangements to go to the U.S. mainland, but as he wrote, "On March 20th there was a change in the law, and I was prohibited to go to America. . . . We were planning to go on April 9th; however, the rule . . . came on the 20th of March."[107]

Although the Japanese government continued to allow its citizens to leave to work on Hawaii's sugar plantations, it was growing more aware of the anti-Japanese movement in the United States. It saw the migration of workers to the west coast as unnecessary and possibly dangerous for Japanese-American relations. This was one of the reasons it accepted the Gentlemen's Agreement.

In the Gentlemen's Agreement, the Japanese government promised to stop issuing passports to "laborers" who wanted to travel to America. In other words, the only Japanese immigrants who were granted passports were former residents and parents, wives, and children of Japanese living in the United States. Finally on 24 February 1913 a Presidential Order ruled that the President could prevent foreign residents on American insular possessions from entering the United States mainland if their entrance proved to be a threat to mainland workers.

Japanese government officials tried to prevent this movement of workers to the U.S. mainland in other ways as well. A public notice issued by Yamanashi prefectural authorities in October of 1905 warned potential emigrants about traveling to the mainland United States after a stop in Hawaii.[108] The consulate in Honolulu cooperated with the sugar planters and issued notices that publicized wage increases on the plantations. Officials also warned the Japanese workers about the risk of going to California and not finding jobs. For example, in March of 1903 they issued a "Notice to Emigrants Intending to go to the Mainland of the United States," which warned about the large number of complaints filed in their office by people who felt they had been cheated. The notice went on to say that "some of the complainants were robbed of the entire amount entrusted to these men to cover the cost of passage to the United States, while others were cheated out of a large portion of their deposit."[109] Finally, to help unify the efforts to halt the migration out of Hawaii, the consulate helped establish the Central Japanese League.

Eventually the number of Japanese leaving Hawaii began to decrease, particularly after 1907. This was despite the fact that the sugar planters could not match the wages offered on the mainland. In the end, it was the restrictions on passports and visas instituted by the governments of Japan and the U.S. that proved to be the major factors that halted this migration.

The last option open to workers whose contract periods had ended or had been canceled after June of 1900 was to move off the plantations and look for other jobs in Hawaii. Many of them migrated to Honolulu and other urban centers, while some became independent farmers. This movement indicated a change in the thinking of many of the Japanese immigrants. They began to see themselves as permanent members of Hawaiian society, a significant departure from the traditional dekasegi rōdō perspective. *The Report of the Commissioner of Labor on Hawaii, 1901* summarizes the gradual infiltration of these people into what had been non-Japanese industries and enterprises. The following are excerpts from that report:

> Japanese fishermen have practically driven the Hawaiians out of this business in the vicinity of the larger towns. They constituted less than 7 percent of those reported in this occupation in 1896 and more than 25 percent in 1900.
>
> Sailors employed upon the local shipping have always been Hawaiian but Japanese are also getting a foothold in this occupation.
>
> The Japanese are undoubtedly making some inroads into fields of employment in the building trades that have hitherto been reserved for white mechanics. They monopolize all the work for their own countrymen. . . .
>
> The clothing trades are almost entirely in the hands of Orientals.
>
> The food, liquor, and restaurant trades employ chiefly Asiatic labor. . . .
>
> Caucasians and Hawaiians predominate in the metal-working and foundry trades, though the Japanese are competing actively and opening small, independent establishments, wherever they have the skill and capital to do so.
>
> The Japanese are crowding into the stevedore and wharf work to an

extent that is causing friction and even influencing local politics in Honolulu.[110]

The same report pointed out that there were 328 Japanese-run mercantile establishments in 1901; that 870 individuals were paying real estate taxes; and that 26,560 Japanese were paying taxes on $1,250,000 worth of property in that same year. By 1910 they held real property valued at $255,810 and liquid assets of $1,664,402.[111] Although the sugar plantations were still the major source of jobs for these immigrants, particularly those just arriving from Japan, the move into the larger Hawaiian community had clearly begun. The establishment of a permanent secondary population had taken place.

There were other indicators that a growing number of Japanese planned to settle permanently in Hawaii. As was said earlier, a number of workers who had left for Japan after their contracts expired came back to stay because of the higher wages; others may have done so because of family members who had stayed in Hawaii. Between 1908 and 1915, 4,307 Japanese returned to the islands.[112] Others went directly to the U.S. mainland to work or to join families. They and more than 11,000 others landed in San Francisco and Seattle between 1908 and 1911.[113]

Another indication that Japanese immigrants intended to settle down in Hawaii was the *yobiyose* (call or summon) phenomenon. The Japanese already living in Hawaii "called" family members or spouses to join them. For example, of those who applied in April of 1912 for passports to enter Hawaii, 118 were women who wanted to join their husbands; 107 were sons of immigrants, 57 of whom were eldest sons; and 37 were daughters.[114] Lastly, 53 parents (mostly fathers) and foster children wished to travel to Hawaii to join their families. This was not in keeping with the traditional dekasegi rōdō pattern whereby family members remained at home; nonetheless Japanese in Hawaii had been calling for their wives and other family members since the earliest days of overseas migration. On the third shipment of workers which left Yokohama for Honolulu early in 1886, fifty of the passengers were yobiyose, passengers, that is, relatives of those who had left less than a year before.[115] During the 1908 to 1915 period the number of yobiyose immigrants to Hawaii and the U.S. mainland can be seen in Table 26.

A large number of women (as compared to men) were called overseas to balance the uneven sex ratio in a predominantly male community. Most of these women were wives who had been left behind in

TABLE 26
Yobiyose Immigrants Entering Hawaii and the Mainland United States, 1908–1915

	Immigrants Entering Hawaii		*Immigrants Entering U.S. Mainland*	
Year	*Men*	*Women*	*Men*	*Women*
1908	1,325	1,282 (755)[a]	341	573
1909	191	784 (436)	105	343
1910	349	1,195 (658)	101	527
1911	503	1,752 (865)	217	972
1912	1,159	2,687 (1,285)	234	1,456
1913	1,032	2,461 (1,572)	363	1,705
1914	705	1,877 (1,407)	605	2,112
1915	626	1,655 (1,050)	848	2,106
Totals	5,890	13,693 (8,028)	2,814	9,794

Sources: Compiled from Gaimushō tsūshōkyoku, *Ryoken kafusū,* pp. 190–204, and Okahata, *Japanese in Hawaii,* p. 165.
[a]Figures in parentheses are the number of picture brides that entered Hawaii in a given year.

Japan or were "picture brides" *(shashin hanayome).* Women who were the latter used a modern version of the traditional custom of relying on intermediaries to negotiate marriages. They became betrothed to men who did not return to Japan through a process that involved an exchange of photographs. For many of the young women arriving in Honolulu, the thought of marrying a stranger and of beginning a new life in a foreign land caused considerable anguish. Yamaguchi Tsuru spoke of her feelings at the time: "[The Bureau of Immigration] had all the people who'd been sent for [as picture brides] sit on a couch. The people who came to get us saw us. . . . "I'm being taken away by a man today," I thought, frightened at the idea. Those who came as picture brides with me were holding me down; I was trembling so much, scared . . . but the more experienced women who were holding on to my shaking legs were saying, "When they come to get us, we'll all be taken away so don't be scared."[116]

Immigration officials in both Hawaii and on the U.S. mainland were reluctant to allow these women to enter the country, being particularly concerned that in most cases these brides had never met their husbands before. The relatively young age of some of the couples also upset the immigration inspectors. At one point, the consulate in San Francisco felt compelled to explain in a letter that in Japan the minimum age for marriage (with parental permission) was fifteen for females and seventeen for males.[117]

This explanation did not satisfy many of the American inspectors who had formed their impressions of Japanese women quite early. An American official wrote in 1899 that, "It is a fact . . . believed by all the immigration officers . . . that at least 75 per cent of the women who come to the United States are lewd, or at least of such a low quality of virtue that they are easily overcome by the conditions which they find in this country."[118]

According to the U.S. Department of Immigration, of the total number of women who were called to Hawaii, picture brides made up more than 58 percent, as can be seen in Table 26. A U.S. government official commenting on this phenomenon which began around 1900 reported that while 17.9 percent of the Japanese leaving the islands were women, they made up 39.3 percent of those arriving. He concluded that, "This change in the character of Japanese may indicate that the people of that nationality are beginning to take root in the Territory to a greater extent than heretofore. . . ."[119]

Two other signs point to the growing realization among the Japanese that their stay in Hawaii would be long if not permanent. The first was the establishment of Japanese language periodicals, which ranged from daily newspapers to monthly literary journals. Thirty-eight different newspapers and magazines started operations between June of 1892 and the end of 1907.[120] Most were published in Honolulu, with local newspapers available on the outer islands of Hawaii, Maui, and Kauai. Four newspapers played particularly important roles in the early years: *Hawai Nichi Nichi Shinbun* (established in 1901), *Shin Nippon* (1897), *Hawai Shinpō* (1894), and *Nippu Jiji* (1895). They were later joined in 1912 by *Hawai Hochi.* These newspapers served not only as the means of communication between the plantation camps and small towns in rural Hawaii but also as the spokesmen for the Japanese community. They were in the frontline of every political and social issue that confronted members of this community.

The second sign was the large number of children born to Japanese families in Hawaii. The number of Japanese school-age children grew at a much faster rate than those of other ethnic groups. From 1900 to 1901 the rate of increase was 47 percent, while the same rate for all nationalities in Hawaii was 13 percent.[121] As the number of children rose, Japanese language schools also multiplied. By 1915 more than 13,500 children were studying the language and traditions of their parents' home country in 135 privately run schools.[122] This was the beginning of the second generation of Japanese in America.

CHAPTER 8

The End of the Emigration Companies

THE success of the government-sponsored emigration of the previous ten-year period inspired the private companies established after 1894 to expand their operations. They saw the migration of thousands of Japanese to Hawaii's sugar plantations as the underpinning of a stable system that "begged" for private management. All of the companies that entered this field assumed that financial success lay ahead and it seems many had attained it, since twenty-nine companies shipped 10,355 workers to Hawaii in 1905 and thirty companies sent 24,887 the following year.[1] Yet after 1908, mainly as a result of the Gentlemen's Agreement, no emigrants, contract or free, used the services of private agents to enter the islands.[2] The emigration company period in Hawaii had ended that year, marking the close of an era for the Japanese community there. The story of how these emigration companies tried to survive in the complex, multinational arena of overseas emigration points out the weaknesses inherent in private enterprise ventures. In other words, the successful government-sponsored venture became one based on company profits and losses in the hands of emigration companies.

The emigration companies had specific internal weaknesses that limited their effectiveness in dealing with large groups of workers, and they also fell victim to events occurring outside their own sphere. In other words, events in Japan, Hawaii, and the United States eventually limited the activities of the companies that tried to send workers to these areas. In addition, international events also affected attempts to send laborers to Canada, Australia, the Philippines, and Latin America.

In order to survive, these companies needed a foreign market that was seeking Japanese workers and a dekasegi rōdō system at home. A temporary work system meant that the companies could continue to send new people year after year since those who returned to Japan had to be replaced. Whenever possible, company officials preferred a labor contract system in which they were guaranteed commissions before the workers even left their homes. Such a system tied individuals to their written agreements and thus made it easier for the company agents to obtain contracts with overseas employers, who wanted above all a stable labor force they could count on for several years.

A successful private emigration system also required a large pool of potential emigrants who were willing to work abroad. Providing an adequate supply of workers was not a problem for the companies as long as sugar planters in Hawaii could offer high wages and agents did their jobs.

Also, changes in government policy on the part of Japan or Hawaii could mean either success or failure for the companies. Unfortunately one of the assumptions the companies operated under was that there would be unrestricted and unlimited movement of workers to the Hawaiian islands.

It is understandable why these companies failed to anticipate the changes that took place in 1900 when Hawaii became an American territory. Their only concerns from month to month were to send as many workers abroad as possible and to receive their commissions. For the same reason, they were not able to respond to their own government's policies—particularly those that restricted the number of Japanese traveling to Hawaii. They also did not try to counter the U.S. government's efforts to restrict the immigration of "laborers," other than to send as many of them as possible before the deadlines. All of these factors contributed to the demise of the emigration companies.

The Weaknesses of the Emigration Companies

During the 1885 to 1894 period the main concern of Japanese officials was sending workers overseas in as safe and stable a way as possible. As was mentioned previously, the government did not expect to make a profit from shipping emigrants abroad and saw the benefits of this migration as being long-term. They hoped that emigration would help the countryside by reducing the number of people there and at the same time encourage an accumulation of foreign capital through overseas remittances.

The private companies could not afford to adopt such an attitude because unless profits could be made in a short time, they would either go bankrupt or be closed by the government. Competition being the basis of the free enterprise system, companies vied for workers, labor contracts with the sugar planters, and cooperative arrangements with boardinghouses and shipping companies. As a result, companies and their agents used whatever means were necessary to reduce expenses and increase profits. Government documents show that the large majority of the cases involving violations of the Emigrant Protection Law took place after 1900, when the competition for sending workers to Hawaii had increased.[3]

Competition between companies led to advertising violations, broken promises, illegal rebates, and questionable ties with boardinghouses, shipping agents, banks, and insurance companies. This in turn left companies subject to close government scrutiny and control and created a bad image in the press. Also, a growing number of workers began to travel to Hawaii without labor contracts or decided not to use the services of the emigration companies. The result was, of course, even more competition for the remaining workers and quota slots.

In Hawaii the criticism against these companies eventually resulted in the formation of the Japanese Reform Association in 1905. The companies were at the height of their activity when the very workers they had shipped began to oppose their practices. The Japanese foreign ministry responded to the workers' position by restricting the activities of the company agents. Faced with the Japanese community's opposition, something that they themselves had created, the emigration companies gave up trying to send workers to Hawaii after the Gentlemen's Agreement in 1908.

Events in Hawaii that Affected Company Activity

Although aware of the sugar planters' need for workers, Hawaiian society found it difficult to absorb large numbers of Chinese and Japanese immigrants. Government authorities and the sugar planters expected them to return to their home countries after the contracts had expired. When thousands of Asian workers chose to remain, efforts were made to limit nonplantation jobs through legal restrictions based on the fact that these immigrants were legally classified as "aliens."

From 1887 the laws of the Hawaiian Kingdom prevented Asians from obtaining citizenship.[4] The constitution of the republic in 1894 forbad the naturalization of Japanese, and a law in the same year required incoming immigrants to have in hand a labor contract or $50.

In an attempt to restrict Japanese and Chinese from entering the fishing industry, government authorities announced in 1902 that "aliens must pay duty of one cent a pound on fish caught in sea waters off Hawaii."[5] Asians met discrimination again when they were not allowed to hold certain public service jobs. Also in that same year, the Superintendent of Public Works in Honolulu stated one specification for road repair crews that, "No Asiatic labor to be employed on this work under penalty of forfeiture of contract."[6]

Other restrictions placed on Japanese occur in the "Act to Provide a Government for the Territory of Hawaii." Section 100 of the 1899 act provided that naturalization was possible only after five years of residence.[7] Another section reserved homestead public land for citizens, and section 452 provided that land could not be acquired or held by or for the benefit of any alien. The Hawaiian government also tried to control the number of Japanese entering Honolulu by preventing ships from landing "more than seven hundred (700) steerage passengers at the port of Honolulu or any other port of the Hawaiian Islands at any one time."[8]

These were but a few examples of how Hawaii viewed immigrants from Asia; their labor was needed on a short-term basis, but their presence over a long period was something to be prevented. Government officials had tried for years to encourage the sugar planters to import non-Asian workers but with little success. At one time the government tried to maintain the status quo on the plantations by announcing in 1899 that, "no further immigration permits for Japanese shall be approved by Executive Council except to maintain on each plantation a force of Japanese employees equal in number to the other employees on such plantation."[9] The problem was that while efforts to find "cheap" white workers failed again and again, thousands of Japanese were willing to work in Hawaii for the wages offered them. The attempt to hold down the number of workers from Japan was complicated by the fact that plantation supervisors preferred them to workers of other nationalities. When a representative of the Bureau of Immigration asked plantation managers about their preference of workers, twenty-three of fifty-nine managers said Japanese.[10] Two others named both Japanese and Portuguese as their choices.

After Hawaii became a part of the United States, the sugar planters realized that they still needed cheap labor and so asked to be exempted from U.S. government restrictions on importing Asian workers. They asked for permission to import not Japanese but Chinese workers for the plantations. The planters argued: "the United States exclusion laws shut out this nationality [Chinese] from Hawaii as soon as annexation became an accomplished fact, and our sole dependence is now placed in Japan for such intermittent supply of labor. . . ."[11] The planters did not obtain permission, but it is clear that even as late as 1923, the Hawaiian sugar planters wanted to reinstitute Chinese immigration rather than use workers from Japan.[12]

The Hawaiian islands became a part of the United States after the passage of the Organic Act and its ratification by its citizens. Section Ten of the "Contracts of Employment—Alien Labor" provision of the act read in part:

> All contracts made since August twelfth, eighteen hundred and ninety-eight, by which persons are held for service for a definite term, are hereby declared null and void and terminated, and no law shall be passed to enforce said contracts in any way . . . .
>
> The Act approved February twenty-sixth, eighteen hundred and eighty-five, "To prohibit the importation and migration of foreigners and aliens under contract or agreement to perform labor in the United States, its Territories and the District of Columbia," [is] hereby extended to and made applicable to the Territory of Hawaii.[13]

In this way, the law originally restricting the immigration of Chinese contract laborers was extended to apply to Japanese workers traveling to and living in Hawaii. This major event affected Japanese immigration to Hawaii and later played an important part in the emigration companies' decision to begin operating in other countries.

The Hawaiian republican government and several of the sugar planters had been in disagreement over the issue of annexation.[14] From the point of view of the authorities, annexation meant political stability in the islands and protection from a major power. The majority of sugar planters, however, had been opposed to the idea since the early days of the republic. They realized that the contract labor system, which was the basis of their plantations, would have to be sacrificed in return for any benefits of annexation. Furthermore they questioned whether a free laborer system would be stable enough to support the plantations if they expanded operations in order to take full advantage of the prospects of increased sugar exports to the rest of the United States.

There is some doubt whether Japanese government officials realized what would happen to the contract workers being sent to Hawaii. A telegram sent from the Japanese minister in the U.S. to the foreign ministry in 1898 erroneously stated that "Laborers' contracts concluded before the above date [July 4, 1899] will remain valid."[15] This misinformation about contracts remaining legal after Hawaii became annexed led to the Japanese government's decision to allow a large number of contract workers—29,592—to be shipped to Hawaii in 1898 and 1899.

Did the emigration companies understand that these workers would all be released from their contracts and be allowed to leave the plantations in 1900? At least one company realized the implications of this act and the probable effects on its business. In 1898 Tōyō imin gōshigaisha wrote as follows to the Hawaiian attorney general: "the act of annexation will be carried out ere long. Then the U.S. Government will . . . stop the immigration of contract laborers . . . there will be only a small number of the men who will land in the Islands as *bona fide* [emphasis in original] free laborers and hence there will hardly be any prospect of these being able to meet the demands of the planters. . . . In view of the reasons stated above, should you be inclined to invite our free laborers into the Islands . . . our kaisha [company] would be willing to supply whole lot of such laborers as may be demanded by all the planters."[16]

In a prospectus attached to the above letter, this company went on to promise that these immigrants would come of "their free and voluntary consent" and under no labor agreement or contract.[17] At first glance this seemed to comply with U.S. laws governing contract labor. However, this prospectus, which was presented to government authorities and the sugar planters, went on to state that the company would "*guarantee* that such employees who are accepted will contrive to work *at least* to such length of time which may be required to mature and harvest two consecutive crops of sugar cane."[18] (Emphasis added.)

Even if the emigration company issued such a guarantee, they could never have enforced it; guaranteeing that the arriving immigrants would work at least until two crops of sugar cane were harvested was a violation of federal law. Prohibition of contract labor meant that the incoming workers had a free choice of jobs, hence the term "free emigrants." As soon as the Japanese landed in Hawaii after June of 1900, they were legally free individuals and under no job constraints.

Several companies ignored federal regulations and shipped contract workers to both the Hawaiian Islands and the mainland United States. In the case of the latter, even before 1900 a number of workers carrying labor contracts were rejected by U.S. immigration officials in both San Francisco and Seattle. Examples include twelve men on the steamship *Australia* who were prevented from landing in San Francisco in July of 1893.[19] In August of 1897 sixteen Kobe immigrants were discovered aboard the S.S. *Walla Walla* with sealed contracts for agricultural work issued by Kōsei imin kabushikigaisha.[20] According to San Francisco officials, the Japanese had traveled on the S.S. *Coptic* from Kobe to Yokohama, then on the S.S. *Columbia* to Victoria, and finally on the S.S. *Walla Walla*. Government authorities claimed the incoming Japanese "had in their possession labor contracts which were to be used in the United States."[21]

American authorities felt these incidents were not exceptions and that emigration companies had allowed Japanese to sign illegal contracts to work in the United States. The commissioner of immigration in San Francisco added that the "non-labor" contracts between emigration companies and immigrant workers were in themselves vague and suspicious. He wrote: "If the company is organized to do nothing but what is expressed in this contract—*if there is not some suppressed understanding between this company and its clients* [emphasis in original]—there it seems to me that the organization is a farce. . . . "[22]

Many companies shifted their emphasis to free emigrants. Before 1900 they had sent a few people of this category to Hawaii. Between 1894 and 1900 only 2,948 of the 43,634 Hawaii-bound emigrants were free of labor contracts.[23] However, during the first seven years after labor contracts were prohibited, company agents sent more than 92 percent of the free immigrants entering Hawaii as can be seen in Table 10.[24]

Even while they were able to send thousands of free workers to Hawaii, the emigration companies realized that they were fighting a losing battle. Not bound to labor contracts with the sugar planters, many Japanese chose to bypass the islands and travel directly to Canada or the U.S. mainland where wages were higher. Then as a result of international negotiations, no "laborers," most of whom were in fact company emigrants, were allowed to go to Hawaii. Thus although the companies managed to ship 46,042 workers between 1905 and 1907, the following year they sent only 450 and none after that.

It may be that the companies may have been able to overcome the commonly held prejudice against Japanese immigrants in Hawaii, because, in the final analysis, they were essential to Hawaii's plantation-based economy. However, when Hawaii became a part of the United States and contract labor was prohibited and international agreements such as the Gentlemen's Agreement became applicable to Hawaii, further company activity became unprofitable.

Events in Japan that Affected Company Activity

The Japanese government used two methods to control the number of companies in the emigration business. A number of individuals were refused permission by government authorities to establish businesses. Also, the government enforced the Emigrant Protection Law which included a provision that required companies to send workers abroad within the first six months of operation at penalty of having their licenses revoked.

After 1900 the foreign ministry set monthly quotas on the number of emigrants that would be allowed to travel abroad through each company. In July of 1901 it announced its policy for Hawaii: each company could send there twenty-five emigrants a month.[25] The only exceptions to this rule were family members of those already living overseas. In addition, ships with Hawaii-bound passengers were prevented from carrying more than sixty workers each, although this did not include wives and children. Because some individuals tried to pass as family members, government officials required that passengers carry copies of their family registers *(koseki tōhon)*.

In 1902 the foreign ministry continued to limit the number of free emigrants bound for Hawaii, but it made some important changes.[26] Unlike the previous year's general allotment of twenty-five emigrants for all companies, officials set specific quotas for each company; for example, three companies had twelve slots, another company seventy-two; twenty others were allowed thirty-six workers a month. In all, the thirty-five active companies sent a total of 1,254 emigrants a month. It is not clear how the government decided on this graded quota system. Why was San'yō imin gōshigaisha allowed seventy-two slots, while Nippon Yoshisa imin gōshigaisha, Murayama Yasuhisa, and Ōno Den'ei only twelve per month? A large company like Morioka Immigration Company was given monthly quota of forty-eight, but so was Kaneo Masatoshi, a much smaller one. The limit of thirty-six was also placed indiscriminately on Japan Emigration Company, which eventually shipped almost 8,000 emigrants overseas, and Mitsunaga Kyūta, which sent only 350.

Whatever the reasoning behind this new system, there is no doubt that it placed an enormous burden on the smaller companies. Limited by this burden, they had no legal way of increasing their revenue and competing with the larger, more financially stable companies. The results were predictable: by September of 1903 seven small companies went bankrupt.[27] They had not been able to survive because the commissions from less than forty clients, the limit of their quotas, did not cover even their monthly expenses.

These quotas were also changed from time to time, making long-range financial planning impossible. For example, in 1902 the government limited Kumamoto Emigration Company to forty-eight emigrants a month.[28] In March of 1904 this was lowered to forty and lowered again to twenty a year later. Foreign ministry officials raised this company's allotment to forty-two in September of 1905, but lowered it again to twenty-one two years later. Even for a company like Nippon Yoshisa imin gōshigaisha, which was the first company to send workers overseas regularly, it was no easier to survive because in 1905 it could send only six emigrants a month to Hawaii.

The quotas placed on the companies depended on the number of workers requested by the sugar planters. For example, in 1905, as Consul General Saitō reported in a telegram to the foreign ministry, "Planters want 600 laborers every month in future possibly with a good number of their wives."[29] So the twenty-nine companies operating at the time divided the total allotment of 600, with only the new Transoceanic Migration Company getting permission to ship as many as 92 workers a month.[30]

The ban on contract laborers in Hawaii and the monthly quotas imposed by the foreign ministry were not the only major problems for the companies. They also had difficulty in cooperating with each other because for years they had been in competition.

In May of 1899 three of the largest companies in Hawaii attempted to work together as partners. The motivation for this was, however, less to satisfy a spirit of cooperation and more to eliminate other competitors. Japanese Emigration Company of Hiroshima, Kumamoto Emigration Company, and Morioka Immigration Company announced that they were "doing business together as partners, for the purposes of this Agreement under the name Japanese Immigration Bureau."[31] This was not a merger but an attempt to use the resources of the three companies to establish a monopoly in the Hawaiian emigration business.

The Japanese Immigration Bureau deposited a bond of $42,000 with Hawaiian banks and established an office in Honolulu.[32] With Matsuoka Tatsusaburō, an employee of the Japanese Emigration Company of Hiroshima, as the manager and several agents, the Bureau quickly signed contracts in which they promised five sugar planters 2,943 workers.[33] These were for a three-month period. In August of that year the Bureau signed agreements with six planters to provide an additional 9,741 workers.[34] These activities not only strengthened the position of the three companies but also weakened the positions of the others, as the case of Tokio Immigration Company shows. On 16 August it signed a contract with the plantation company Theo. H. Davies for 350 male workers.[35] Five days later, this sugar planter canceled that agreement and signed with the Bureau for those 350 workers.

The companies also made several attempts to regulate themselves. The Japanese government had always encouraged a system of self-regulation, as it had done with the boardinghouses in the Japanese port cities.[36] The companies first attempt to this end came in 1902 with the establishment of Imin toriatsukai rengō jimusho, or the Union of Emigration Agents Office.[37] It issued a set of guidelines concerning company and agent activities and established offices in Kumamoto, Hiroshima, Fukuoka, and Yamaguchi prefectures.

The Union of Emigration Agents Office failed to gain the cooperation of many of the companies, however, and so in 1905 Imin toriatsukainin dōmeikai, or the Alliance of Emigration Agents, was formed.[38] The two founders of this group were Saitō Chūtarō, the head of Tokio Immigration Company, and Mugita Saisaburō of Japanese Emigration Company of Hiroshima. Like the Union, the Alliance did not gain the confidence of the majority of companies and failed to set up a central organization.

A final effort to create a central administrative structure for emigration companies was made in November of 1907 at the Zenkoku imingaisha rengō taikai, or the National Convention of the Union of Emigration Companies.[39] This meeting had been initiated by members of Morioka Immigration Company and Kōkoku shokumingaisha. Although a full slate of officers was chosen, the convention ended with the delegates in disagreement over the question of profits and illegal rebates from shipping companies.[40] One faction made up of the larger companies called itself Seigiha (justice faction). The other consisted of former members of the Alliance of Emigration Agents and called themselves Kyūdōmeiha (former Alliance faction).

None of these attempts to establish a regulatory body for the emigration companies succeeded, and the problem of too many companies in competition was solved only when some began to drop out of the business. Because the companies also had no solution to the problems of the foreign ministry's quotas on emigration to Hawaii and the U.S. government's demand to limit Japanese immigration, their only recourse was to seek their fortunes in other countries.

International Events that Affected Company Activity

North America held little hope for the emigration companies. This despite the fact that an estimated 107,253 Japanese migrated to the United States mainland before 1930.[41] This figure does not include a significant number who entered illegally either by jumping ship in San Francisco or Seattle, or by crossing the border from Canada or Mexico.[42] An American official estimated that up to 90 percent of the Japanese who arrived in Canada entered the United States within two weeks.[43] This figure also does not include the thousands of workers moving between Hawaii and the U.S. mainland before restrictions were placed on this travel.

The companies themselves shipped only a small number of legal emigrants to the U.S. mainland. Six of the larger companies sent a total of 165 Japanese workers there through the year 1898; foreign ministry figures show that five individuals used other companies in that same year.[44] They also indicate that the only others who were sent legally were twenty-six workers in 1901.[45] It is impossible to estimate the number who entered the United States illegally, either through a company or on their own, secretly holding labor agreements. The Immigration Commission set up by Congress in 1907 estimated that

Table 27
Number of Company and Non-Company Emigrants to Canada, 1898–1908

Year	*Company Emigrants*	*Non-Company Emigrants*
1898	1,151	—
1899	1,193	533
1900	1,425	1,285
1901	—	—
1902	—	35
1903	—	178
1904	—	159
1905	—	196
1906	—	442
1907	1,658	1,095
1908	10	591
Totals	5,437	4,514

Source: Gaimushō tsūshōkyoku, *Ryoken kafusū,* pp. 142–163.

between 1896 and 1909 about 900 Japanese were refused entrance into the country because they had labor contracts.[46]

Another possibility for the companies was Canada, where jobs in mining, the lumber and fishing industries, and railroad construction were available. Between 1891 and 1898 more than 3,400 emigrant passports were issued by the Japanese government for travel there.[47] Most of those who went after 1894 did so as company emigrants. Between that year and 1900 seventeen companies sent 4,048 workers to Canada, with Kobe Immigration Company, Kōsei imin kabushikigaisha, and Kyushu imin kabushikigaisha sending the majority.[48] As can be seen in Table 27, the number of company emigrants decreased after 1898, except in 1907 when a final attempt to send workers was made immediately before restrictions were placed on emigration.[49] None of the workers who went after 1908 used private companies because it was then that the Canadian government put restrictions on the number and types of immigrants it would allow, just as the U.S. government had done.

The companies also saw the South and West Pacific regions as potential destinations for workers.[50] Japanese farmers were sent to Guam as early as 1868. The first emigration company to be established in Japan, Nippon Yoshisa imin gōshigaisha, sent 600 workers to New Caledonia to work in French-owned nickel mines in 1891.[51] This company also sent 305 workers to Fiji in April of 1894; however, because of sickness, only 194 survivors returned on a ship sent by the government to rescue them.[52] The company suffered a financial loss of more than 203,000 yen after this its only attempt to send anyone there.

Several individuals in Australia requested Japanese workers as early as 1876. By 1898 the number of Japanese residents there had risen to more than 3,000.[53] Over 1,500 workers traveled to the Australian continent during the 1898 to 1905 period, mostly through private companies.[54] Many signed labor contracts to work for three years and six months on sugar cane plantations.[55] The establishment of the Australian federal government and the passage of that government's Immigration Restriction Act in December of 1901 made it difficult for Japanese to enter areas as they could before when these were under the control of local governments.[56] In 1902, the Settlers' Limitation Law restricted the number of Japanese entering the country.[57]

Emigration to the Philippines had begun in 1899, but was suspended for a short period.[58] Then it began again in 1903 and from that year to 1904 fifteen companies sent more than 4,500 workers to these islands.[59] Most of them helped to build roads and worked on large construction projects, but this came to an end in 1905.[60]

A small number of Japanese emigrants also traveled to a number of places around the world during this period, including French Indo China, Thailand, the East Indies, India, Borneo, Tahiti, and the cities of Hong Kong, Macao, and Singapore.[61] However, none of these places offered the ideal combination of large-scale labor projects, liberal immigration laws, and a willingness to accept large numbers of Japanese workers. In the end, the only region that promised some hope for the companies was Latin America.

Latin America and the End of the Emigration Company Period

The only Japanese emigrants who went to Latin America before 1899 were the 119 workers who went to Mexico in 1892.[62] While some of these men intended to work in Mexican mines, others planned to cross Mexico's border and enter the United States illegally. A Japanese official who later surveyed the situation in Mexico reported to his superiors that many were being recruited for work in coal mines and agriculture by "the Toyo Imin Kaisha (Oriental Emigration Company) [and] the Tairiku Imin Kaisha (Continental Emigration Company) [among] others . . . ."[63]

In 1894 foreign ministry officials compiled a handbook on the trip of Nemoto Tadashi to Mexico.[64] Also, Nemoto discussed the possibility of emigration to that region in the introduction of another foreign ministry work, published in 1895, on Brazil and other Latin American countries.[65] By 1895 considerable interest was stirred among foreign ministry officials about the possibility of emigration to Latin America.

Large-scale emigration to Latin America began in 1899 when 790 Japanese workers went to Peru.[66] This was done with the help of Morioka Makoto of Morioka Immigration Company, and all who were sent were company emigrants who had signed labor contracts.[67] Emigration to Brazil started in 1908, and, as in the case of Peru, the contract workers had been recruited by private company agents. This was the general pattern of emigration to Latin America until 1920.

By that year Japan had sent 11,549 workers to Mexico, 20,168 to Peru, and 28,661 to Brazil.[68] Gradually the number of Japanese sent to Brazilian coffee plantations increased. Emigration to Argentina also began and by the start of World War II, Japan had sent 244,946 emigrants to various countries in Latin America, the largest number, 188,985, going to Brazil.[69]

Despite this prospect of sending Japanese workers and their families to Latin America, the number of emigration companies dwindled after 1908. The 1902 to 1908 period saw an average of thirty companies sending workers abroad each year.[70] However, in 1908 eighteen companies folded, and only Morioka Immigration Company, Nippon shokumin kabushikigaisha known as Nippon Colonization Company, Tōyō imin gōshigaisha, Meiji shokumin gōshigaisha, and Bōchō imin gōshigaisha remained in operation by 1909.[71] In the following year, the last two went out of business and the remaining three companies were joined by the new Takemura Yoemon. Another that entered this business was Nanbei shokumin kabushikigaisha, which operated between 1916 and 1918. Takemura Yoemon and Kōkoku shokumin kabushikigaisha merged to form this company.[72]

Kaigai kōgyō kabushikigaisha (known overseas as International Development Company Ltd.), which began operations in 1917, merged with Tōyō imin gōshigaisha, Nippon Colonization Company, and Nanbei shokumin kabushikigaisha.[73] Ultimately it became Morioka Immigration Company's only competitor. By 1920 Morioka merged with its formidable rival. With considerable Japanese government subsidies, it was able to continue to send emigrants to Latin America, particularly to Brazil and Peru, until the beginning of World War II. Postwar emigration did not begin until 1952, and in the following years Brazil, Paraguay, Argentina, and Bolivia received the most immigrants.[74]

CHAPTER 9

The Legacy of the Emigration Companies

THE immigration of large numbers of Japanese citizens to the Hawaiian Islands and subsequently the mainland United States was an important event but one whose full significance is apparent only from historical study. Furthermore, the meaning of events occurring between 1894 and 1908 becomes understandable in a historical context if one realizes how overseas migration can be both a linkage and a process at the same time.

By looking at the link between Japan and Hawaii, one can see events unfolding on both sides of the Pacific Ocean at the same time. One can understand how events in one country can cause things to happen in the other. Thus, for example, different "push" and "pull" factors, their relative values, and their relationships with each other become a little clearer. One can see that the link between the Japanese immigrants in Hawaii and their homeland was maintained over a period of several decades. This is evidenced by the contributions they made to a developing Japan by sending money home. Also revealed is the attitude of America, the host country, toward the immigration of large numbers of Japanese workers.

The process of emigration and eventual settlement not only underwent transformation as government policies, economic conditions, and societal reactions changed; as the years passed, it evolved into a more sophisticated process and its structure became more defined. Furthermore it began to build upon itself and led to the migration of family members and new brides in addition to those who sought work overseas. Thousands of Japanese families settled in the Hawaiian Islands and struggled for economic security and political justice. As a result, new generations of Japanese were born in America.

Causation in Emigration

Before examining the legacy of emigration from the perspectives of individuals as well as from both Japan and the United States, it is necessary to address the arguments concerning causation in the emigration–immigration process. The following questions are important to this discussion: What were the most important factors in determining whether a Japanese farmer chose to work overseas or to live his life out on a farm? Were economic factors—the state of the agricultural economy, the price of rice, and the prevalence of tenancy—most responsible? Or were noneconomic considerations—the role of government officials and emigration company recruiters—more important? Did national events occurring in Japan and America have more impact than what was happening on the local level? The answers involve a complicated series of events in both countries.

Perhaps the easiest method of understanding the complex relationships and series of events involved is by visualizing an inverted triangle with the following six levels (from top to bottom): international, national, prefectural, county and city, town and village, and individual. Certain events have to occur and specific decisions have to be made on all levels of this model in order to have sustained emigration over a period of time.

At the highest level, the Kingdom of Hawaii established formal relations with Japan, which was necessary to pave the way for an immigration convention. It was also essential that the labor market in Hawaii offer wages substantially higher than those offered in Japan. Relatively unrestricted travel and entrance into the host country was also important, as the fact that, when the U.S. government began to impose various restrictions on this travel, the system fell apart proves.

On the national level, what contributed to the success of this system was the state of the economy in Japan, particularly in its countryside. Unless the economic reality in Japan and promise in Hawaii were in sharp contrast, Japanese farmers would have had no incentive to leave their country. Thus certain economic indicators—daily wages, the price of rice, tenancy, and any signs of economic dislocation—are significant *only* if these elements affected the overall state of the Japanese economy during the years of major emigration to Hawaii. Also, the traditions of internal migration and of seeking temporary work away from home prepared a foundation for social patterns that were important in the emigration process.

Different prefectures prepared their residents for work and travel overseas in different ways. Some saw emigration as a solution to local economic problems, while others found different solutions. Early on in the emigration period government officials decided in which prefectures emigration would make an important contribution.

Even within these prefectures, emigration was encouraged in some counties and cities but not in others. This took place because of local economic conditions and the activities of certain local authorities. Even something as simple as the issuing of official notices encouraging travel to Hawaii made a significant difference.

The same was true for smaller towns and villages. One village might have sent many residents, while another several miles away might not have sent any. The reason for this variation was that each village's background with respect to emigration was unique, as was its physical environment, which of course determined its economic situation. Thus to understand these differences, one must ask the following about each village: How much land was available to be cultivated? What were the soil conditions there like? Was water supply a problem? What secondary crops or cottage industries were available to the farmers? Was there already established a tradition of migration in some form? Did a government or private emigration company recruiter stop there to disseminate information about emigration? Was there a village official there who encouraged people to go to Hawaii? Had others from this area gone abroad and become successful?

All of these considerations came into play when individuals (at the bottom level of the triangle) made their final decisions. The reason some villages and towns would ultimately have many people traveling overseas is that all of the above factors were presented and together they led farmers, fishermen, and laborers to believe this option was reasonable and logical. For perhaps the first time in their lives they saw before them a chance to earn some money and to better their lives, and many chose to do so.

The Legacy for Individuals

In any study that reviews the process by which thousands of people moved from one country to another, generalizations about that process and its participants are inevitable; and often, how migration affected the lives of specific families over several generations is ignored. However, there is no basis to the idea that significant lessons of history can only be learned from a study of large groups and not from a study of individuals, if only because the latter is part of the former. In fact, in many cases, the broader themes of history can be seen with more clarity in accounts of individuals who actually went through the experience of a particular historical event themselves. The following is the story of how five Japanese—Yamano Akizō, Moriyama Goichi, Yamaguchi Masato, Kuwashima Iseno, and Yamano Matsuno—emigrated to Hawaii and eventually ended up in one family.

In the history of Japanese overseas migration and settlement, a few villages became known as "emigrant villages." They had several characteristics in common, the most important of which was an unusually high percentage of residents going overseas. People from these villages continued to emigrate over a long period so that there were family members of several generations abroad at the same time. These villages also tended to send large numbers of workers and their families only to one country. Therefore in Hawaii not only were prefectures represented by groups of workers *(kenjinkai)* but also groups based on county *(gunjinkai)*, village *(sonjinkai)*, and even ward *(kujinkai)* ties.

One emigrant village, Kuchida in Hiroshima prefecture, had over 10 percent of its population residing abroad during the 1898 to 1916 period.[1] A 1925 survey taken of Jigozen (in the same prefecture) showed an average of two emigrants per household, or 50 percent of its residents overseas.[2] A group of villages on Yamaguchi prefecture's Ōshima island sent almost a third of the total number of those in the first government-sponsored emigration shipment to Hawaii in 1885.[3] Emigration from the village of Miho in Shizuoka prefecture was set in motion with the return of Kawaguchi Genshichi. When he came back in 1889 after working for seven years in Hawaii he encouraged others to follow his example. Between 1906 and 1913 almost 600 villagers went overseas.[4] Another village, Mio in Wakayama prefecture, sent hundreds of fishermen to work in the town of Steveston in British Columbia.[5]

Niojima, a village on an island near Hiroshima city, sent many workers to Hawaii during the government-sponsored emigration period. Migration from this area was spawned by the construction of the new Ujina port. The port was completed in November of 1889, despite stong protests by residents who feared the loss of valuable fishing grounds, which meant the loss of their means of livelihood.[6] Niojima fishermen signed up in large numbers, and this continued for decades. In 1910, 14.6 percent of Niojima's population was overseas; this was the fourth highest percentage in its prefecture.[7]

In 1885 Yamano Akizō, the son of a Niojima farmer, Yamano

Kinzō, was twenty-three years old.[8] Kinzō had died at a young age and his widow later remarried into the Yamane family. The young Akizō had been brought up in the family of his grandfather Yamano Kinta. Akizō lived in a farming household which grew rice and barley. Families living in the Hiroshima bay area typically made their living fishing and selling *nori* (dried seaweed) door to door. Akizō worked on the farm and aboard a fishing boat, and he received little formal education. In 1883 he married Yamashiro Ishi, the second daughter of Yamashiro Ichiemon, and by 1888 they had two children.

Since a large number of Niojima villagers were going overseas, it was not unusual that Akizō, at the age of twenty-six, decided to leave his young wife and two children and emigrate to Hawaii. He and some friends signed a three-year labor contract and left Yokohama on 20 May 1888 aboard the *Takasago Maru.* This ship was carrying the fifth government-sponsored shipment of workers to Hawaii and it arrived in Honolulu on 1 June.[9] Although there were 1,062 workers aboard the ship, Akizō spent most of his time with the 109 men from his home village.[10]

From the port of Honolulu Akizō was sent to Paauhau plantation on the Hamakua coast of the island of Hawaii.[11] His first job in the sugar cane fields there was "water boy" for the more experienced workers. After his initial three-year contract, Akizō moved to Kula on the island of Maui and leased a small section of land on which he raised corn and other vegetables. He often thought of his wife and children back in Japan and after he established himself in Hawaii, Akizō summoned his wife and daughter to join him on the island of Maui. Three years later, his seventeen-year-old son Hatsutarō also left his young bride and child in Niojima village and went to Hawaii. Two more children, Matsuno and Isao, were born to Akizō and Ishi. By this time the Yamanos had settled into the life of a plantation family, with both Akizō and Hatsutarō working for the local sugar planter. Ishi opened a small store and bakery for other plantation families. Their lives changed suddenly when Hatsutarō fell ill. In 1907 the entire family returned to Japan to find better medical care for him. For Akizō, the return to Niojima village came after spending nineteen years in Hawaii.

In the small mountain village of Koya (also known as Kiya), in the southern part of Fukuoka prefecture, the family of Moriyama Ichihachi celebrated the birth of their sixth child and fifth son, Goichi, on 25 October 1884.[12] He would be the last child in that farming family.

Later, Koya, along with the surrounding mountainous areas, was incorporated into the town of Kuroki; but during the early Meiji years, the village stood alone along the Yabe river. In 1894 at the beginning of the emigration company period, Goichi was only ten years old. He had never heard of Hawaii and expected to live his entire life in Koya. But then he began to notice how crowded his family was on the small leased farm. Few families at this time were able to raise five sons and a daughter as the Moriyama family had done without having any die at birth or during childhood. However, having five sons to work on a small farm was not always a blessing.

In early 1906 Goichi, by then twenty-two, decided to go to Hawaii because he had heard other tenant farmers were achieving success there. A number of company agents passed through the village and talked about people being able to save 400 yen in three years in Hawaii. Finally Goichi and fourteen others from Fukuoka prefecture paid their commissions and signed up as free emigrants with Imperial Emigration Company, which operated out of Okayama city.[13] This particular company, the only one based in Okayama prefecture, was started by Nishizaka Kazuyoshi, Takeuchi Tadashi, and Suzuki Hideo with 30,000 yen in capital. It operated for nine years, between 1898 and 1907.[14] During those years it shipped about 5,800 emigrants overseas. It recruited workers in the southwestern area of Japan, from Aichi to Okinawa prefectures.

Goichi received official permission to leave and obtained a passport signed by Foreign Minister Saionji Kinmochi, on 14 April 1906. After traveling to Yokohama with the others from Fukuoka, Goichi left Japan on 5 May aboard the *Hong Kong Maru*. Like the typical Japanese emigrant at the time, he was young, single, and, in the tradition of dekasegi rōdō, expected to return after a few years abroad. However, like Akizō, Goichi decided to remain overseas after his initial years in Hawaii.[15] Working on a sugar plantation as a carpenter, Goichi eventually settled on the island of Oahu and became one of the growing number of immigrants who became settlers in the Hawaiian Islands. He lived in the plantation camp barracks and, like other bachelors in such camps, he had his meals prepared and his laundry done by wives of the fortunate few who had come with their families.

A major road runs from Hiroshima city on the coast of the Inland Sea northeast to the border of Shimane prefecture as it had during the Meiji period. The road parallels the Mita river, and both pass through a mountainous region in Takada county. Ichikawa, a small mountain village located just west of this road, later became a part of Shiraki town and then a part of the larger Hiroshima metropolitan area. Yamaguchi Masato, born on 1 October 1888, was the second son and the fourth child of Yamaguchi Masajirō and Katō Kuma.[16] The family lumber business in Ichikawa was fairly successful, and later Masato would be followed by five brothers and sisters. Unlike Akizō and Goichi, Masato did not need to work away from home because the family business was prosperous. The young Masato had heard stories of Japanese going overseas and thus it was more for adventure than economic need that he decided at the age of eighteen to travel to Hawaii in 1906.[17]

Masato paid his fees and signed a ship passage contract with Morishima Hisao, an emigration company that worked out of Tokyo. The company was named after its president. It sent 2,369 workers abroad between 1902 and 1907, and with assets of 50,000 yen it concentrated on recruiting in Kyushu.[18] In his application, Morishima claimed he was able to send workers to Hawaii, Canada, America, Australia, and Mexico. Masato signed up along with seven others from Hiroshima prefecture. After he received permission to leave and obtained a passport, he left Japan aboard the *Siberia Maru* on 16 August 1906. Upon arrival in Honolulu, Masato was sent to work for a sugar planter on the island of Hawaii.

He became dissatisfied with his job because he had not traveled thousands of miles just to be a sugar plantation worker.[19] Masato left the plantation and during the next thirteen years held an assortment of jobs. His knowledge of English was limited and he sought work that gave him a chance to meet with other racial groups. Thus he was at one time a bartender and another a mechanic. He eventually found his way back to Honolulu by 1919. Masato had decided by this time that his future lay in Hawaii, and he asked his family back in Ichikawa to start searching for a suitable bride for him.

On 25 March 1890 a baby girl, Iseno, was born the only child to Ushijima Shōichi and Ōtsubo Seki.[20] Seki had been married to Shōichi for less than a year before they were divorced. She then married Kuwashima Matakichi and gave her newborn daughter a new family name. The Kuwashima family lived on a small leased farm in the village of Koya in Fukuoka prefecture, only a short distance from the Moriyama family.

At this time there were only a few options available to rural families who faced economic distress. One was to seek a better life elsewhere. Seki's older stepbrother chose this option and took his family to begin a new life in the Okinawan islands. Other families sent sons to cities to work, hoping that they would be able to send money home. Second and third sons reaching adulthood expected to leave the home to establish branch families, and daughters of marriageable age hoped to find husbands and leave the family. Because rural villages were quite a distance from one another, marriage among the villagers was a common practice. For the male emigrant living abroad marriage had to be arranged by his family and friends back home.

Moriyama Goichi asked his family to find someone willing to travel to Hawaii as his wife. The Kuwashima family became interested in this proposition because their daughter, Iseno, was twenty-two years old and still without a husband. After negotiations took place between the families, photographs were exchanged. Iseno registered at the village office as the wife of Goichi and sought permission to emigrate as a relative of a worker already residing overseas. Having obtained this permission from local authorities, Iseno left Yokohama on 27 February 1912 as a third-class passenger on the *Chiyo Maru.*

When Akizō and the Yamano family returned to Japan in 1907, Matsuno was ten years old.[21] For her and her younger brother, Japan was a new experience. It was in Niojima that the entire Yamano family was together for the first time. They were brought together by Hatsutarō's illness, which lasted for some time until his death. Nonetheless the family prospered, and the two younger children were able to further their education. Matsuno was sent to a school for women and Isao a military school in Tokyo. Although she enjoyed her studies and her life in Japan, Matsuno never forgot that she had been born in Hawaii and longed for the day she might return.

The opportunity to do so came as a result of her advanced schooling. One of Matsuno's teachers was a relative of the Yamaguchi family of Ichikawa and had heard that Masato was seeking a wife. Although Matsuno knew she had a good chance of securing a teaching position in Japan, she agreed to go to Hawaii as a picture bride.

She left Hiroshima and traveled from Kobe to Yokohama by ship in the summer of 1919. From Yokohama it was a thirteen-day trip aboard the *Tenyō Maru* to Honolulu. When she arrived in Hawaii and met Masato for the first time, Matsuno realized what financial situation she was marrying into when her husband failed to hold a wedding reception party for his new bride.

Life in Hawaii was not easy for two newly wedded couples. Goichi and Masato would both hold a variety of jobs and move their growing families a number of times. Goichi never had a chance to return to Japan and died at the age of fifty-one in 1936. He did not get to see his eldest son give a series of lectures around Japan on Japanese-American relations. Masato became a successful car salesman who saw the birth of seven grandchildren before he passed away in 1960. Unlike Goichi, Masato had once revisited his home; he accompanied a young Japanese American baseball team to Japan.

In addition to giving birth to and raising seven children, two of whom died at an early age, Iseno worked at a number of jobs throughout her life. More than forty-five years after she arrived in Hawaii, her young grandson asked her, "Why did you come to Hawaii, *Obāchan* [grandmother]?" Iseno, who never learned English, tried to tell her story by using simple Japanese words and a map of Japan. All her grandson would later remember were her fingers tracing the route from Fukuoka prefecture to the port of Yokohama and the tears in her eyes when she talked about Japan. Iseno passed away in 1970, leaving behind five children and eight grandchildren.

Matsuno was known in the community in Hawaii for her work as a teacher at Japanese language schools and for her poetry, which was published in the local Japanese newspapers. She has seen the birth of eight grandchildren and seven great-grandchildren. During her last trip to Japan she visited her grandson. He had remembered the tears of his other grandmother, and was studying in Japan, having in a sense returned home.

The Legacy for Japan and America

The major chapters of this study have concentrated on the story of Japanese immigrants to Hawaii and their experiences there; this story is linked to that of their countrymen who chose to live on the U.S. mainland. There are several reasons for this. As has been mentioned, the Republic of Hawaii became a part of the United States when large numbers of Japanese were entering the islands. Thereafter federal laws on immigration became applicable in Hawaii, affecting Japanese who wanted to work there. In addition, when Japanese workers traveled freely from the islands to the mainland, their move had a direct effect on the growing anti-Japanese movement there. For this reason, many of the important questions concerning the role of the Japanese immigrant in a western society are just as pertinent to the western United States as they are to Hawaii.

Of course, there are differences between the experiences of Japanese workers in the respective societies, but there also are similarities. Although the Japanese in Hawaii dominated the Hawaiian scene in terms of numbers, they were as much a minority group as their fellow countrymen working in the western United States; that is, they did not have any power—a solid economic base, political presence, or the possibility of coalition building—to speak of. It was only after twenty-five years of sustained immigration to the islands that the large Japanese labor force was able to organize a lengthy strike that involved more than one plantation. In addition, while the anti-Japanese movement was more open, sophisticated, and organized on the mainland, Japanese in Hawaii also faced discrimination. For these reasons, I have chosen not to make a distinction between Hawaii's experience and that of the mainland's; so "America" or "the United States" will be used to refer to both Hawaii and the mainland.

In an examination of the Japanese overseas emigration process and of the immigration experience in the host country that followed, these questions should be addressed: What was the influence of overseas emigration on the development of modern Japan? How can the study of the Japanese immigrant contribute to the understanding of the political, economic, and social structures of the host country?

The first question is significant because the emigration companies sent workers to Hawaii during the Meiji period, a time of rapid change in all sectors of Japanese society. It would not be sound reasoning to say that the thousands of individuals who went through the experience of traveling abroad did so without being affected or without influencing those left behind in the villages. This influence could have manifested itself in specific economic terms or in more subtle ways.

The Japanese government "created" new industries in the early Meiji period in order to further the interests of the nation. As one such industry, overseas migration was "enriching the country" because it helped to solve some of the problems that were usually present in rural areas—small plots of land, a dependency on rice, tenancy, and so forth. It was also helping by channeling foreign currency into the economy. As was mentioned, at times emigrants' remittances made up almost 2 percent of the total yearly value of the nation's exports, this in addition to the large amounts of money carried back. With overseas markets being created for Japanese products as well, it is clear that the emigrants abroad were contributing to the modernization of Meiji Japan.

Further examination of the history of these companies offers some insights into the workings of Japan's government bodies, particularly the foreign ministry. By 1894 it was so confident about the emigration system it had established and the Emigrant Protection Law it had drawn up that it was willing to turn this business over to private groups. Government officials had every reason to believe that they had created a successful Meiji-period business enterprise.

The change from a public to a private system did not work out as planned, however. The emigration companies managed to operate successfully in Hawaii for only fifteen years before they were literally driven out of the islands. The Japanese government had failed in two ways. First of all, although the provisions of the Emigrant Protection Law were designed to protect the interests of workers going abroad, they were obviously inadequate. From the viewpoint of the Japanese workers, the history of this period was characterized by illegal rebates, corruption, and scandal. Second, authorities failed to anticipate the effects changes in foreign government policy would have on the private companies. Company officials did not understand the implication of Hawaii's becoming a part of the United States in 1900 and consequently could not adapt themselves to the change that was inevitable.

A common assumption about the role of the Japanese government in these affairs has been that, from the beginning, it understood the possibilities and benefits of large-scale emigration. Thus, the argument goes, authorities did everything possible to encourage and promote this option. While it is true that they were happy about the *results* of the overseas migration, foreign ministry documents show that its staff members had to be persuaded by overseas employers to send workers abroad. Only after many requests were received and a labor convention was signed did workers receive permission to go to Hawaii in 1885. Furthermore, a large number of overseas requests were received before the government allowed private companies to enter this field. In later years, Japan's officials were quick to respond to complaints from abroad about the growing number of immigrants entering Hawaii and the mainland United States. They were more than willing to place limits on this travel regardless of the disastrous consequences for the private companies and the disappointment of those Japanese who still wanted to go abroad.

The development of modern Japan could not have taken place without certain segments of the population sacrificing themselves for the common good. These included teenaged girls working for low wages in textile mills and mine and factory laborers working under poor conditions. They enabled the nation to both increase its exports and to compete in the international marketplace. Farmers were expected to increase production even though the average size of farms had shrunk, and many were forced into tenancy. Overseas emigrants were another group helping to provide, in a limited sense, the capital necessary for the industrialization of the country.

Although none of the emigrants had been forced to leave their homeland, they could see that their futures were limited in the small farming villages. These individuals gambled that they could earn a decent living overseas. Although very unfamiliar with foreigners, there being so few in Japan, they were willing to travel thousands of miles to work and live in an alien country. Finally most of them had to be adaptable enough to succeed in a society where customs, laws, and languages were alien to them. Perhaps these individuals represent the best examples of the "Meiji spirit," which helped transform Japan from an isolated feudal country into a modern nation.

As far as the second question posed at the outset is concerned, the study of any immigrant group is significant only if it can contribute to a better understanding of the larger host society. There is, of course, value in the study of these immigrants independent of these broader concerns, particularly from the points of view of the individuals involved and their descendants. A sense of one's identity and place in society can be gained from historical study. Still, unless larger lessons are learned, the importance of the study disappears with the demise of the group or with its absorption by the larger society. The history of the Japanese emigration companies and their activities offers some lessons that are appropriate for all Americans.

Research and studies of the Japanese immigrant in the United States have for the most part been limited to the story of the assimilation of an alien minority group into a larger society. Yet the more important lessons that Americans can learn from their experiences have yet to be explored. For example, the history of the Japanese immigrant in

America was one filled with prejudice, discrimination, and finally exclusion. The most popular school of analysis has stressed racial differences as the basis for this prejudice and discrimination. Another school emphasizes the economic competition with white workers as being the underlying reason for anti-Japanese sentiments. Further studies of Japanese-American relations point to yet a third view, that in the early 1900s Americans grew increasingly fearful of Japan's military strength. After the victory in the Russo-Japanese War, the Japanese immigrant was characterized as being a veteran soldier in disguise. This negative image of the Japanese immigrant led to alien land laws, miscegenation ordinances, and exclusion.

Undoubtedly all three theories are correct to some degree and they are to some extent related. Yet deciding which, if any, was the major factor in shaping the character of the anti-Japanese movement in the United States could have a great deal of implication for a multiracial and multiclass America.

This question is complex as even an examination of the Japanese on the Hawaiian sugar plantations shows. While the wage scale may reflect that racial discrimination was practiced, the most important consideration of the sugar planters was an economic one. Reference has been made to the experiences of a number of white workers from Australia. It is clear that while the sugar planters preferred non-Asian workers, they expected them to labor under similar conditions as those from Asia. Thus immigrants from Australia became just as resentful of their working and living conditions as the Japanese had become. This is one example that illustrates how economic factors played a part in what seemed like pure racial exploitation.

The history of the Japanese immigrant in America has other implications. For example, the generally positive relationship Japan had with the United States began to change in the early decades of the twentieth century. Of the different issues that created a rift between Tokyo and Washington, a major one was the treatment of Japanese residing in the United States. The laws restricting immigration, forbidding intermarriage, withholding the right to own land, as well as the limitations put on the jobs that could be had by Japanese and on citizenship were particularly offensive to the government and the people of Japan. Newspapers gave more and more coverage to these topics along with anti-Japanese incidents and demonstrations. In this way, the emigration of Japanese workers to the United States before 1924 helped create misunderstandings and tension, which were intensified in the 1930s.

Another insight into the American economic and social structure is apparent through the study of the history of Japanese immigrant women. Although little attention has been given to this particular group, they played a more important role than previously thought. That they have largely been ignored is somewhat understandable since women were not hired as company employees and did not invest in emigration company ventures. Those going to Hawaii were listed as either wives or daughters of emigrants. Also, the number of females was limited for a long time to 25 percent of the total number leaving Japan. Still, it must be made clear that they held important jobs on the plantations, working both in the fields and in the mills. They also tended to the needs of unmarried men in addition to those of their own families. Working wives were vital to the economic welfare of their families because the wages they earned often made the difference between ending the year with a profit or in debt. In this sense, these women can be likened to the thousands of others who worked in the textile mills and on the farms in Japan. They were part of the "invisible work force" on which the larger economy was dependent; yet they were never acknowledged.

The experience in the United States of these immigrants reveals other interesting things. For example, many Americans had and still have the impression that the incoming Japanese were diseased, uneducated, and poor. Many held this negative image—sometimes even the members of the immigrant community. Yet as we have seen there is much evidence that suggests the contrary: (1) Japanese were required to pass two sets of physical examinations, one in Japan and the other in the United States, and those found ill were refused entrance; (2) the educational level of the average incoming Japanese worker was among the highest of all immigrant groups; and (3) the average Japanese entered the country carrying more money than most European immigrants. Americans nevertheless continue to hold this unsubstantiated and negative image and attribute the later success of this immigrant group to factors inherent in the United States.

One of the most significant ways in which the Japanese immigrant to America was a model of a striving spirit was the way in which he identified and confronted important political and economic problems. It has been shown that the immigrant community in Hawaii was willing to stand up to major Hawaiian and Japanese institutions, including the emigration companies, which it felt to be oppressive and unfair.

This type of thinking is not characteristic of a community made up of immigrants living only temporarily in Hawaii, but of a community of people establishing permanent roots in a foreign land. This was the beginning of the transformation of the Japanese dekasegi rōdō emigrant into a Japanese American.

Appendix 1

Contract for Government-Sponsored Emigrants (1887)

This Memorandum of Agreement between the Hawaiian Government, represented by ROBERT W. IRWIN, His Hawaiian Majesty's Minister Resident and Special Agent of the Hawaiian Bureau of Immigration, party of the first part, and .... a Japanese subject, party of the second part; Whereas, the said party of the second part, has expressed a desire to proceed from Yokohama to Hawaii as an agricultural laborer; And whereas His Imperial Japanese Majesty's Government have given their consent thereto; And whereas, the Hawaiian Government has agreed to furnish the wife and two children of the said party of the second part, if they accompany him, free transportation to Hawaii, and upon arrival there to secure for the said party of the second part agricultural employment, and employment for his wife; And whereas, it has been determined by and between the parties hereto, in order to avoid any misunderstanding which might otherwise arise, to conclude at once a contract for the purposes hereinbefore recited. Now therefore this Agreement witnesseth:

The Hawaiian Government, in consideration of the stipulations hereinafter contained, to be kept and performed by the said party of the second part, convenants and agrees as follows:

I.—To furnish steerage passage, including proper food, from Yokohama to Honolulu, to .... his wife .... and to his two children, if they accompany him, which fact is to be noted at the bottom of this Agreement, and also to procure proper transportation for the said party of the second part and his family from Honolulu to the place where such labor is to be performed. The vessel in which such passage from Yokohama to Honolulu is furnished to be subject to the approval of the Chiji of Kanagawa.

II.—On arrival at Honolulu, the Hawaiian Government agrees to obtain employment for the said party of the second part, as an agricultural laborer, for the full period of three years, from the date such employment actually begins, and also proper employment for the wife of the said party of the second part. Until such employment is obtained, the Hawaiian Government will cause to be provided for the said party of the second part, and his family, lodgings commodious enough to secure health and a reasonable degree of comfort. The Hawaiian Government will, during the continuance of the contract, cause to be furnished to the said party of the second part and his family, fuel for cooking purposes free of expense.

III.—The Hawaiian Government guarantees to the said party of the second part, wages at the rate of fifteen dollars per month, and to his said wife at the rate of ten dollars per month, payable in United States Gold Coin, with lodgings, and an allowance of one dollar per month for each of the said two children. The said party of the second part shall furnish blankets and bed-clothing for himself and his family.

IV.—The Hawaiian Government agrees to cause to be provided for the said party of the second part and his family medicines free of cost and good

Mill and Sugar House, shall, within the meaning of this Agreement, constitute one month's service as an agricultural labour. Work over-time exceeding thirty minutes to be paid for at the rate of twelve and one half cents per hour to the said party of the second part, and eight cents per hour to his wife.

VI.—The Hawaiian Government guarantees to the said party of the second part and his family, the full, equal, and perfect protection of the laws of the Hawaiian Kingdom, and agrees that, during the continuance of this Contract, the said party of the second part and his family shall be exempt from all and every kind of personal tax.

VII.—Fifteen per cent. of the sum payable to the said party of the second part, and to his wife, as wages, shall be remitted monthly by the employer directly to the Japanese Consulate-General at Honolulu in the name of the said party of the second part. The amount so remitted to be deposited by the said Consul-General in the Imperial Treasury at Tokio, and for all amounts so remitted the said Consul-General shall issue receipts to and in favour of the party of the second part. All deposits so made in the Treasury to bear interest at the rate of.........per cent. per annum.

VIII.—The Hawaiian Government, having guaranteed employment and wages to the said party of the second part, shall have the right to assign, withdraw, and re-assign the said party of the second part to such plantations for labor as it may see fit. In case of such withdrawal and re-assignment, all the expenses incidental thereto shall be paid by the Hawaiian Government.

IX.—The said party of the second part agrees to proceed to Honolulu by the vessel provided for him in accordance with this Agreement.

X.—On arrival at Honolulu, the said party of the second part agrees to accept such employment as the Hawaiian Government may, under this Contract, assign to him, provided no valid objection thereto exists. In the matter of any such objection he agrees to abide by the decision of the Bureau of Immigration.

XI.—The party of the second part acknowledges to have received from the Hawaiian Government, the sum of seventy five dollars United States Gold to meet his necessary expenses and for other purposes, and he agrees to repay the said sum in monthly instalments after his employment actually begins, not exceeding three dollars United States Gold Coin each month until the said sum is paid, which payments shall be made by the employer to the Board of Immigration; but in the event of sickness protracted over twenty days in any one month, the instalment for such month shall be deferred.

XII.—During the continuance of this Contract the said party of the second part agrees to fulfil all the conditions of this Agreement, and to observe and obey the laws of Hawaii, and he further convenants and agrees to diligently and faithfully perform all lawful and proper labor which may, under this Agreement, be assigned to him by the Hawaiian Government, during the full period of three years from the date such labor actually begins.

Signed and sealed in triplicate in the English and Japanese languages, at Yokohama, this...........................November A.D. 1887. One copy to be retained by each of the parties hereto, and one to be left in the custody of the Chiji of Kanagawa.

Source: JFMAD 3.8.2.3, vol. 5.

Appendix 2

Imperial Emigration Company Labor Agreement

(Note: Handwritten notations appear on the original agreement.)

This Agreement. Made this ......23rd...... day of ......May...... A.D. 189
by and between the IMPERIAL EMIGRATION COMPANY, of Japan, an emigration compan organized and existing under the laws of the Empire of Japan, and doing business in Hawaii, for th purpose of introducing laborers into Hawaii for the Planters, hereinafter called the COMPANY party of the first part, and ......Palawai Development Association......, a corporation doing business under the laws of the Hawaiian Islands, hereinafter called the PLANTER, of the second part.

Witnesseth,

1. The Planter hereby requests the Company to furnish to it in Honolulu ......— 75 —...... able-bodied male Japanese agricultural laborers and .... female able-bodied Japanese agricultural laborers, within ......three months from the date hereof, upon the terms hereinafter set forth.

2. Upon the arrival or such laborers in Honolulu, the Planter agrees to immediately cause the to be examined by a competent physician, appointed by the employer, for the purpose of determini whether they are able-bodied and fit to perform agricultural labor, and to accept as agricultural lab rers all who shall be found to be so able-bodied and fit, and to pay the Company for each such lab rer so furnished by the Company the sum of Thirty Dollars ($35.00) gold coin of the United State and for each female laborer so furnished by the Company the sum of Twenty-Five Dollars ($25 30) gold coin of the United States of America.

3. Such payment shall cover all expenses of recruiting such laborers in Japan, their passa money to Honolulu, commission for securing them, and all incidental expenses up to the time of riving in Honolulu.

4. The Planter shall pay all Hawaiian quarantine expenses, hospital tax, medical examinat expenses and all local transportation and other charges after the arrival of such laborers in Honolu

5. The Planter hereby agrees that it will furnish employment, either as an agricultural laborer or other employment connected with sugar or coffee cultivation or production, to all the laborers furnished to it by the Company, during the term of three years from the date of the arrival of such aborers in Honolulu, and will also provide for such laborers, free of charge, unfurnished lodging, uel, water for domestic purposes, medical attendance and medicines for the laborer and his family, nd will pay all personal taxes of such laborers.

6. And also that he will pay to each male laborer furnished by the Company under this agreenent the sum of Fifteen Dollars ($15.00) per month, and to each female laborer furnished by the Company under this agreement the sum of Ten Dollars ($10.00) per month as wages. The entire vages of such female laborers shall be paid to them at the end of each month, but the Planter shall t the end of each month deduct Two Dollars and Fifty Cents ($2.50) from the wages due to each nale laborer, paying remaining Twelve Dollars and Fifty Cents ($12.50) to the respective laborers ntitled thereto. The Two Dollars and Fifty Cents ($2.50) per month so deducted from the wages of ach male laborer shall be immediately remitted to the Company, which shall hold the same in trust for ach of said laborers. Out of the accumulation of the said Two Dollars and Fifty Cents ($2.50) per nonth to the credit of each male laborer, there shall be paid by the Company at the expiration of aid term of three years, his return passage to Japan if he desires to return, and any surplus after the ayment of said passage shall be paid to such laborer in cash.

7. The Planter also agrees that if any such laborers shall work over-time, each male laborer so orking over-time shall be paid therefor at the rate at of ten cents per hour, and each female laborer hall be paid therefor at the rate of seven cents per hour.

8. It is mutually agreed that, for the purposes of this agreement, one month shall consist of venty-six (26) working days of ten (10) hours each actual work in the field, or twelve (12) hours each ctual work in and about the sugar mill or sugar house.

9. And also that each of said laborers shall work at night and rest during the day when so reuested by the Planter.

10. And also that following holidays shall be allowed to each of such laborers, viz: New Years ay, Christmas, the Third of November, Sundays, and all United States national holidays.

11. In consideration of foregoing agreements on the part of the Planter, the Company hereby grees to furnish to the Planter within the said period of three months 75 able-bodied Japanese male agricultural laborers, and .... le-bodied female Japanese agricultural laborers, at Honolulu, upon the terms and conditions herebefore set forth, subject to the approval of the governments of Japan and Hawaii.

12. And also that each of said laborers shall faithfully work for the Planter for the term of three ars from date of arrival of said laborer in Honolulu as aforesaid, as an agricultural laborer, or at ler employment connected with sugar or coffee cultivation or production.

13. And the Company hereby further agrees that if any laborer furnished by it, either as original laborer or as a substitute for deserters, under this agreement to the Planter, shall discontinue his rvice for said Planter, or absent himself from his employment for a period of thirty days, for er cause than sickness or death, the Company shall immediately after receiving notice from Planter that such laborer has discontinued his services or absented himself from his ployment for a period of Thirty Days for other cause than sickness or death, or

because of assault of the laborer by the Planter or any of its servants or agents, but the said Planter shall within seven days give notice in writing of such absence of the laborer to the Company and of its intention to claim for same under sections 13 and 14. Provided it is possible to recruit additional laborers in Japan and to introduce the same into Hawaii, the Company will replace such laborer who has discontinued his service or absented himself from the employment of the Planter as aforesaid, by another laborer who shall pass a physical examination similar to the one hereinbefore specified for the original laborer, provided such examination is required by the Planter, for which furnishing of such additional laborer no charge shall be made by the Company to the Planter.

14. In case the Company is unable for any cause to furnish the Planter with such additional laborer in the place of the laborer discontinuing or absenting himself from the employment of the Planter aforesaid, within ninety days, it hereby agrees to immediately pay to the Planter, as liquidated damages for such failure to furnish such laborer, the sum of Thirty Dollars (~~$30.00~~ 35.00) for each male laborer and Twenty-Five Dollars (~~$25.00~~ 30.00) for each female laborer discontinuing service or absenting himself or herself as aforesaid from the employment of said Planter.

PROVIDED, HOWEVER, that it is not intended that the Company shall at its option pay said sum of Thirty or Twenty-Five Dollars in lieu of furnishing such additional laborers to take the place of any laborer discontinuing or absenting himself from the employment of the Planter, but it is intended that the Company shall furnish such substitute laborer if it is possible to do so, paying such liquidated damages only in case of its inability to furnish such substitute laborers.

15. It is hereby further mutually agreed that at the end of said period of three years the Planter shall have the option to re-engage the laborers furnished to it by the Company upon the payment by it to the Company of an additional sum of Thirty Dollars (~~$30.00~~ 35.00) for each male laborer so re-engaged, and Twenty-five Dollars (~~$25.00~~ 30.00) for each female laborer so re-engaged, provided such laborer agrees thereto, upon the same terms and conditions hereinbefore set forth.

PROVIDED, HOWEVER, that the Planter shall have the right at the end of the term of three years and before the re-engagement of such laborers, to cause them to pass a physical examination similar to that provided for above, and to reject any laborer who fails to comply with the physical conditions hereinbefore required concerning such laborer.

16. The Company hereby further agrees upon execution of this Agreement to place with Messrs. Bishop & Company, as Trust for the Planter and for other Planters, who have entered or may enter into contracts with the Company, similar to this one, cash deposit of Thirty Dollars ($30.00 per head until there is a sum of Ten Thousand Dollars ($10.000.00) in their hands, conditioned fo the faithful execution and observance by it of the foregoing agreements by it made, and withi ......Ninety...... days from the date hereof to deposit with Messrs. Bishop & Company, i Honolulu, the said sum, which shall be held by the said banking house subject to the conditions of thi agreement.

Any payments which may become due by the Company to the Planter, under the terms of thi agreement, shall be paid by said banking house to the Planter therefrom either upon the written con sent of the Company as to each such claim; or in case of refusal of such consent, upon the sai banking house being satisfied by proper investigation that said sum is due to the Planter under th terms of this agreement.

IN WITNESS WHEREOF, the said parties hereto and to two other instruments of like date and even tenor set their hands and seals the day and year first above written.

Executed and delivered in presence of }

Palawai Development Ass'n
H. N. Parr
Treasurer
Imperial Emigration Co.
Y. Hamano
Agent

awaiian Islands)
) ss.
sland of Oahu.)

On this twenty-fourth day of May A.D.1899, personally ppeared before me, Y. Hamano,satisfactorily proved to me to be the erson who executed the within instrument on behalf of the Imperial migration,by the oath of G. Nakamura,a credible witness for that purpose o me known and by me duly sworn,and the said Y.Hamano, did acknowledge o me that he is the agent of the Imperial Emigration Company,that the eal affixed to said instrument is the corporate seal of said corporation d that said instrument was signed and sealed in behalf of said cor-ration by authority of its rules,and said Y. Hamano acknouledged said astrument to be the free act and deed of said corporation.

Lyle A. Dickey.

Notary Public.

---

rce: *JFMAD 3.8.2.84.*

Appendix 3

Tokyo Emigration Company Labor Contract

LABOR CONTRACT.

This Agreement, made entered into this .... day of ....

A. D. 189........, by and between ....

a corporation duly created and existing under the laws of the Hawaiian Islands, party of the first part, and

.... a Japanese subject, party of the second part, and Tokyo Emigration Co., Ltd., party of the third part:

WHEREAS, the party of the second part has come to the Hawaiian Islands from Japan to engage as an agricultural laborer for said party of first part; and,

WHEREAS, the said party of the first part has agreed to furnish said party of the second part, and his wife, if she accompanys him, free transportation from Japan to Hawaiian Islands; and

WHEREAS, the said party of third part have contracted with the said party of the first part that in case of desertion of the said party of the second part before the expiration of his term of service, to repay said party of the first part a pro rata sum of the advancement for passage and costs of the said party of the second part from Japan to the place of labor; and

NOW, THEREFORE, the Agreement witnesseth:

The said party of the first part, in consideration of stipulations hereinafter contained to be kept and performed by the said party of the second part and said party of the third part, covenants and agrees as follows:

I. To furnish free steerage passage from Japan to Honolulu to said party of the second part, and his wife if she accompanys him, subject however, to the conditions hereinafter contained, and provide proper food during said passage, and proper accommodation in said Honolulu, upon his or their arrival from Japan, and also furnish proper transportation from said Honolulu to the place where such labor is to be performed.

II. To employ said party of the second part and his wife, if she accompanys him, as agricultural laborers for the full period of three years from the date of this contract.

III. To well and truly pay, or cause to be paid, to said party of the second part compensation or wages at the rate of Twelve and 50-100 Dollars ($ 12.50) per month, and to his wife if she works, at the rate of Seven and 50-100 Dollars ($ 7.50) per month, payable in U. S. Gold Coin.

IV. To provide said party of the second part and his wife, if she accompanys him unfurnished lodgings, commodious enough to secure health and a reasonable degree of comfort, free of expense.

V. To furnish said party of the second part and his wife, if she accompanys him, sufficient fuel and water for domestic purposes and all necessary medical attendance free of cost.

VI. To hold the said party of the second part and his wife, if she accompanys him, exempt from any Government assessment for personal taxes and military services.

VII. To allow the said party of the second part and his wife, if she accompanys him, holidays to be observed as follows: New Year, Christmas, 3rd November, Sundays end Hawaiian National Holidays.

Said party of the second part in consideration of the stipulation herein contained, to be kept and performed by the said party of the first part and the said party of the third part, covenants and agrees as follows:

VIII. To faithfully and diligently perform, as become a good workmen, such agricultural labor in said Hawaiian Islands as the said party of first part, its agents and overseers, shall direct for the period of three years from the date of this contract.

IX. And it is mutually agreed between the said parties of the first and second parts, that a month's service or employment shall consist of twenty-six days of ten hours each, actual work in the field, or twelve hours each in and about the sugar mill and sugar house, and to work at night and rest during the day if required.

Work overtime exceeding thirty minutes to be paid for at the rate of 10 cents per hour to said party of the second part, and 7 cents per hour to his wife.

X. And it is further agreed between all the parties hereto the Two Dollars ($2.00) for and during *first twelve months* and one dollar ($ 1.00) for and during next twenty four months, of such contract period shall be retained by the employer out of the said wages of the party of second part, and remitted monthly by such employer to said party of third part, to be by them deposited in the bank of savings, and the aggregate thereof to be paid by parties of the third part to the said party of second part in the case of his return to Japan or removal to some other country at the expiration of his term of service, *Provided, however*, should the said party of the second part desert service during said term, then, and in such case, the said party of the third part shall pay, or cause to be paid, to the said party of the first part, from said amount, the sum due under their certain bond to the said party of the first part, to refund to the said party of the first part, in case of desertion of the said party of the second part, a pro rata amount of the passage money advanced and cost of transportation to the place where service is to be performed by the said party of the first part.

And it is further agreed by the party of the second part that no recourse can be had upon the party of the first part for such sums as may be deposited with the party of the third part.

IN CONSIDERATION WHEREOF, the parties have hereunto set their hands and seals this ....

days of .... A. D. 189——, and to a duplicate of like tenor date.

.... (SEAL.)

....

....

Source: *JFMAD 3.8.2.84.*

Appendix 4

Kobe Immigration Company Labor Contract

(Note: Handwritten notations appear on the original contract.)

LABOR CONTRACT.

This Agreement made and entered into this 22 day of August A. D. 1896, by and between Laupahoehoe Sugar Co. party of the first part, and Saiki Tounetaro, party of the second part, and **KOBE IMMIGRATION COMPANY,** party of the third part:

Whereas, party of the second part has come to Hawaii from Japan to engage as an agricultural laborer for the said party of the first part; and,

Whereas, the said party of the first part has agreed to furnish the said party of the second part free transportation from Japan to the Hawaiian Islands; and,

Whereas, the said party of the third part has agreed to the said party of the first part to furnish a superior class of Japanese laborer; and,

Now, Therefore, this agreement witnesseth:

The said party of the first part in consideration of the stipulations hereinafter contained, to be kept and performed by the said party of the second part, and the said party of the third part, covenants and agree as follows:

[1] To pay to the said party of the third part or their accredited agent the sum of THIRTY DOLLARS ($30.00), U. S. Gold Coin, for the said party of the second part as his passage money from Japan to Honolulu.

The said sum to be divided into six parts, and each part (that is $5.00) due and payable at the end of six months, provided that,

When satisfactory proof is furnished that the party of the second part has deserted his contract, the said party of the first part will be entitled to suspend the payment of the said sum for the unexpired term.

[2] To pay for the transportation of the said party of the second part from Honolulu to the plantation and furnish proper food to them while awaiting transportation at Honolulu.

[3] To employ said party of the second part and his wife if she accompany him as agricultural laborers for the full period of three years from the date of this contract.

[4] To pay or cause to be paid to the said party of the second part, compensation or wages at the rate of TWELVE DOLLARS ($12.00), U. S. Gold Coin, per month for the first and the second years, and THIRTEEN DOLLARS ($13.00), U. S. Gold Coin, per month for the third year, and to his wife at the rate of SEVEN DOLLARS ($7.00), U. S. Gold Coin, per month for the first and the second years, and EIGHT DOLLARS ($8.00), U. S. Gold Coin, per month for the third year (if she works).

[5] To furnish said party of the second part and his wife, if she accompany him, with suitable unfurnished lodgings, fuel for cooking purposes, water, necessary medical attendance free of cost, and also to hold said party of the second part and his wife harmless from any Government assessment for personal taxes.

Expired Aug 22/99
Laupahoehoe Sugar Co
per C. A. Lehman

[6] To guarantee to the said party of the second part and his wife if she accompany him, the full and equal protection of the laws of the Hawaiian Islands.

The said party of the second part, in consideration of the stipulation herein contained, to be kept and performed by the said party of the first part and the said parties of the third part, covenants and agrees as follows:

[7] To work faithfully and diligently on any part of the Hawaiian Islands and to perform such labor as may be required by the said party of the first part or its agent, for the period of three years from the date of this contract.

[8] And it is mutually agreed between the said party of the first part and second parts, that month's service or employment shall consist of twenty-six days of ten hours each for actual work in the field, and twelve hours each for actual work in or about the sugar mill and sugar house (meal hour excepted) and to work at night and rest during the day when called upon to do so.

Overtime work exceeding thirty minutes shall be paid for at the rate of ten cents per hour to the said party of the second part and seven cents per hour to his wife.

Holidays recognized by Hawaiian Government and Japanese Emperor's birthday to be excepted from working days.

[9] And it is further mutually understood between the said party of the first part and the said party of the second part that renewal contract would be made upon same terms and conditions if the said both parties mutually desire to do the same at the expiration of term of this contract.

[10] And it is mutually agreed between all the parties hereto, that, ONE DOLLAR ($1.00) per month be retained by the said party of the first part for and during whole term of this contract out of the said wages of the said party of the second part for every month he works, and the said sum to be paid to the said party of the third part or their accredited agent, to be by them deposited in the savings bank in Honolulu, as trustee for the said party of the second part and to be sent per three months to the family of said party of the second part in Japan for the purpose of support; provided, however, that if the said party of the second part has no family in Japan, he will be entitled to draw the sum deposited to his credit.

In consideration whereof, the parties have hereto set their hands and seals this 22 day of August, A. D. 189...., and to a duplicate of like tenor and date.

Kobe Immigration Co.
Per B. Ushimizu

佐倍 [illegible]

IN THE PRESENCE OF

....

....

LAUPAHOEHOE SUGAR CO.

THEO. H. DAVIES & CO. Limited
[illegible signature]
Treasurer

Source: JFMAD 3.8.2.88.

Appendix 5

Japanese Immigration Bureau Labor Contract

(Note: Handwritten notations appear on the original contract.)

This Agreement made this 21st day of August A. D. 1899, by and between the JAPANESE EMIGRATION COMPANY of Hiroshima, the KUMAMOTO EMIGRATION COMPANY, and MORIOKA AND COMPANY, all emigration companies organized and existing under the laws of the Empire of Japan and doing business together as partners, for the purposes of this Agreement, under the firm name of "The Japanese Immigration Bureau" hereinafter called "The Bureau," party of the first part, and Theo. H. Davies & Co. Ltd. a corporation doing business under the laws of the Hawaiian Islands, hereinafter called "the Planter," party of the second part.

WITNESSETH:

1. The Planter hereby requests the Bureau to furnish to it in Honolulu Three Hundred Fifty able-bodied male Japanese agricultural laborers and Eighty Seven female able-bodied Japanese agricultural laborers within four (4) months from the date hereof upon the terms hereinafter set forth.

2. Upon the arrival of such laborers in Honolulu the Planter agrees to immediately cause them to be examined by a competent physician appointed by it for the purpose of determining whether they are able-bodied and fit to perform agricultural labor, and to accept as agricultural laborers all who shall be found to be so able-bodied and fit, and to pay to the Bureau for each such male laborer so furnished by the Bureau the sum of Thirty-five Dollars ($35.00) United States gold coin, and for each female laborer so furnished by the Bureau the sum of Thirty ($30.00) Dollars United States gold coin.

3. Such payment shall cover all expenses of recruiting such laborers in Japan, their passage money to Honolulu, commissions for securing them and all incidental expenses up to the time of arriving in Honolulu.

4. The Planter shall pay all Hawaiian quarantine expenses, hospital tax, medical examination expenses and all local transportation and other charges after the arrival of such laborers in Honolulu.

5. The Planter hereby agrees that it will furnish employment either of an agricultural character or other employment connected with sugar or coffee cultivation or production, to all of the laborers furnished to it by the Bureau, during the term of three years from the date of the arrival of such laborers in Honolulu, and will also provide for such laborers free of charge, unfurnished lodging, fuel, water for domestic purposes, medical attendance and medicines for the laborer and his family, and will pay all personal taxes of such laborers.

6. And also that he will pay to each male laborer furnished by the Bureau under this Agreement the sum of Fifteen Dollars ($15) per month, and to each female laborer furnished by the Bureau under this Agreement, the sum of Ten Dollars ($10) per month as wages. The entire wages of such female laborers shall be paid to them at the end of each month, but the Planter shall at the end of each month deduct Two Dollars and fifty cents ($2.50) from the wages due to each male laborer, paying the remaining Twelve Dollars and fifty cents ($12.50) to the respective laborers entitled thereto. The Two Dollars and fifty cents ($2.50) per month so deducted from the wages of each male laborer shall be immediately remitted to the Bureau which shall hold the same in trust for each of said laborers.

Out of the accumulation of the said Two Dollars and fifty cents ($2.50) per month to the credit of each male laborer, there shall be paid by the Bureau at the expiration of said term of three years, his return passage to Japan, if he desires to return, and any surplus after the payment of such passage shall be paid to each such laborer in cash.

7. The Planter also agrees that if any of such laborers shall work overtime each male laborer so working overtime shall be paid therefor at the rate of ten cents per hour and each female laborer shall be paid therefore at the rate of seven cents per hour.

8. It is hereby mutually agreed that, for the purposes of this agreement, one month shall consist of twenty-six (26) working days of ten hours (10) each actual work in the field, or twelve hours each actual work in and about the sugar mill or sugar house.

9. And also that each of said laborers shall work at night and rest during the day when so requested by the Planter.

10. And also that the following holidays shall be allowed to each of said laborers, viz: New Year's Day, Christmas, the 3rd of November, Sundays, and all United States National Holidays.

11. In consideration of the foregoing agreements on the part of the Planter, the Bureau hereby agrees to furnish to the Planter within the said period of *Four (4)* months *350* able-bodied Japanese male agricultural laborers and *87* able-bodied female Japanese agricultural laborers at Honolulu upon the terms and conditions hereinbefore set forth, subject to the approval of the Government of Japan and Hawaii.

12. And also that each of said laborers shall faithfully labor for the Planter for the term of three years from the date of their arrival in Honolulu as aforesaid, as agricultural laborers, or at other employment connected with sugar or coffee cultivation or production.

13. And the Bureau hereby further agrees that if any laborer furnished by it either as original laborer or as a substitute therefor shall discontinue his service for said Planter or absent himself from his employment for a period of 15 days for other cause than sickness or death, or because of assault on the laborer by any agent or servant of the Planter, the Bureau shall within ninety (90) days after receiving notice from the Planter that such laborer has so discontinued his services or absented himself from his employment as aforesaid, provided it is possible to recruit additional laborers in Japan and to introduce the same into Hawaii, replace such laborer who has discontinued his service or absented himself from the employment of the Planter as aforesaid, by another laborer who shall pass a physical examination similar to the one hereinbefore specified for the original laborer, provided such examination is required by the Planter, for which furnishing of such additional labor no charge shall be made by the Bureau to the Planter.

14. In case the Bureau is unable for any cause to furnish the Planter with such additional laborer in the place of the laborer discontinuing or absenting himself from the employment of the Planter as aforesaid, within the said period of ninety days, it hereby agrees to immediately pay to the Planter as liquidated damages for such failure to furnish such laborer, the sum of Thirty-five Dollars ($35.00) for each male laborer and Thirty Dollars ($30.00) for each female laborer discontinuing service or absenting himself or herself as aforesaid from the employment of said Planter.

PROVIDED HOWEVER, that it is not intended that the Bureau shall at its option pay Thirty-five Dollars or Thirty Dollars in lieu of furnishing such additional laborer to take the place of any laborer discontinuing or absenting himself from the employment of the Planter, but it is intended that the Bureau shall furnish such substitute laborer if it is possible to do so, paying such liquidated damages only in case of its inability to furnish such substitute laborers.

15. It is hereby further mutually agreed that at the end of said period of three years the Planter shall have the option to re-engage the laborers furnished to it by the Bureau upon the payment by it to the Bureau of an additional sum of Thirty-five Dollars ($35.00) for each male laborer so re-engaged, and Thirty Dollars ($30.00) for each female laborer so re-engaged, provided such laborer agrees thereto; upon the same terms and conditions hereinbefore set forth.

PROVIDED HOWEVER, that the Planter shall have the right at the end of the term of three years and before the re-engagement of such laborers, to cause them to pass a physical examination similar to that provided for above, and to reject any laborer who fails to comply with the physical conditions hereinbefore required concerning such laborer.

16. The Bureau hereby further agrees upon the execution of this Agreement to give to ....Geo. R. Carter....................as Trustee for the Planter, ~~and for other Planters who have entered or may enter into contract with the Bureau, similar to this one,~~ a bond in the sum of $5205.00 ....conditioned for the faithful execution and observance by it of the foregoing agreements by it made, and within 6 months... days from the date hereof to deposit with Claus Spreckels Co. & The Bank of Hawaii in said Honolulu the sum of Five thousand two hundred fifty Dollars which shall be held by the said Claus Spreckels Co. & The Bank of Hawaii subject to the conditions of this Agreement, and of said Bond.

Any payments which may become due by the Bureau to the Planter, under the terms of this Agreement and of said Bond, shall be paid by said... Bureau direct .... or to said trustee for Planter ....to the Planter from the said deposit either upon the written consent of the Bureau as to each such claim, or, in case of refusal of such consent, upon the said ....Trustee..being satisfied by proper investigation that said sum is due to the Planter under the terms of this Agreement and of said Bond.

IN WITNESS WHEREOF the said parties have hereto and to two other instruments of like date and even tenor set their hands and seals the day and year first above written.

Executed and delivered
in presence of }

Source: *JFMAD 3.8.2.84.*

Appendix 6

Dollar Exchange Rate for 100 Yen, 1884–1908

1885	$84.78
1886	78.88
1887	76.26
1888	74.24
1889	75.28
1890	82.12
1891	78.01
1892	69.84
1893	62.12
1894	50.79
1895	51.21
1896	52.75
1897	49.31
1898	49.11
1899	49.80
1900	49.35
1901	49.50
1902	49.85
1903	49.81
1904	49.16
1905	49.41
1906	49.50
1907	49.54
1908	49.50

Source: Keizai kikakuchō chōsakyoku tōkeika, *Nihon no keizai tōkei,* p. 274.

Appendix 7

The Emigrant Protection Law

LAW FOR THE PROTECTION OF IMIN

Law No. 70, the 7th April, 29th year of Meiji (1896).
As amended by Law No. 23, the 34th year of Meiji (1901),
Law No. 4, the 35th year of Meiji (1902), and Law No.
33, the 40th year of Meiji (1907).

CHAPTER I
Imin

ARTICLE I. By the term "Imin" in the present Law are meant persons who emigrate for the purpose of labour to foreign countries other than China and Korea, and such members of their families as accompany them or emigrate to their place of residence.

The descriptions of the labour mentioned in the preceding clause shall be determined by Ordinance.

ARTICLE II. No *Imin* shall, without the permission of the Administrative Authorities, emigrate to a foreign country.

The permission to emigrate shall be invalidated by failure to depart not later than six months from the date at which such permission was granted.

ARTICLE III. The Administrative Authorities may, according to the conditions of the place to which an *Imin* desires to emigrate, require him, if he proposes to emigrate without the agency of an *Imin Toriatsukainin,* to appoint as his sureties not less than two persons whom they deem to be satisfactory.

Such sureties shall, in case the Imin falls sick or is otherwise in distress, give him assistance or cause him to return; and if he has been assisted or brought home by the Administrative Authorities, they shall reimburse the expenses incurred on his account.

ARTICLE IV. The Administrative Authorities may, with a view to the protection of Imin or maintenance of public peace, or if they deem it necessary having regard to foreign relations, suspend the emigration of Imin or revoke the permission granted therefor.

The term of such suspension of emigration shall not be included in the period specified in the second clause of Art. II.

Chapter II
Imin Toriatsukainin

ARTICLE V. By the term "Imin Toriatsukainin" in the present Law is meant a person, who, under any denomination whatever, makes it his business to collect Imin or make arrangements for their emigration.

An Imin Toriatsukainin may, with the permission of the Administrative Authorities, engage in business directly connected with Imin.

ARTICLE VI. A person who desires to become an Imin Toriatsukainin must obtain the permission of the Administrative Authorities.

The permission to become an Imin Toriatsukainin shall be invalidated by failure to commence business not later than six months from the date at which such permission was granted.

ARTICLE VII-1. Only a Japanese subject or a commercial company whereof the partners or shareholders are all Japanese subjects, with the principal office established in the Empire, may become an Imin Toriatsukainin.

The qualifications required for an Imin Toriatsukainin, in addition to those mentioned in the preceding clause, shall be determined by Ordinance.

ARTICLE VII-2. The Imin Toriatsukainin shall, with respect to the Imin for whose emigration he has made arrangements, bear for the period of full ten years from the date of departure of such Imin, the obligations of sureties prescribed in the second clause of Art. III.

ARTICLE VIII. In case any act of an Imin Toriatsukainin is in violation of Laws or Ordinances or is deemed to be prejudicial to public peace, and in case he fails to deposit the security required of the Imin Toriatsukainin, the Administrative Authorities may suspend his business or revoke the permission granted therefor.

ARTICLE IX. The Imin Toriatsukainin shall not, even during the suspension or temporary cessation of his business, arrest the fulfilment of contracts in respect of those Imin whom he has already sent abroad.

ARTICLE X. An Imin Toriatsukainin, who desires to appoint an agent to conduct his business, must, according to provisions to be made by Ordinance, obtain the permission of the Administrative Authorities.

ARTICLE XI. The Imin Toriatsukainin shall not send an Imin to a place where he has not resident a managing partner, a director, or an agent.

ARTICLE XII. The Imin Toriatsukainin shall not make arrangements for or collect any persons for emigration unless they intend to emigrate as Imin.

ARTICLE XIII. The Imin Toriatsukainin shall, in making arrangements for or collecting Imin for emigration under a labour contract, make written contracts with such Imin and obtain therefor the approval of the Administrative Authorities.

The necessary terms of the contracts mentioned in the preceding clause shall be determined by Ordinance.

ARTICLE XIV. The Imin Toriatsukainin shall not, under any pretext whatever, receive from the Imin money or articles other than his fees; and the amount of such fees must be previously approved by the Administrative Authorities.

ARTICLE XV-1. When it is proposed to collect Imin, the Imin Toriatsukainin shall previously fix and notify the date of their departure; and in the event of his failing without sufficient reason to send them abroad by the date so fixed, he shall bear the expenses incurred by the Imin by reason of such delay.

ARTICLE XV-2. The Administrative Authorities may, if they deem it necessary, order the Imin Toriatsukainin to establish a business guild.

The business guild shall be a juridical person.

Regulations relating to the business guild shall be determined by Ordinance.

Chapter III
Security

ARTICLE XVI. The Imin Toriatsukainin shall not commence business until he has deposited a security with the Administrative Authorities.

The amount of the security shall be not less than ten thousand (10,000) yen and the actual amount shall be determined by the Administrative Authorities.

ARTICLE XVII. The Administrative Authorities may, if they deem it necessary, raise or reduce the amount of the security; they shall not, however, bring it below the amount mentioned in the preceding article.

ARTICLE XVIII. If the Administrative Authorities deem that the Imin Toriatsukainin has failed to carry out his contract with the Imin or to perform the obligations of surety as prescribed in Art. VII-2, they may assist or bring home such Imin and defray the expenses thereof out of the security.

ARTICLE XIX. Even in the event of the business of an Imin Toriatsukainin being discontinued through his death, the dissolution of his firm, the revocation of the permission to carry on his business, or any other cause, the Administrative Authorities may, so long as they deem it necessary, retain the whole or a part of his security.

ARTICLE XX-1. While the Imin Toriatsukainin is carrying on his business and during the time the Administrative Authorities deem it necessary to retain the security as mentioned in the preceding article, no person whatever can make a claim upon the security for recovery of debts, except in the case where the Imin or their heirs exercise their rights in virtue of the contract concluded in accordance with the present Law.

Chapter IV
Emigrant ship (imin unsosen)

ARTICLE XX-2. By the term "Emigrant ship (Imin Unsosen)" in the present Law is meant a vessel which carries on board not less than fifty Imin emigrating to the localities to be designated by Ordinance.

ARTICLE XX-3. The conveyance of Imin by an emigrant ship shall not take place without the permission of the Administrative Authorities.

The person who has obtained the permission mentioned in the preceding clause shall deposit a security in a manner to be determined by the Administrative Authorities.

ARTICLE XX-4. In the event of any act of a person who has obtained the permission mentioned in the preceding article being in violation of the Laws or Ordinances or of the conditions on which such permission was granted, or being deemed to be prejudicial to the interests of the Imin, the Administrative Authorities may revoke the said permission.

ARTICLE XX-5. A person who desires to convey Imin by an emigrant ship must previously obtain the approval of the Administrative Authorities with respect to the passage-money.

ARTICLE XX-6. The Administrative Authorities may designate the ports of departure and destination of emigrant ships.

ARTICLE XX-7. The Administrative Authorities may cause the master of an emigrant ship to report on various matters relating to the Imin carried on board.

Chapter V
Miscellaneous Provisions

ARTICLE XX-8. A person engaged in the business of money-lending, who proposes to lend to an Imin his passage expenses and other expenses required in preparing for the passage, must previously obtain the approval of the Administrative Authorities with respect to the terms of such loan.

ARTICLE XX-9. A person who desires to engage in the business of lodging Imin at the port of departure, must obtain the permission of the Administrative Authorities.

A person to whom the permission mentioned in the preceding clause has been granted, must previously obtain the approval of the Administrative Authorities with respect to the arrangements for lodging Imin, their maintenance and lodging charge, and other items which may become a charge upon them.

ARTICLE XX-10. A person other than an Imin Toriatsukainin, who desires to make arrangements relative to the embarkation of Imin, must obtain the permission of the Administrative Authorities.

A person to whom the permission mentioned in the preceding clause has been granted, must previously obtain the approval of the Administrative Authorities with respect to the manner of making arrangements for the embarkation of Imin and other items which may become a charge upon them.

ARTICLE XX-11. In case any act of a person, to whom the permission mentioned in the preceding two clauses has been granted, is in violation of Laws or Ordinances, or is deemed to be prejudicial to the interests of Imin, the Administrative Authorities may suspend his business or revoke the permission granted thereof.

Chapter VI
Penal Provisions

ARTICLE XXI. An Imin who emigrates without permission, after obtaining permission by falsely reporting his place of emigration, or in violation of orders suspending emigration, shall be liable to a fine of not less than five yen but not more than fifty yen.

ARTICLE XXII. An Imin Toriatsukainin or his agent, who makes arrangements for the emigration of an Imin who has violated Laws or Ordinances, or sends abroad any Imin during the suspension of emigration, shall be liable to a fine of not less than fifty yen but not more than five hundred yen.

ARTICLE XXIII. A person who acts as an Imin Toriatsukainin without obtaining the permission of the Administrative Authorities and an Imin Toriatsukainin or his agent who collects Imin or makes arrangements for their emigration during the suspension of his business shall be liable to a fine of not less than two hundred yen but not more than one thousand yen.

The provision of the preceding clause shall also apply to an Imin Toriatsukainin who, without obtaining the permission of the Administrative Authorities, engages in the business mentioned in the second clause of Art. V.

ARTICLE XXIV. An Imin Toriatsukainin who causes to act as his agent one for whom such permission has not been obtained from the Administrative Authorities shall be liable to a fine of not less than twenty yen but not more than two hundred yen; such agent shall be liable to a similar fine.

ARTICLE XXV. An Imin Toriatsukainin or his agent who violates the provisions of Art. XI, Art. XII, Art. XIII, Art. XIV, or Art. XVI, Clause I, of the present Law shall be liable to a fine of not less than fifty yen but not more than five hundred yen.

ARTICLE XXVI-1. An Imin Toriatsukainin or his agent who, by means of false representations, collects Imin or makes arrangements for their emigration, shall be liable to major imprisonment for a term of not less than one month but not more than one year.

ARTICLE XXVI-2. A person who violates the provision of Art. XX-3 shall be liable to a fine of not less than five hundred yen but not more than ten thousand yen.

ARTICLE XXVI-3. A person who violates the provision of Art. XX-5 shall be liable to a fine of not less than two hundred yen but not more than three thousand yen; and in case the ports of departure and destination of an emigrant ship have been designated by the Administrative Authorities, a person who acts contrary to such designation shall be liable to a similar fine.

ARTICLE XXVI-4. A person who fails to make the reports when so ordered by the Administrative Authorities under the provision of Art. XX-7, shall be liable to a fine of not less than fifty yen but not more than three hundred yen.

ARTICLE XXVI-5. A person who violates the provisions of Art. XX-8, Art. XX-9, or Art. XX-10 shall be liable to a fine of not less than one hundred yen but not more than one thousand yen.

ARTICLE XXVII. The penal provisions of the present Law shall, in the case of a commercial company, apply to the managing partner or director thereof, who is guilty of the acts mentioned in the respective articles of this Chapter.

Chapter VII
Supplementary Provisions

ARTICLE XXVIII. An Imin Toriatsukainin who has, prior to the coming into force of the present Law, been engaged in his business with the permission of the Proper Authorities, may, in conformity with the provisions of the present Law, continue such business without being required to obtain permission specially at the time the Law comes into force; in case, however, he discontinues his business, the provisions of this Law shall apply to the security which he has already deposited.

ARTICLE XXIX. The present Law shall not apply to Imin who emigrate by virtue of a special treaty concluded by the Empire or to their Toriatsukainin.

ARTICLE XXX. The Detailed Regulations necessary for the enforcement of the present Law shall be determined by Ordinance.

ARTICLE XXXI. The present Law shall come into force on the first day of the sixth month of the Twenty-ninth year of Meiji (1st June, 1896).

The Regulations for the Protection of Imin, promulgated by Imperial Ordinance No. 42 of the Twenty-seventh year of Meiji (1894), shall cease to be binding from the date at which the present Law takes effect.

Appendix 8

Japanese Consuls General in Honolulu, 1886–1908

Andō Tarō (term began 14 February 1886)
Torii Tadafumi (Deputy; 3 December 1889)
Masaki Taizō (Deputy; 22 May 1890)
Masaki Taizō (26 June 1891)
Fujii Saburō (26 November 1892)
Narita Gorō (Representative; 12 November 1894)
Shimamura Hisashi (5 January 1895)
Shimizu Seisaburō (Deputy; 10 January 1895)
Hirai Shinzō (Deputy; 13 July 1898)
Saitō Miki (Deputy; 9 September 1898)
Okabe Saburō (Deputy; 23 August 1902)
Saitō Miki (19 March 1903)
Matsubara Kazuo (Deputy; 23 December 1905)
Saitō Miki (7 September 1906)
Abe Yoshihachi (Deputy; 6 August 1908)
Ueno Sen'ichi (1 October 1908)

Source: Gaimushō gaikō shiryōkan, *Nihon gaikōshi jiten*, supplement, pp. 384–385.

Appendix 9

Emigration Companies that Failed to Meet the Six-Month Deadline, 1894–1902

Yokohama kaigai shokumin gōshigaisha (date of operation, 1894)
Dainippon imin kabushikigaisha (1895)
Chinzei imin kabushikigaisha (1896)
Kimoto Shunkichi (1896–1897)
Kobe yūsen imin kabushikigaisha (1897–1898)
Nippon shokumin kabushikigaisha (1897–1898)
Kyōdō imin gōshigaisha (1899–1900)
Niigata shokumin kabushikigaisha (1899–1900)
Shinobe Matsujirō (1900)
Osaka tokō gōshigaisha (1900)
Shinjō Rokyō (1900)
Murata Tamekichi (1900–1901)
Ōkura gumi (1900–1901)
Shinoda Saburobē (1900–1901)
Shibuya Kinshirō (1902)

Source: JFMAD files. See references listed in note 30, chapter 4.

Appendix 10

Business License Applicants Turned Down by the Foreign Ministry, 1896–1906

Fukuyasu Shikanosuke (year applied, 1896)
Matono Hansuke (1900)
Asaoka Iwatarō (1900)
Suzuki Hideo (1900)
Nagawa Mitsugu (1901)
Okabe Hiroshi (1902)
Amagi Isahiko (1902)
Ogiso Masajirō (1902)
Nakamura Taroku (1903)
Miyake Hikoemon (1903)
Imanashi Rinzaburō (1903)
Ariyama Hikokichi (1903)
Wakao Tamizō (1903)
Dezaki Kōsuke (1906)

Source: JFMAD 3.8.2.54.

Appendix 11

Agents in the U.S. and Canada and the Emigration Companies They Represented, 1899

Shinobe Takejirō, San Jose: Kobe Immigration Company
Takaya Tanichi (Taneichi?), San Francisco: Japan Emigration Company, Morioka Immigration Company
Hamano Kisuke (Keisuke?), San Francisco: Japanese Emigration Company of Hiroshima
Nishihata Eikichi, San Francisco: Kōsei imin kabushikigaisha
Takahashi Kinsuke (Kinosuke?), Vancouver: Kobe Immigration Company, Kōsei imin kabushikigaisha, Japanese Emigration Company of Hiroshima
Kayashi Kawanichi (Hayashi Kannichi?), Vancouver: Kyushu imin kabushikigaisha
Mito Masatarō, Vancouver: Japan Emigration Company
Minami Jinnosuke (Ginnosuke?), San Francisco: Japanese Emigration Company of Hiroshima
Nishihata Y., San Francisco: Kōsei imin kabushikigaisha

Source: W. M. Rice, Commissioner of Immigration, to the Commissioner-General of Immigration, 24 April 1899, *AH Bureau Letters (1897–1900).*

Appendix 12

Japanese Inspectors, Interpreters, and Doctors Hired by the Hawaiian Government

Inspectors and Interpreters

Akisu Nagamitsu (also listed as a doctor)
Fukushima Takeji
Igarashi Naomasa (also listed as a doctor)
Itō Chōjirō
Katsunuma Tomizō
Katsura Keigorō
Kimura Saiji
Nacayama G.O.
Nagano Keijirō
Okkotsu Kanezō
Onome Bunichirō (Bunichi)
Osada Kitarō
Sakiyama Yoshitada
Satō Yoshisuke
Seya Masaji (Setani Shōji)
Tanaka Naokata

Doctors

Akiyama
Asano Mitsuya
Iwai Teizō
Katsuki Ichitarō
Kawada Moriyuki (Moriyasu)
Kimishima Keizō
Kobayashi Kōan
Koga Seisan (Seisen)
Komai K.
Mitamura Toshihide
Mōri Iga
Muraura Seishichirō
Nakazawa Shigetomo
Noda S.
Satō K.
Takenouchi Morisuke
Toki Hisaki
Uchida Jūkichi
Wada S.
Yamamoto S.
Yamashita Matsuzō
Yoshida Kōsai

Status Unclear

Yamamoto Hiroshi

Source: JFMAD and HSA documents and Kihara, *Hawai Nipponjinshi.*

Appendix 13

Agents in Hawaii

Adachi S.
Hamanaka Yatarō
Hamano Yonetsuchi
Hasegawa Harumasa
Hayashi Takisaburō
Hinata Takeshi
Hirayama Katsukuma
Inoue Keijirō
Katsunuma Tomizō
Kobayashi Kiroku
Kobayashi Unosuke
Koizumi Sakutarō
Kuramoto Yūgo
Masuda Tomojirō
Matsumoto Santarō
Matsuoka Tatsusaburō
Mitsutome Yoshisuke
Mizuno Hamon
Mōri Iga
Nagatani Yūzō
Onodera Hisao
Ozaki Sanshichi
Ozawa Kenzaburō
Ozawa Tadamoto
Sasaki Kōjirō
Sawano Chūzō
Shimizu B.
Shinozawa Chūzaburō
Sukie Ryōji
Tainaka Kusuemon
Tasaka Yōkichi
Tokunaga Isatarō
Tsumura Shikao
Uchida Jūkichi
Wada Morisaburō
Watanabe Kanjūrō
Yamaguchi Yūya
Yamashita Fujitarō
Yokogawa Shūsan
Yokogawa Yūji

Sources: Report from the Consulate to the Foreign Ministry, 1904, *JFMAD 3.8.2.168.* Some names from other sources. See also Sōga, *Gojūnenkan,* pp. 12–107.

Appendix 14

Major Boardinghouses in Honolulu and Their Owners

FUKUOKAYA	Ichikawa Kumatarō
MIZUHAYA (also as Haramoto ryokan)	Haramoto Taichi
NIIGATAYA (also as Nishimura ryokan)	Nishimura Shūsuke
KAWASAKIYA (also as Kawasaki ryokan)	Kawasaki Kiyozō
KUMAMOTOYA	Udō Yoshinori
GEISHŪYA (also as Yamashiroya)	Yamashiro Matsutarō
KYUSHUYA	Fukushima Hatsutarō
IZUMIYA (also as Hawaiya, Kobayashiya)	Kobayashi Unosuke
CHŪGOKUYA (also as Komeya ryokan)	Komeya Miyotsuchi
KŌRIYA (also as Higoya)	Takaki Gentarō
YANAIYA	Hirano Takejirō
HIROSHIMAYA	Nishikida Naotarō
ŌSHIMAYA	Nishimura Shūsuke
SHINSHŪYA	Imanaka Kitarō
KANJŌ RYOKAN	Yasumura Harutada
KOMATSUYA	Satō Yoshisuke
SUMIYA KYUSHUTEI	?
IWAKUNIYA	?

Sources: 1903 list is attached to a 2 December 1903 letter from the Consulate to the Foreign Ministry, in *JFMAD 3.8.2.168;* Sōga, *Gojūnenkan,* p. 141; Kihara, *Hawai Nipponjinshi,* p. 482; Okahata, *Japanese in Hawaii,* p. 161; and *JFMAD 3.8.2.198.*

Appendix 15

San Francisco Boardinghouse Owners and Agents

Iki K.
Nanko S.
Suzuki M.
Kamai K.
Takano A.
Toriuchi N.
Emoto C.
Shōno K.
Sakai
Nagatani Yūji
Negoro Motoyuki
Haga K. (Kanjō Hotel)
Kuroishi Seisaku
Tōyō Bōekigaisha
Wakamoto Yoshizō (Meijiya)
Aikawa Torakichi (Meijiya)
Sasai Shikanosuke
Hoshide Yasujirō
Ebisuya
Fuse Torazō
Uozumi Utarō (Echigoya ryokan)
Yamamoto Masajirō (Echigoya ryokan)
Murakami Suetsuchi (Nishikuya ryokan)
Fujii Shōtarō (Nishikuya ryokan)
Tajeri (Tajiri?) R.

Sources: See list, 1902, *JFMAD 3.8.2.168.* See also *JFMAD 3.8.2.198.*

Notes

Introduction

1. See Daniels, "American Historians and East Asian Immigrants," pp. 449–472; Daniels, "Westerners from the East," pp. 373–383; and the Introduction of *A Buried Past,* compiled by Ichioka et al., pp. 3–15.

2. Kokusai kyōryoku jigyōdan, *Kaigai ijū tōkei,* pp. 66–67. Although most works on this topic have figures for emigrants leaving Japan, the most accurate are those issued by the Japanese foreign ministry. Until recently, Japanese historians usually have relied on Gaimushō tsūshōkyoku, *Ryoken kafusū oyobi imin tōkei,* which I believe is reasonably accurate, although it does not offer figures for years prior to 1898. In terms of overall emigrant figures, I have chosen whenever possible to use *Kaigai ijū tōkei* because its figures were compiled from *Teikoku tōkei annai*; Gaimushō tsūshōkyoku, *Ryoken kafusū;* Gaimushō tsūshōkyoku, *Kaigai ijū tōkei;* Takumushō takumukyoku, *Takumu tōkei;* and Gaimushō Amerikakyoku, *Imin tokōsha tōkei.*

3. Suzuki, *Japanese Immigrant in Brazil,* vol. 1, pp. 286–287. The figures were calculated from statistics from the foreign ministry's *Overseas Migration Statistics—Ministry of Foreign Affairs,* 1964.

4. Ibid. I am differentiating between emigrants and colonizers. To countries under the Japanese government's control, Japanese settlers were colonizers.

5. The Japanese term is *kan'yakuimin.* At times during this period, the foreign ministry also used *dekaseginin* when they mentioned emigrants. This word refers to a type of outside labor Japanese farmers engaged in during the Tokugawa and succeeding periods.

6. The definition given in a 1912 English version of the Emigrant Protection Law was as follows: "By the term 'Imin Toriatsukainin' . . . is meant a person who . . . makes it his business to collect Imin or makes arrangements for their emigration." See Bureau of Commercial Affairs, *Japanese Laws,* p. 2.

7. The reason for the popular usage of this word was that almost all of the toriatsukainin were incorporated and were in a legal sense operating as companies.

8. In Japanese the term is *kaishaimin.*

9. There is no particular Japanese term for "independent emigrants." Rather, they

were referred to as *imin toriatsukainin ni yorasaru mono,* or "emigrants not using emigration companies." See Gaimushō tsūshōkyoku, *Ryoken kafusū,* pp. 142–181.

10. In Japanese these contract emigrants were known as *keiyakuimin,* while free emigrants were called *jiyūimin.*

11. Article, "Foreigners in Tokyo," *Japan Times,* 22 March 1897.

12. "Four hundred yen in three years" is *sannen de yonhyakuen* in Japanese. See Kaigai ijū jigyōdan, *Kaigai ijū jigyōdan jūnenshi,* p. 5. Returning clad in brocade is in Japanese *kokyō ni nishiki o kazaru.*

Chapter 1
The Background in Japan and Hawaii

1. Gaimushō hyakunenshi hensan iinkai hen, *Gaimushō no hyakunen,* p. 857.

2. For accounts of this episode in English, see Watanabe, "Diplomatic Relations" (unpublished M.A. thesis), pp. 20–33; Conroy, *Japanese Frontier,* pp. 15–33; Masaji Marumoto, " 'First Year' Immigrants to Hawaii and Eugene Van Reed," in Conroy and Miyakawa, eds., *East Across the Pacific,* pp. 5–39; and Okahata, *Japanese in Hawaii,* pp. 37–62. Japanese sources cover this topic more extensively. For a recent and detailed treatment see Imai, "Kindai Nihon," pp. 1–11. Matsunaga deals with the departure from Yokohama in "Yokohama shuppatsu," pp. 98–110. Also useful are Yamashita, *Gannen mono;* Watanabe, "Nikkei," pp. 109–119; Yagisawa, "Iminshi no issetsu," pp. 41–61; Irie, "Meiji gannen," pp. 158–167; and the first installment of Matsunaga, "Mitsui Bussan." Because 1868 was the first year of the Meiji period, these emigrants were known as *Gannen mono,* or "first year people."

3. David I. Lee, M.D., to the Board of Immigration, 19 June 1868, *Archives of Hawaii* (hereafter cited as *AH*) *Department of the Interior-Miscellaneous Files, Immigration: Japanese - 1868–1900.* Occasionally other figures are given, but foreign ministry documents include a list of only 141 men. *Japanese Foreign Ministry Archival Documents* (hereafter cited as *JFMAD*) *3.8.2.1,* vol. 1 has the list in an enclosure dated May, n. p. As will be apparent from these footnotes, most of my research for this book was done at the Diplomatic Record Office in Tokyo. There the materials of the Meiji through Shōwa periods are cataloged in files. In almost all cases, there are no page numbers and so the tables of contents are of little use. They consist of brief summaries of the contents of the file in the order that they appear. The materials consist of internal foreign ministry memos and reports, letters, enclosures, reports from overseas officials, newspaper clippings, reports submitted by emigration companies, and others.

4. Foreign Ministry (always of Japan unless otherwise indicated) to the American Consul in Japan, 16 June 1868, *JFMAD 3.8.2.1,* vol. 1; see letters, June–October 1868, *JFMAD 3.8.2.1,* vol. 1; U.S. Minister Resident in Japan to the U.S. Minister Resident in Hawaii, 20 October 1869, *JFMAD 3.8.2.1,* vol. 1.

5. See Gaimushō ryōji ijūbu, *Waga kokumin* (honpen), p. 126.

6. Ibid. There have been several fictional accounts about Okei, who served as a nursemaid for the Schnell family until her death. See for example Saotome, *Okei.* For more information on Schnell's relationship with the Tokugawa Shogunate, see Tanaka, "Suneru no sujō," pp. 14–27.

7. Nakamura, *Economic Growth,* p. 54. (Translated from *Senzen Nihon keizai seichō no bunseki* [Tokyo: Iwanami shoten, 1971].)

8. Ibid.

9. Ibid., p. 58.

10. Waswo, *Japanese Landlords,* p. 14.

11. Ibid., pp. 19–20.

12. Rosovsky, *Capital Formation in Japan,* p. 85.

13. Mundle and Ohkawa, "Agricultural Surplus Flow in Japan," pp. 247–265.

14. See Beasley, *Meiji Restoration,* p. 63 for information on samurai stipends. See Ono, *War and Armament Expenditures of Japan,* p. 263 for details about government expenditures in the Satsuma rebellion. See also Nakamura, *Economic Growth,* p. 61.

15. Nakamura, *Economic Growth,* p. 51.

16. Shindo, "Inflation," pp. 51–56.

17. Waswo, *Japanese Landlords,* p. 48.

18. Nakamura, *Economic Growth,* p. 61; Waswo, *Japanese Landlords,* p. 19.

19. Ike, "Taxation," p. 175.

20. Nakamura, *Economic Growth,* p. 56.

21. Ono, *Gendai Nippon bunmeishi,* vol. 9, pp. 178–181.

22. Nakamura, *Economic Growth,* p. 51.

23. This is the basis of an ongoing argument among the historians, economists, and sociologists writing in this field. Generally both Japanese and American scholars have been divided into two schools of thought. Briefly stated, one school sees this period (particularly after 1881) as one of low agricultural production, severe economic and social dislocation, widespread tenancy (due to economic factors), parasitic landlords, and peasant uprisings (see Ike, "Taxation"; Hane, *Peasants;* Norman, *Japan's Emergence*). The other school has a more positive view of the Meiji economy, citing as evidence a higher rate of agricultural production, little dislocation in the countryside, and an evenhanded landlord-tenant system that though complex is based on mutual benefits (see Nakamura, *Economic Growth;* Waswo, *Japanese Landlords*). On this topic, Richard Smethurst's manuscript "From Peasant to Farmer: Agricultural Development and Tenancy Disputes in Japan, 1870–1940" shows tenancy resulted from several factors and that accounts of the level of severity of the lives of tenants have been overdrawn. I am grateful for his comments on this. Japanese chose to migrate overseas for economic and noneconomic reasons. A discussion of the latter would involve such topics as the role of government officials, active recruitment, the role of private emigration companies, and the influence of previous emigrants. These will be discussed in detail in later chapters. The major arguments concerning the level of severity of the life of the Meiji peasant are important, in this particular case, only as support for the claim that there was a wage differential between what was possible to earn in Japan and what was promised in Hawaii. Even the most optimistic observer of the Meiji agricultural economy will not argue that the income level of the majority of farmers in *any* region of Japan even closely approached the wages offered by sugar plantations in Hawaii.

Furthermore national conditions including rice production rates, the level of tenancy, the amount of acreage farmed, and so forth are far *less* significant than the particular historical, economic, and social factors on the prefectural, local, and village levels. We will see in chapter 2 how events on these levels, whether it be the construction of a breakwater in a small bay, the fertility of soil on one part of an island, or the activities of one village official could become the deciding factor in starting emigration from a particular area.

24. For information on cash crops, see Kodama Masaaki, "Kaigai e no imin" (hereafter cited as "Kaigai e") in Hiroshima-ken hen, *Hiroshima-ken shi kindai ichi,* pp. 988–1035. For information on the value of cottage industry production (214,000,000 yen in 1884 compared to 6,500,000 yen worth of factory products), see Nakamura, *Economic Growth,* p. 80.

25. See Morisaki, *Karayukisan;* Yamazaki, *Sandakan hachiban shokan;* Miyaoka, *Shofū—kaigai ruroki—;* Yamazaki, *Sandakan no haka;* Ichioka, "Ameyuki-San: Japanese Prostitutes," pp. 1–21.

26. Hanley and Yamamura, *Economic and Demographic Change,* pp. 254–255.

27. For information on this topic see Kajinishi et al., *Seishi;* Hosoi, *Jokō aishi;* and Yamamoto, *Aa nomugi tōge.*

28. Waswo, *Japanese Landlords,* p. 68.

29. For a case study of how this dekasegi rōdō pattern began and led to overseas emigration from a specific area (Ōshima island in Yamaguchi prefecture) see Miyamoto, "Shima," pp. 136–150.

30. Okahata, *Japanese in Hawaii,* p. 277; Glick, *Sojourners and Settlers,* p. 18; Nagai, ed., *Nichi-Bei bunka kōshōshi,* vol. 5, p. 350.

31. Alan Moriyama, "The 1909 and 1920 Strikes of Japanese Sugar Plantation Workers in Hawaii" (hereafter cited as "1909 and 1920 Strikes") in Gee, ed., *Counterpoint,* pp. 169–180. See Liebes, "Labor Organization in Hawaii" (unpublished M.A. thesis), p. 11; Johannesson, *Hawaiian Labor Movement,* p. 74; and Kuykendall, *Hawaiian Kingdom,* pp. 116–141.

32. Ibid. See also Aller, "Evolution of Hawaiian Labor Relations" (unpublished Ph.D. dissertation), p. 134; Morgan, *Hawaii,* p. 188; and Russ, "Hawaiian Labor," pp. 207–222.

33. Lind, "Economic Succession" (unpublished Ph.D. dissertation), p. 268.

34. Charles Bishop to Robert M. Brown, H.H.M.'s Charge d'Affaires and Consul General for the Empire of Japan, 2 January 1874, *AH Foreign Office Letter Books,* p. 30.

35. Irie, "Senkakusha no keifu," no. 270. This was one of a series of articles under this title by Irie for *Kaigai ijū.* See also Kuykendall, *Hawaiian Kingdom,* pp. 154–155.

36. Chief Secretary of South Australia to the Japanese Foreign Ministry, 19 September 1876, *JFMAD 3.8.2.2,* vol. 1; Japanese Foreign Office to Wilton Hack (the individual seeking Japanese workers), 27 February 1877, *JFMAD 3.8.2.2,* vol. 1.

37. Telegraph message from Sakurada Chikayoshi, Charge d'Affaires of Japan in the Netherlands to Foreign Minister Inoue, 10 September 1883, *JFMAD 3.8.2.2,* vol. 1; Inoue to Sakurada, 11 September 1883, *JFMAD 3.8.2.2,* vol. 1.

38. Report from the Governor of Kanagawa prefecture to the Foreign Ministry and the Home Ministry, 5 July 1884, *JFMAD 3.8.2.6.*

39. Governor of Kanagawa prefecture to the Foreign Ministry, 19 June 1885, *JFMAD 3.8.2.6.*

40. Internal Foreign Ministry report, 9 July 1885, *JFMAD 3.8.2.6;* report from the Governor of Kanagawa prefecture to the Foreign Ministry, 21 September 1885, *JFMAD 3.8.2.6.*

41. Report from the Governor of Kanagawa prefecture to the Foreign Ministry, 11 September 1885, *JFMAD* 3.8.2.6.

42. See Gaimushō ryōji ijūbu, *Waga kokumin* (honpen), p. 127. No passport figures are given in Kokusai kyōryoku jigyōdan, *Kaigai ijū tōkei,* pp. 66–67. Information was also obtained through an interview with Oshimoto Naomasa of the Emigration Service Department, Japan International Cooperation Agency, July 1981. These thirty-seven workers were carrying labor contracts.

43. Kuykendall, *Hawaiian Kingdom,* pp. 159–161.

44. Matsunaga, "Mitsui Bussan," particularly the first two installments.

45. Ibid. See Conroy, *Japanese Frontier* and Yuriko Irwin and Hilary Conroy, "R. W. Irwin and Systematic Immigration to Hawaii" (hereafter cited as "R. W. Irwin") in Conroy and Miyakawa, eds., *East Across the Pacific,* pp. 40–55.

46. During the 1869–1882 period the Japanese government had taken the responsibility to colonize its northernmost island of Hokkaido. It was official policy to subsidize farmers willing to travel to Hokkaido by offering them free passage, free farm equipment, exemptions from land taxes, and at times, free land. Authorities oversaw this colonization venture through the *Kaitakushi* (Colonization Office). See Harrison, *Japan's Northern Frontier,* pp. 74–75.

Chapter 2
The Government-Sponsored Emigration Period

1. Commissioner of Labor, *Third Report,* p. 145.

2. Hawai Nihonjin iminshi kankō iinkai, *Hawai Nihonjin iminshi,* pp. 99–100. The English translation is the previously cited Okahata, *Japanese in Hawaii.* Okahata claims that 29,069 immigrants arrived during this period.

3. Report from the Consulate to the Foreign Ministry, 22 November 1902, Gaimushō, *Nihon gaikō bunsho* (hereafter cited as *NGB),* vol. 35, pp. 328–389.

4. Enclosure, 20 April 1891 (1891–1894 figures later added in pencil), *AH Board of Immigration Letters* (hereafter cited as *Board Letters*), p. 13. The Board was usually referred to as the Bureau of Immigration during the Hawaiian Kingdom and the Board of Immigration during the Hawaiian Republic. I will try to keep this distinction, although on occasion they were used interchangeably.

Any study of large-scale emigration depends on the accuracy of statistical data, but unfortunately few historians in this particular field agree on the exact number of Japanese who went to Hawaii. Conroy's ground-breaking work *The Japanese Frontier in Hawaii* gives as a total for the ten years 28,691 (p. 154). Given that there were undocumented births and deaths, and illegal passengers aboard the ships, not to mention errors in counting, we probably will never be able to settle this issue, particularly for the early shipments.

5. Conroy, *Japanese Frontier,* pp. 148–150. In both the English-language and Japanese documents of this period, there were spelling and typographical errors. I have made the corrections in these cases and did not change the intended meaning.

6. Commissioner of Labor, *Third Report,* p. 147.

7. Conroy, *Japanese Frontier,* pp. 148–150.

8. *Daily Bulletin,* 8 December 1886, *JFMAD 3.8.2.5 Bessatsu muyakutei;* Irwin to

Inoue, 21 January 1887, *JFMAD 3.8.2.5 Bessatsu muyakutei;* Inoue to Irwin, 21 January 1887, *JFMAD 3.8.2.5 Bessatsu muyakutei.*

9. Commissioner of Labor, *Third Report,* p. 146.

10. Ibid., p. 145.

11. Undated enclosure, *AH Bureau Letters 1893–1897,* p. 194.

12. Enclosure attached to report from the Consulate to the Foreign Ministry, 15 May 1886, *JFMAD 3.8.2.5 Bessatsu tōgyō.*

13. Yoshida, "Meiji shoki," pt. 1, pp. 260–264.

14. Kodama, "Meijiki," pp. 73–100.

15. Tōgō, *Nippon shokuminron,* pp. 137–143.

16. Ibid. The national average was 55 percent.

17. Kodama, "Meijiki," pp. 76–83 and Kodama, "Kaigai e," in Hiroshima-ken hen, *Hiroshima-ken shi kindai ichi,* pp. 988–1035.

18. Doi, *Hawai,* pp. 16–17. Wakatsuki, "Japanese Emigration," pp. 415–417.

19. Miyamoto, "Shima," pp. 136–140. See also Doi, *Hawai,* pp. 22–48 for information on the role of Ōshima county officials and Hino Norisuke.

20. For Irwin's relationship with Masuda, see note by Irwin 27 January 1885, *JFMAD 3.8.2.5 Bessatsu zatsu no bu,* vol. 1. Irwin's relationship with Inoue is described by Yuriko Irwin and Hilary Conroy's "R. W. Irwin," in Conroy and Miyakawa, eds., *East Across the Pacific,* pp. 40–55.

21. Wakayama-ken, *Wakayama-ken iminshi,* p. 479.

22. Kawazoe, *Imin hyakunen,* p. 93. See also Doi, *Hawai,* p. 13 and Matsunaga, "Mitsui Bussan," installment one.

23. Matsunaga, "Mitsui Bussan," installment six. See also Doi, *Hawai,* pp. 14–15 for the appropriate excerpt from Masuda's autobiography.

24. Conroy, *Japanese Frontier,* pp. 82–83.

25. Kajinishi et al., *Seishi,* p. 50.

26. Lorrin A. Thurston, Minister of the Interior and President of the Bureau of Immigration, to Irwin, 8 September 1887, *JFMAD 3.8.2.360.*

27. Ishikawa, "Jigozen-son," pp. 75–91; "Kuga-son," pp. 25–38; "Kuchida-son," pp. 33–52. I have used figures given for the 1885–1887 period. For later years, the data does not distinguish between emigrants going to Hawaii and those going directly to the mainland United States.

28. This statement was included in a circular issued by the Bureau of Immigration and is referred to in the 27 February 1885 issue of the *Daily Pacific Commercial Advertiser.*

29. Japanese workers were able to bring in a larger percentage of women than other Asian groups. Thus the growth of the Chinese, Korean, and Filipino communities was also delayed.

30. Yoshida, "Meiji shoki," pt. 1, pp. 258–259.

31. Minutes, Bureau of Immigration meeting, 27 July 1887, *AH Board Minutes* 1879–1899.

32. See Ishikawa, "Jigozen-son," "Kuga-son," and "Kuchida-son."

33. Gaimushō ryōji ijūbu, *Hyakunen no ayumi,* p. 22. The author of this work is Irie Toraji.

34. Ishikawa, "Kuchida-son," p. 41; "Jigozen-son," p. 83; and "Kuga-son," p. 33. For another viewpoint see Staniford, "Nihon ni itemo sho ga nai: The Background, Strategies and Personalities of Rural Japanese Overseas Immigrants," n. p.

35. Paul Neumann to Charles N. Spencer, Minister of the Interior, 18 March 1891, *AH Bureau Misc. Files* document 10. The documents in this file are loose but in chronological order so I have numbered them arbitrarily.

36. Ishikawa, "Jigozen-son," p. 85.

37. Kaigai ijū jigyōdan, *Jūnenshi,* p. 5.

38. Kodama, "Kaigai e" (see note 17), p. 993.

39. Doi, *Hawai,* p. 16.

40. *Japan Weekly Gazette,* 11 April 1891. Article attached to a letter from H. Marks to the Vice Minister of State for Foreign Affairs, 24 November 1891, *JFMAD 3.8.2.2,* vol. 1. Marks saw himself as an "unofficial agent" for the Japanese government and he tried to raise interest in Australia for Japanese laborers. The occupations in this article were divided into three wage classes.

41. Enclosure attached to a letter from Mie prefectural officials to the Foreign Ministry, 18 June 1885, *JFMAD 3.8.2.5 Bessatsu zatsu no bu,* vol. 1.

42. Article, *Bōchō Shinbun,* 30 November 1884 and Matsunaga, "Mitsui Bussan," installment seven. A sample of articles which appeared in *Bōchō Shinbun* and *Chūgai Bukka Shinpō* dealing with emigration to Hawaii can be found in Doi, *Hawai,* pp. 21–22. Evidence of the use of newspaper advertisements to attract potential emigrants from Kumamoto, Okayama, Fukuoka, Miyazaki, Wakayama, Hiroshima, Kagoshima, Gifu, and Ōita prefectures can be found in *JFMAD J.1.2.0 J 3–4.*

43. Enclosure attached to a report from the Consulate to the Foreign Ministry, 15 May 1886, *JFMAD 3.8.2.5 Bessatsu tōgyō.*

44. I have compiled figures for Ōshima island based on emigrant lists sent by the Kanagawa prefectural governor to the Foreign Ministry, 16 February 1885, *JFMAD 3.8.2.5 Bessatsu meibo,* vol. 1.

45. Ibid. For information regarding the geography of Yamaguchi prefecture, including village *(son)* names, I have relied on Naramoto and Misaka, eds., *Yamaguchi-ken no chimei.*

46. Irie, *Hōjin hattenshi,* vol. 1, p. 57. The Commissioner of Labor in 1905, (*Third report,* p. 147) notes that, "In two provinces 1,400 presented themselves as applicants within two days, and 28,000 men applied for passage. . . ."

47. Foreign Minister Mutsu Munemitsu to Irwin, 3 October 1887 and Irwin to Mutsu, 3 October 1887 (enclosure attached to the letter from Irwin), *JFMAD 3.8.2.3,* vol. 7.

48. Report from the Consulate to the Foreign Ministry, 30 December 1888, *JFMAD 3.8.2.3,* vol. 7. Another estimate of $55 for men and $20 for women is given in a letter from Irwin to Foreign Minister Ōkuma Shigenobu, 11 April 1888, same volume.

49. Viscount Aoki Shūzō to Irwin, 31 July 1890 and Irwin to Aoki, 2 October 1890, *JFMAD 3.8.2.3,* vol. 7.

50. Watanabe, "Diplomatic Relations" (unpublished M.A. thesis), pp. 132–153. Okahata, *Japanese in Hawaii,* pp. 106–108.

51. Kodama, "Meijiki," p. 85.

52. List of emigrants from the Consulate to the Foreign Ministry, March 1885, *JFMAD 3.8.2.5 Bessatsu meibo,* vol. 1. See also a list of emigrants from the Consulate to the Foreign Ministry, September 1885, same volume.

53. Private letter from Irwin to Inoue, 9 April 1886, *JFMAD 3.8.2.9.*

54. Irwin to Ōkuma, 17 March 1888, *JFMAD 3.8.2.3,* vol. 5.

55. Irie, *Hōjin hattenshi,* vol. 1, p. 80.

56. *Ibid.,* pp. 95–96. Although Irie was not able to give a breakdown for the 1885 to 1889 period, he estimated that $830,000 was sent back during those years. See also Yoshida, "Meiji shoki," pt. 1, p. 300. Slightly higher figures are given in Doi, *Hawai,* p. 173.

57. See Ōkubo et al., *Kindaishi,* pp. 300–301.

58. Kodama, "Dekasegiimin," pp. 40–41.

59. Wakatsuki, "Japanese Emigration," p. 451.

60. Kodama, "Dekasegiimin," pp. 40–41.

61. Attachment to a letter from Hiroshima prefectural officials to the Foreign Ministry, 8 November 1892, *JFMAD 3.8.2.5 Bessatsu zatsu no bu,* vol. 2.

62. Wakatsuki, "Japanese Emigration," p. 452.

63. Kawazoe, *Imin hyakunen,* p. 93. I have shortened the passage in my translation. See also Miyamoto, "Shima," p. 139.

64. Irie, *Hōjin hattenshi,* vol. 1, p. 61.

65. Bureau to the Consulate, 30 May 1885, *JFMAD 3.8.2.7.*

66. Public circular issued by the bureau on 10 August 1885. The chief of the special board was G. O. Nacayama (previously and at times as Nakayama). Nacayama was the name used by Nakayama Jōji, a former calvary officer during the Tokugawa period. He had worked for the Italian embassy in Tokyo and came to Hawaii in the first shipment from Japan.

67. Nacayama to Prime Minister W. M. Gibson, 26 October 1886, *AH Bureau Misc. Files,* document 9.

68. Irwin to Inoue, 28 May 1885, *JFMAD 3.8.2.5 Bessatsu niwari.*

69. The Japanese relief fund was called the Japanese Mutual Aid Association, and was organized in October 1887 by the wife of Consul General Andō Tarō and the wife of Nacayama. In 1889 this group began a campaign to build a permanent hospital in Honolulu for Japanese workers. The money for the hospital, which still provides medical services today, came not only from the Japanese workers but also from the Bureau of Immigration and outside contributors. See 4 September 1889 attachment to a letter from the Consulate to the Foreign Ministry, 16 September 1889, *JFMAD 3.8.2.9.*

70. "Proposition in reference to the 25% deposits now made with the Hawaiian Government or to be made hereafter," 6 March 1886, *JFMAD 3.8.2.3,* vol. 5.

71. Private letter from Irwin to Inoue, 22 May 1885, *JFMAD 3.8.2.5 Bessatsu chōhei.*

72. Aoki to Irwin, 29 January 1891, *JFMAD 3.8.2.5 Bessatsu zatsu no bu,* vol. 2. See also Hori, "Japanese Prostitution," pp. 113–124.

73. Report from James H. Blount, Special Commissioner of the United States to W. Q. Gresham, Secretary of State, 1 June 1893, U.S. Congress, House, *President's Message,* pp. 1347–1357.

74. Ibid.

75. Report from the Consulate to the Foreign Ministry, 22 November 1902, Gaimushō, *NGB,* vol. 35, pp. 828–831.

76. Yoshida, "Meiji shoki," pt. 1, pp. 296–297. In the table the total is more than 100 percent because of births. The high percentage of deaths is due to the fact that the survey was taken at least forty-five years after the contracts had expired.

77. Secretary of the Bureau to the President of the Bureau, 8 February 1897, *JFMAD 3.8.4.15.*

78. See Conroy, *Japanese Frontier* and Irwin and Conroy, "R. W. Irwin" (see note 20). Until the disagreement over the salaries of the interpreters and doctors was settled, Irwin himself paid their salaries.

79. See Moriyama, "1909 and 1920 Strikes" in Gee, *Counterpoint,* pp. 169–180.

80. The process of the Meiji government's taking over an industry until it was on a stable economic basis and then turning it over to private enterprises, often at a loss, was not limited to the emigration business. In *Political Change and Industrial Development in Japan* Thomas Smith outlines this process and offers several examples. See also Nakamura, *Economic Growth,* pp. 59–60.

81. Figures calculated from Kokusai kyōryoku jigyōdan, *Kaigai ijū tōkei,* pp. 66–67.

82. Irwin to Foreign Minister Enomoto Takeaki, 28 September 1891, *JFMAD 3.8.8.3.*

83. Report from Kanagawa prefectural officials to the Foreign Ministry, 13 July 1887, *JFMAD 3.8.2.6;* Marks to the Foreign Ministry, 26 September 1887, *JFMAD 3.8.2.2,* vol. 1; Jas. Murdoch to Ōkuma, 31 March 1889, *JFMAD 3.8.2.2,* vol. 1; Japanese Legation in Washington to Romero, 7 May 1889, *JFMAD 3.8.2.2,* vol. 1; Marks to Aoki, 24 March 1890, *JFMAD 3.8.2.2,* vol. 1; see appropriate letters in *JFMAD 3.8.2.2,* vol. 1.

84. Hayashi to Marks, 11 November 1891, *JFMAD 3.8.2.2,* vol. 1.

85. Irie, "Senkakusha," no. 268. Harrison (*Northern Frontier,* p. 75) indicates in a footnote that one private company, Kaishinsha, was established to send workers to Hokkaido.

86. Irie, *Hōjin hattenshi,* vol. 1, p. 102; Kodama, "Imingaisha no jittai," p. 462.

87. For information on the emigration venture to the island of Guadaloupe, see Ishikawa, "Nishiindo Futsuryō Gādorūputō," pp. 113–137.

Chapter 3
The Emigrant Protection Law

1. The Japanese-language version of Ordinance Number 42 can be found in Gaimushō, *NGB,* vol. 27, no. 2, pp. 618–622. For an earlier version see *JFMAD 3.8.1.3,* vol. 1. An English-language version entitled "Regulations for Protecting Imin," which was issued by the foreign ministry, can be found as an enclosure in *JFMAD 3.8.1.3,* vol. 1. The Japanese-language version of the Emigrant Protection Law can be found in Gaimushō, *NGB,* vol. 29, pp. 978–981. For a condensed version see Ishikawa, "Imingaisha," pp. 20–22. An English-language version of this law was found in Bureau of Commercial Affairs, *Japanese Laws.* See *JFMAD 3.8.1.4,* vol. 2.

2. *Emigrant Protection Ordinance* (hereafter cited as *Ordinance*), *JFMAD 3.8.1.3,* vol. 1.

3. *Emigrant Protection Law* (hereafter cited as *Law*), Bureau of Commercial Affairs, *Japanese Laws,* pp. 1–35; *JFMAD 3.8.1.4,* vol. 2.

4. *Law,* Chapter 1, Article 2, p. 1.

5. *Law,* The Regulations for the Enforcement of the Law (hereafter cited as Regu-

lations), Article 1, p. 10. In the Japanese version, the word *doboku* is used and later translated as "engineering." Given the period, a more correct translation would be "construction work."

6. *Law,* Chapter 1, Article 2, p. 1; Article 3, p. 1.

7. *Law,* Chapter 2, Article 5, p. 2.

8. *Law,* Chapter 2, Article 6, p. 2; Article 7–1, p. 2; Article 8, p. 3.

9. *Law,* Chapter 2, Article 7–2, pp. 2–3; Article 9, p. 3; Articles 10 and 11, p. 3.

10. *Law,* Chapter 2, Article 12, p. 3; Article 14, p. 3.

11. *Law,* Chapter 3, Article 16, p. 4. This was later raised to 30,000 yen per company. See secret announcement issued by the Foreign Ministry, 16 October 1901, *JFMAD 3.8.1.8,* vol. 3.

12. *Law,* Chapter 3, Article 18, p. 4; *Ordinance,* Article 6.

13. *Law,* Chapter 4, Articles 20–2 and 20–3, p. 5; Articles 20–5 and 20–4, p. 5; Articles 20–5 and 20–6, pp. 5–6.

14. *Law,* Chapter 5, Articles 20–8 and 20–9, p. 6.

15. *Law,* Chapter 5, Article 20–10, p. 6.

16. *Law,* Chapter 6, Article 21, p. 7; Article 26–1, p. 8.

17. *Law,* Chapter 6, pp. 7–8.

18. *Law,* Regulations, pp. 10–30; *Law,* Chapter 1, Article 2, p. 1; *Law,* Regulations, Chapter 1, Article 2, p. 10.

19. *Law,* Regulations, Chapter 2, Article 5, p. 11.

20. *Law,* Regulations, Chapter 2, Articles 6 and 7, pp. 12–13.

21. *Law,* Regulations, Chapter 2, Article 8, pp. 13–14; Articles 11, 12, and 13, pp. 14–15; Article 14, p. 15.

22. *Law,* Regulations, Chapter 2, Article 18, p. 16; Article 19, pp. 16–17; Article 21, p. 17; Article 23, pp. 17–18; Article 31, p. 19.

23. *Law,* Regulations, Chapter 4, Article 40, pp. 20–22; Articles 44 and 45, pp. 22–23.

24. *Law,* Regulations, Chapter 5, Article 51, p. 24.

25. *Law,* Regulations, Chapter 6, Article 58, p. 25; Article 59, p. 25.

26. *Law,* Rules of Procedure Relative to the Detailed Regulations for the Enforcement of the Law for the Protection of Imin (hereafter cited as Rules), pp. 31–35.

27. *Law,* Rules, Articles 1 and 2, p. 31; Articles 4 and 5, p. 32; Article 10, p. 33.

28. In the beginning, the only port of departure for emigrants was Yokohama; later Kobe was added, and in the end Nagasaki and Moji also became ports for departures.

29. Statement by Harry S. Kawabe, in Itō, *Issei,* pp. 12–13. This book is a translation of the first volume of Itō, *Hoku-Bei hyakunen zakura.*

30. *JFMAD 3.8.2.122,* vol. 6, part 1.

31. Application of Occidental and Oriental Steamship Company, Ltd. to continue operations, 26 June 1907, *JFMAD 3.8.2.237,* vol. 1.

32. Application of Ocean Steamship Company to continue operations 1 July 1907, *JFMAD 3.8.2.237,* vol. 1.

33. Pamphlet titled *Ryoken narabini imin jimu toriatsukai sankōsho,* January 1913, *JFMAD 3.8.1.4,* vol. 3, fourth pamphlet, p. 239.

34. Article (15 December 1906, Tokyo edition of *Asahi Shinbun*) attached to a Foreign Ministry memo 17 December 1906, *JFMAD 3.8.2.57,* vol. 2; report from Kana-

gawa prefectural officials to the Foreign Ministry, 30 November 1906, *JFMAD 3.8.2.122,* vol. 6, part 1.

35. Tsurutani, *Amerika,* pp. 72–73. Governor of Niigata prefecture to the Foreign Ministry, 10 July 1903, *JFMAD 3.8.2.122,* vol. 4.

36. See *JFMAD 3.8.2.50,* vol. 1.

Chapter 4
Emigration Companies in Japan: The Stage and the Actors

1. The only secondary works in Japanese about the emigration companies are Ishikawa, "Imingaisha"; Kodama, "Imingaisha no jittai"; Kodama, "Shoki," pp. 20–44, which deals with Australia; and Kodama, "Imingaisha ni tsuite no ichi kōsatsu," pp. 12–25. There have been no works in English on this topic.

2. Ishikawa lists forty-six companies operating in the 1898–1920 period, including Nanbei shokumin kabushikigaisha and Kaigai kigyō kabushikigaisha, which were founded after 1908 and which sent emigrants to Latin America. See Ishikawa, "Imingaisha," pp. 25–26. In "Imingaisha no jittai" Kodama (p. 482), says forty-seven companies were operating in the 1898 to 1910 period. Ishikawa and Kodama also disagree about several small companies that later merged with larger ones before sending emigrants abroad. Ishikawa has combined some of these companies in his list. I have generally used Kodama's ranking of the companies. My list of fifty-one companies includes those that operated in the 1891 to 1897 period.

3. A list of the fifteen companies which operated for less than six months and a list of the fourteen companies that were not allowed to begin business can be found in Appendixes 9 and 10.

4. I gave a paper titled "Imingaishashi kenkyū no ichi hōhō," on 4 July 1981 at Ryūkoku University in Kyoto. At the time, I used the word *yakusha* for actor and the word *butai* for stage.

5. *Tsūshōkyoku* in Japanese. Until 1885, emigration matters were handled by the trade and commerce section of the foreign ministry. See Gaimushō, *Waga kokumin,* honpen, p. 262.

6. Gaimushō ryōji ijūbu, *Waga kokumin,* honpen, pp. 262–263.

7. Information on the inner workings of the foreign ministry is from various JFMAD files.

8. See for example *JFMAD 3.8.2.122,* vol. 4.

9. Neumann to Spencer, 18 March 1891, *AH Bureau Misc. Files,* document 10.

10. Commissioner of Labor, *Second Report,* p. 36.

11. *Emigrant Protection Ordinance,* Articles 1, 5, 8, and 22, *JFMAD 3.8.1.3,* vol. 1. *JFMAD 3.8.2.57,* vol. 1, has examples of these letters.

12. See *JFMAD 3.8.1.5.* For emigrant lists and forms (1898–1899) see *JFMAD 3.8.2.74,* vol. 1. Status designations were *heimin* (commoners) or *shizoku* (of warrior descent). A report from Hiroshima prefecture to the Foreign Ministry (28 December 1898) has information on home addresses, contract numbers, dates of permission to leave, status, and age. Another report from Niigata prefecture to the Foreign Ministry (16 March 1899) also gives information on emigrant occupations (farming).

13. *JFMAD 3.8.1.5.*

14. For an example of the emigrant lists of 1899 see *JFMAD 3.8.2.74.* In volume 2 are lists that have the status of the emigrants already printed on the forms. In volume 3 the lists have "farming" and "commoner" already printed. For an example see the list attached to a report from Fukuoka prefectural officials to the Foreign Ministry, 14 October 1899. Historian Doi Yatarō has reported that some of the contracts were for two-year periods, but I have found no evidence of this. All contracts that indicate the length of the contract period are for three years. See Doi, *Hawai,* p. 69.

15. Guarantee forms issued by Niigata prefectural officials, 4 August 1894, *JFMAD 3.8.1.5.*

16. See *JFMAD 3.8.1.7,* vol. 1. The Japanese terms are *gun yakusho* (county office), *shi yakusho* (city office), and *machi-mura yakuba* (town and village offices). In the case of a village, the office was usually in the village headman's house. This system of counties, cities, towns and villages was set up in 1888.

17. *JFMAD 3.8.1.7,* vol. 1.

18. See *Emigrant Protection Law,* Regulations, Article 58, Bureau of Commercial Affairs, *Japanese Laws,* p. 25.

19. In addition to the previously mentioned sixty-six companies, there are two or three small companies about which very little is known.

20. Gaimushō, *NGB,* vol. 35, pp. 832–833; Irie, *Hōjin hattenshi,* vol. 1, pp. 143–144. See also *JFMAD 3.8.2.43.* At times emigration companies used what usually were English translations of their Japanese names when operating abroad. In the first reference to such a company in the text, I will give both the Japanese and the English names; thereafter I will use the latter. Most of the emigration companies had only Japanese names. I have tried to select the most common reading of the Japanese characters. When only two readings are possible, I have given both; for example, "Takaki (Takagi)," at first mention only. I have used as references O'Neill's, *Japanese Names* and Araki's, *Nanori jiten.*

21. Irie, *Hōjin hattenshi,* vol. 1, pp. 143–144; see *JFMAD 3.8.2.52.* A *kabushiki-gaisha* is a joint-stock company or corporation. In *Nipponjinshi* (p. 478), Kihara writes of a company called Nan'yusha, which he claims sent about 960 emigrants to Hawaii in October of 1894. Okahata (*Japanese in Hawaii,* pp. 141–142), also writes of this episode. I have not found evidence of this venture in JFMAD files. Okahata (p. 150) also claimed that this company, Ogura shōkai, and Itōhan shōkai were already in Honolulu importing Japanese goods by 1891.

22. In Gaimushō, *NGB,* vol. 35, pp. 832–833 gives as the figure for Japanese Emigration Company of Hiroshima in 1895 1,106. The same source claims that 209 of the workers sent by Ogura shōkai to Hawaii went without labor contracts, and 401 of those shipped by Kobe Immigration Company and 51 by Japanese Emigration Company of Hiroshima were also without contracts. A *gōshigaisha* is a limited partnership.

23. Gaimushō tsūshōkyoku, *Ryoken kafusū,* pp. 142–181. The figure 13,248 is from Gaimushō ryōji ijūbu, *Hyakunen no ayumi,* pp. 42–43. The figures by year are 1,329 for 1894, 2,416 for 1895, 6,217 for 1896, and 3,286 for 1897. This is certainly possible because the total number of passports issued for Hawaii according to Gaimushō tsūshōkyoku (*Ryoken kafusū,* pp. 5–6) by year is as follows: 4,036 in 1894, 2,445 in 1895, 9,486 in 1896, and 5,913 in 1897. The non-emigrant passports had been issued to former government-sponsored emigrants, *yobiyose* (those summoned

by family members) emigrants, businessmen, government officials, visitors, and students. Irie (*Hōjin hattenshi,* vol. 1, pp. 143–144) mentions 9,920 for the 1894 to 1896 period.

24. Several different types of non-emigrants traveled to Hawaii during this period and Irie believed that some emigrants traveled there without the help of the companies. See Irie, *Hōjin hattenshi,* vol. 1, p. 101.

25. Kodama, "Imingaisha no jittai," p. 482. Ishikawa, "Imingaisha," pp. 25–26. A *gōmeigaisha* is an unlimited partnership and a *kabushiki gōshigaisha* is a joint-stock limited partnership.

26. *JFMAD 3.8.2.46, 3.8.2.69,* and *3.8.2.105.*

27. See Rowland, "The United States and the Contract Labor Question," pp. 265–266.

28. Ishikawa, "Okinawa-ken," p. 61.

29. *Law,* Chapter 2, Article 6, p. 2.

30. *JFMAD 3.8.2.40, 3.8.2.52, 3.8.2.59, 3.8.2.58, 3.8.2.66, 3.8.2.77, 3.8.2.107, 3.8.2.120, 3.8.2.128, 3.8.2.127, 3.8.2.138, 3.8.2.129, 3.8.2.132, 3.8.2.140, 3.8.2.142, 3.8.2.160.*

31. *JFMAD 3.8.2.36; JFMAD 3.8.2.151.* The last three names have appeared as representatives of emigration companies during the 1903 to 1905 period. Hiruma had worked to set up Imperial Emigration Company, Morita had helped to start Bansei imin gōshigaisha, and Yamaguchi had worked for Kumamoto Emigration Company in its earliest days.

32. Gaimushō tsūshōkyoku, *Ryoken kafusū,* pp. 142–181.

33. *JFMAD 3.8.2.194.*

34. For Morioka Immigration Company, see *JFMAD 3.8.2.46, 3.8.2.69,* and *3.8.2.105.* For Japanese Emigration Company of Hiroshima, see *JFMAD 3.8.2.35, 3.8.2.62,* and *3.8.2.117.* For Kumamoto Emigration Company, see *JFMAD 3.8.2.64, 3.8.2.76, 3.8.2.95, 3.8.2.96,* and *3.8.2.99.* For Japan Emigration Company, see *JFMAD 3.8.2.61, 3.8.2.113,* and *3.8.2.65.* For Tokio Immigration Company, see *JFMAD 3.8.2.57, 3.8.2.74,* and *3.8.2.103.*

35. See Irie, *Hōjin hattenshi,* vol. 1, p. 445. The use of this term was probably inspired by the "Big Five" sugar plantation companies in Hawaii. I will refer to them later.

36. See applications in: *JFMAD 3.8.2.76* and *JFMAD 3.8.2.64; JFMAD 3.8.2.226; JFMAD 3.8.2.63;* Kawazoe, *Imin hyakunen,* p. 149. This was, of course, because the company was based in Hiroshima.

37. Applications: January 1897, *JFMAD 3.8.2.70;* February 1902, *JFMAD 3.8.2.162,* vol. 1; March 1907, *JFMAD 3.8.2.231* (a similar pattern of local investment in "new industries" can be seen in the cotton spinning enterprises in the late 1890s [see Nakamura, *Economic Growth,* pp. 58–59]); November 1901, *JFMAD 3.8.2.153,* vol. 1; April 1902, *JFMAD 3.8.2.164;* September 1903, *JFMAD 3.8.2.194,* vol. 1.

38. *JFMAD 3.8.2.186.*

39. Application, October 1903, *JFMAD 3.8.2.196.*

40. The designation of shizoku or heimin was printed beside the signature on the application. One American observer wrote of these men: "The managers and stockholders are among the leading business men and politicians of Japan, and are a formi-

dable power when cooperating together." See letter from W. M. Rice, Commissioner of Immigration, to the Commissioner General of Immigration, 24 April 1899, U.S. Congress, House, *Letter from the Secretary of the Treasury,* p. 6. See also Kodama, "Shoki," p. 35.

41. Application, September 1906, *JFMAD 3.8.2.223,* vol. 1. Other shizoku were using their money to enter the new banking and textile spinning industries. See Nakamura, *Economic Growth,* pp. 105–106.

42. Applications: March 1897, *JFMAD 3.8.2.77;* June 1898, *JFMAD 3.8.2.97,* vol. 1.

43. See applications in the following: *JFMAD 3.8.2.196; JFMAD 3.8.2.149,* vol. 1; *JFMAD 3.8.2.109;* and *JFMAD 3.8.2.124.*

44. Sasa, "Imingaisha to chihō seitō," pp. 61–80.

45. Applications: December 1901, *JFMAD 3.8.2.157;* July 1901, *JFMAD 3.8.2.149;* November 1901, *JFMAD 3.8.2.162;* June 1906, *JFMAD 3.8.2.57,* vol. 1.

46. Applications: November 1901, *JFMAD 3.8.2.27,* vol. 1; November 1901, *JFMAD 3.8.2.156,* vol. 1; July 1894, *JFMAD 3.8.2.35,* vol. 1; November 1896, *JFMAD 3.8.2.63.*

47. Kodama, "Shoki," pp. 42–43.

48. Application, October 1894, *JFMAD 3.8.2.46,* vol. 1.

49. Applications: September 1903, *JFMAD 3.8.2.194,* vol. 1 and April 1898, *JFMAD 3.8.2.95,* vol. 1.

50. Application, November 1896, *JFMAD 3.8.2.63.*

51. Application, July 1894, *JFMAD 3.8.2.35,* vol. 1.

52. Application, October 1894, *JFMAD 3.8.2.46,* vol. 1; *JFMAD 3.8.2.69;* and *JFMAD 3.8.2.105.*

53. *JFMAD 3.8.2.194,* vol. 1. American government official Rice was sent to Japan to investigate the emigration companies. He wrote, "it is a matter of general repute that they are the most profitable enterprises in Japan." See letter from Rice to the Commissioner General of Immigration, 24 April 1899, U.S. Congress, House, *Treasury,* p. 7.

54. Calculated from JFMAD documents cited in note 30.

55. *JFMAD 3.8.2.114.* For the other companies, see *JFMAD 3.8.2.231; JFMAD 3.8.2.123;* and *JFMAD 3.8.2.135.*

56. The Japanese term for office workers in Japan was *naichi gyōmu dairinin.* Agents in Hawaii were referred to as *Hawai ni oite gyōmu dairinin.*

57. *JFMAD 3.8.1.4,* vol. 4, pp. 917–918. See also Gaimushō tsūshōkyoku dai sanka, *Ryoken sankōsho,* pp. 97–98.

58. Kodama, "Shoki," pp. 34–35.

59. *JFMAD 3.8.2.162,* vol. 1; *JFMAD 3.8.2.165; JFMAD 3.8.2.182; JFMAD 3.8.2.188* and *JFMAD 3.8.2.194,* vols. 1–4.

60. Information on Ehime prefecture emigrants from an interview with Murakawa Yōko, 22 January 1983, Tokyo.

61. See for example the role played by Doi Tsumoru in Kodama, "Shoki," pp. 42–43. Information on commissions found on p. 42. Doi was a village headman during the period that he was employed by Nippon Yoshisa imin gōshigaisha and Tōyō imin gōshigaisha (1891–1902).

62. *JFMAD 3.8.2.109.*

63. *JFMAD 3.8.2.194,* vol. 1; *JFMAD 3.8.2.231.*

64. *JFMAD 3.8.2.97,* vols. 1–4.

65. For Morioka Immigration Company, see *JFMAD 3.8.2.46,* vols. 1–5; for Transoceanic Migration Company, see *JFMAD 3.8.2.194,* vol. 1–4.

66. *JFMAD 3.8.2.97,* vols. 1–4; *JFMAD 3.8.2.95,* vols. 1–2; see agent applications, 15 April 1904–1 November 1907, *JFMAD 3.8.2.71,* vol. 5; for Morioka Immigration Company, see *JFMAD 3.8.2.46,* vols. 1–5; for Transoceanic Migration Company, see *JFMAD 3.8.2.194,* vols. 1–4; *JFMAD 3.8.2.44,* vols. 1–6.

67. See Harrison, *Northern Frontier,* pp. 84–85.

68. Agent applications, 12 May 1902, *JFMAD 3.8.2.154,* vol. 1.

69. For Taiheiyō shokumingaisha, see *JFMAD 3.8.2.177;* for Mitsunaga Kyūta, see *JFMAD 3.8.2.171.*

70. Ibid. Information on agents working for several companies at the same time in Japan can be found in Kodama, "Imingaisha no jittai," p. 477.

71. Emigrant lists attached to a letter from Fukuoka prefecture to the Foreign Ministry, 24 January 1899, *JFMAD 3.8.2.96,* vol. 3.

72. For place names I have relied extensively on Ōnishi, *Jitsuyō teikoku chimei jiten.*

73. The distance was about one *ri* which is about 2.44 miles. The map of Fukuoka prefecture I have used was printed in 1917.

74. Irie, *Hōjin hattenshi,* vol. 1, p. 109.

75. Emigrant lists attached to a letter from Hiroshima prefecture to the Foreign Ministry, 23 December 1898, *JFMAD 3.8.2.96,* vol. 1. The map of Hiroshima prefecture I have used was printed in 1910.

76. Kodama, "Shoki," p. 25.

77. Emigrant lists attached to a letter from Wakayama prefecture to the Foreign Ministry, 3 October 1899, *JFMAD 3.8.2.96,* vol. 3.

78. Emigrant lists attached to a letter from Wakayama prefecture to the Foreign Ministry, 6 September 1899, *JFMAD 3.8.2.102.*

79. See for example Kodama, "Shoki," p. 27.

80. Ibid., p. 26.

81. Nakamura, *Economic Growth,* p. 131.

82. Ōkubo et al., *Kindaishi,* p. 398.

83. Kodama, "Dekasegiimin," p. 42.

84. Nakamura, *Economic Growth,* pp. 132–133.

85. Ōkubo et al., *Kindaishi,* p. 390.

86. Itō, *Issei* (English source), p. 22.

87. Ibid., p. 17.

88. See Iwasaki, "Kii hantō" part one and part two (three parts).

89. I have spoken on this topic at the 26th International Conference of Orientalists (8 May 1981) in Tokyo under the title "To-Bei Annai: Japanese Emigration Guides to America, 1885–1905."

90. Although there are copies of twenty-five guidebooks in the Japanese American Research Project collection at UCLA, the most extensive holding of these books is in a special collection at the National Diet Library of Japan.

91. Katayama, *To-Bei.*

92. See in particular Akiyoshi, *To-Beisha hikkei.*

93. See Mitsunaga, *Konnichi* (p. 14) and Katayama, *To-Bei* (p. 11).

94. The figures for the 1894 to 1896 period were obtained from Irie, *Hōjin hatten-shi,* vol. 1, pp. 143–145. For the 1898 to 1908 period I have used Gaimushō tsūshō-kyoku, *Ryoken kafusū,* pp. 142–181. I have done the calculations.

95. Wray Taylor, Secretary of the Board of Immigration, to C. Brewer and Company, 13 December 1897, *JFMAD 3.8.2.84.*

96. My own calculations drawn from Gaimushō tsūshōkyoku, *Ryoken kafusū,* pp. 142–181.

97. Enclosure, 12 May 1898, *JFMAD 3.8.2.84.*

98. Emigrant lists attached to a letter from Yamaguchi prefecture to the Foreign Ministry, 16 September 1898, *JFMAD 3.8.2.62,* vol. 5. For another example, see the lists attached to a letter from Kumamoto prefecture to the Foreign Ministry, 13 September 1898 in the same volume. In this instance, eight of sixty-five emigrants were nineteen years old or younger. The government generally allowed individuals between the ages of fifteen and fifty to leave as emigrants. The exceptions were family members of emigrants. See announcement, 15 August 1896, *JFMAD 3.8.1.8,* vol. 1.

99. Gaimushō tsūshōkyoku dai sanka, *Ryoken sankōsho,* p. 95.

100. Emigrant lists attached to a letter from Niigata prefecture to the Foreign Ministry, 10 February 1899, *JFMAD 3.8.2.74,* vol. 2.

101. Draft agreement, 1898, *JFMAD 3.8.2.71,* vol. 6.

102. Circular, January 1898, attached to a letter from Inoue Keijirō of Kumamoto Emigration Company to the Consulate, 14 May 1898, *JFMAD 3.8.2.84.*

103. Kodama, "Shoki," p. 27.

104. Prefectural reports to the Foreign Ministry, 1903, *JFMAD 3.8.2.159,* vol. 2. The number of companies operating in other prefectures during that year was as follows: Miyagi, 3; Yamanashi, 2; Iwate, 2; Fukui, 11; Gumma, 2; Niigata, 6; Kanagawa, 2; Shizuoka, 6; Aichi, 5; Gifu, 1; Wakayama, 11; Shiga, 8; Osaka, 5; Okayama, 19; Shimane, 4; Ehime, 1; Kagawa, 7; Kōchi, 1; Saga, 7; Ōita, 9; Kagoshima, 6; and Okinawa, 1.

105. Itō, *Issei* (English source), p. 62.

106. Report from Keihin Bank to the Foreign Ministry, 14 November 1903, *JFMAD 3.8.2.93.*

107. Itō, *Issei* (English source), p. 22.

Chapter 5
Emigration Companies and the Emigration Process in Japan

1. Itō, *Issei* (English source), pp. 376–377; Commissioner of Labor, *Third Report,* p. 149.

2. Agent applications, 4 July 1899 to 11 August 1900, *JFMAD 3.8.2.109.*

3. Announcement (labeled "secret") from the Foreign Ministry to the emigration companies, 16 October 1901, *JFMAD 3.8.1.8,* vol. 3.

4. Company application, December 1896, *JFMAD 3.8.2.71,* vol. 1.

5. For information on the terms of the proposition, see articles 1 and 2, 1898, *JFMAD 3.8.2.64.*

6. For information on foreign agents, see labor propositions, 1897–1898, *JFMAD 3.8.2.64;* 1897–1899, *JFMAD 3.8.2.84.*

7. Agreement between Imperial Emgiration Company and Palawai Development Company, 23 May 1899 *JFMAD 3.8.2.84.* A copy of this can be found in Appendix 2.

8. Later this was changed so that deposits could be made with banks in Honolulu. Another agreement mentioned the bank of Claus Spreckels and Company (established in 1884) as well as the Bank of Hawaii (established in 1897).

9. Labor contracts by Laupahoehoe Sugar Company, 1896, *JFMAD 3.8.2.88.*

10. "New Plan for Furnishing Laborers to the Planters of Hawaii," December 1895, attached to a letter from the Secretary of the Kobe Kaigai Ijū Kansai Dōshikai to the Home Ministry, 23 April 1896, *JFMAD 3.8.2.23.*

11. Labor contract issued by Japan Emigration Company, 1898–1900, *JFMAD 3.8.2.65,* vol. 1.

12. Details can be found in *Emigrant Protection Law,* Chapter 4, Bureau of Commercial Affairs, *Japanese Laws; Law,* Regulations, Chapter 4; and *JFMAD 3.8.2.237,* vol. 1.

13. Applications of shipping companies, 1 July 1907–2 July 1908, *JFMAD 3.8.2.237,* vol. 1. An application was filed in July of 1907 in the name of Matsukata Kōjirō, but there is no evidence that he shipped emigrants overseas. This may have been because he declared assets of only 10,000 yen, less than the minimum deposit required to obtain permission to operate.

14. Information on assets from applications of shipping companies, 1907–1908, *JFMAD 3.8.2.237,* vol. 1.

15. Nishimukai, "Kaiungyō," p. 82. This is the first of four articles by Nishimukai on this topic.

16. Nishimukai, "Kaiungyō horon," pp. 153–155.

17. *JFMAD 3.8.2.237,* vol. 1.

18. Ibid. Information gleaned from Occidental and Oriental Steamship Company's application. There were first-class, second-class, and third-class (steerage) fares. Almost all of the emigrants went as steerage passengers. Even those returning from Hawaii traveled by the cheapest means available. For example, of the 478 Japanese going to Yokohama in June of 1910, 462 went as third-class passengers, as did all sixty-two sailing to Kobe. See the chart attached to 1 November 1910 internal foreign minstry memo, *JFMAD 3.8.2.263.*

19. Ibid. Information from Pacific Mail and Steamship Company's application.

20. Okahata, *Japanese in Hawaii,* pp. 287–296.

21. Attachment to a letter from B. C. Howard, agent of the Pacific Mail and Steamship Company, to the Foreign Ministry, 3 July 1907, *JFMAD 3.8.2.237,* vol. 1.

22. Article from the *Honolulu Republican,* 17 October 1901, *JFMAD 3.8.2.122,* vol. 2; W. M. Rice to the Commissioner General of Immigration, 24 April 1899, U.S. Congress, House, *Treasury,* p. 7.

23. For information on the relationship between emigration companies and shipping companies during the 1916 to 1926 period, see Oshimoto, "Imingaisha to funagaisha," pp. 74–91; telegram from Consul General Saitō Miki to Foreign Minister Hayashi, 17 October 1906, *JFMAD 3.8.2.122,* vol. 6, pt. 1.

24. Itō, *Issei* (English source), p. 31.

25. Application of Morioka shōkai (for Peru-bound emigrants), 27 February 1908 and application of Takemura Yoemon (for Brazil-bound emigrants), 5 April 1910, *JFMAD 3.8.2.237,* vol. 6, pt. 2.

26. Commissioner of Labor, *Third Report,* p. 150.

27. Itō, *Issei* (English source), p. 15.

28. *JFMAD 3.8.2.122,* vol. 6, pt. 1.

29. In their contracts with emigration companies, free emigrants were referred to at times as "*jiko no hataraki ni yori* (dependent on one's own labor)," while contract laborers were referred to as "*keiyaku dekasegi imin* (contract emigrants)." For the former, see the contract issued by the Japanese Emigration Company of Hiroshima, 17 June 1898 in *JFMAD 3.8.2.62,* vol. 4. For the latter, see the contract used in Ōita prefecture in 1898, attached to a letter from Ōita prefecture to the Foreign Ministry, 11 October 1898, *JFMAD 3.8.2.96,* vol. 1.

30. Attached to a letter from the governor of Shizuoka prefecture to the Foreign Ministry, 16 April 1903, *JFMAD 3.8.2.159,* vol. 2.

31. Ogawa, "Hiramatsu Shinpachi shōden," p. 43.

32. For an example see *JFMAD 3.8.2.62,* vols. 1–4.

33. Gaimushō ryōji ijūbu, *Hyakunen no ayumi,* pp. 42–43.

34. Foreign Ministry notice 436, 4 July 1901, JFMAD 3.8.2.122, vol. 2.

35. For information on these six attempts, see Gaimushō tsūshōkyoku, *Enkaku,* pp. 96–97.

36. Letter from Rice to the Commissioner General of Immigration, 24 April 1899, *AH Bureau Letters* (1897–1900). The names of the agents, their residences, and the companies they represented are included in this letter. I have corrected the names of certain individuals and companies. For example, Minami Jinnosuke is indicated in the letter as representing "Hiroshima Emigration Company." Since Hiroshima imin gōshigaisha was not established until 1901, the reference is probably to Japanese Emigration Company of Hiroshima, which was established in 1894.

37. Ishikawa, "Okinawa-ken," p. 63.

38. Ōkawahira, *Nippon iminron,* pp. 51–52.

39. Editorial in *Hawai Nichi Nichi Shinbun,* 22 June 1905, *JFMAD 3.8.2.122,* vol. 6, pt. 1; Kobe Immigration Company to Hyōgo prefecture, 29 July 1901, *JFMAD 3.8.2.88.*

40. Sōga, *Gojūnenkan,* p. 7; see statement of Kakazu Hashiji in Ethnic Studies Oral History Project, *Uchinanchu,* pp. 483.

41. The name of the bank comes from a combination of the character *kyō* in "Tokyo" and *hama* in "Yokohama." In other words, "Keihin" is a combination of Tokyo and Yokohama, indicating that the bank operated in those areas.

42. Application of Keihin ginkō, attached to a letter from the Finance Ministry to the Foreign Ministry, 11 April 1898, *JFMAD 3.8.2.93.*

43. Wakukawa, *History,* p. 154.

44. Article from *Hawai Shinpō,* 23 January 1905, attached to a letter from the Consulate to the Foreign Ministry, 31 January 1905, *JFMAD 3.8.2.93.*

45. Wakayama-ken, *Iminshi,* p. 280.

46. I have translated this from one of Kawazoe Zen'ichi's newspaper columns originally written in July of 1963 and subsequently included in Kawazoe, *Imin hyakunen,* p. 232.

47. See Kawazoe, *Imin hyakunen,* p. 232 and Okahata, *Japanese in Hawaii,* p. 144. Early in the emigration company period fifty yen was necessary as a deposit. See *JFMAD 3.8.1.8,* vol. 1.

48. Itō, *Issei* (English source), pp. 20–21.
49. Yamato, *Japanese,* pp. 87–88.
50. See Ogawa, *Conscription,* pp. 14–231. There is some evidence that emigrants might have been returned to Japan for conscription purposes during the government-sponsored emigration period. See letter from Irwin to Inoue, 1 February 1886, *JFMAD 3.8.2.5 Bessatsu muyakutei.*
51. Ogawa, *Conscription,* p. 36.
52. Ibid., p. 52.
53. *JFMAD 3.8.1.9.*
54. See statement of Higa Toden in Ethnic Studies Oral History Project, *Uchinanchu,* p. 512.
55. See "Quarantine Regulations," issued by the Department of Foreign Affairs, 19 November 1896, *AH FOLB,* p. 412.
56. Letter from Pacific Mail and Steamship Company, Occidental and Oriental Steamship Company, and Tōyō kisen kabushikigaisha to the Foreign Ministry, 11 May 1903, *JFMAD 3.8.2.122,* vol. 4.
57. See *JFMAD 3.8.2.122,* vol. 6, pt. 2.

Chapter 6
Emigration Companies in Hawaii: The Stage and the Actors

1. Adler, *Spreckels,* p. 7. Kuykendall, *Hawaiian Kingdom,* pp. 74–78.
2. Wakukawa, *History,* p. 16; Kuykendall, *Hawaiian Kingdom,* pp. 74–78.
3. Notice attached to inside cover, "An Act to Reconstruct the Board of Immigration," 1868, *AH Board Minutes.*
4. See undated newspaper clipping, *AH Board Minutes,* p. 106.
5. Joseph Marsden, Secretary of the Board, to H. Hackfeld and Company, 29 May 1895, *AH Bureau Letters* (1893–1897), p. 147. Marsden was secretary pro. tem. of the board. The regular secretary was Wray Taylor who was being paid wages of $100 a month in 1895.
6. Taylor to H. Hackfeld and Company, 9 August 1895, *AH Bureau Letters* (1893–1897), p. 155; Taylor to H. Hackfeld and Company, 24 March 1896, *AH Bureau Letters* (1893–1897), p. 199; attachment to a letter from Taylor to Kobe Immigration Company, 1 December 1896, *AH Bureau Letters* (1893–1897), p. 235.
7. King, President of the Board, to the sugar plantation companies, 23 May 1899, *AH Bureau Letters* (1897–1900), p. 87.
8. Applications from the sugar planters to the Board, 2 August 1897, *JFMAD 3.8.2.84;* letters from the Secretary of the Board to H. Waterhouse and Company, 2 August 1897 and W. G. Irwin and Company, 5 November 1897, *JFMAD 3.8.2.84.*
9. Article, *Daily Pacific Commercial Advertiser,* 27 February 1885, *JFMAD 3.8.2.5 Bessatsu meibo,* vol. 1.
10. Taylor to Captain Ahlbara, Manager of Pioneer Mill Company, 24 March 1896, *AH Bureau Letters* (1893–1897), p. 198; Taylor to Nacayama, 6 July 1895, and Taylor to Bishop and Company, 10 July 1895, *AH Bureau Letters* (1893–1897), pp. 151–152; Tōyō imin gōshigaisha to W. O. Smith, Attorney General, 26 July 1898, *AH Bureau Misc. Files,* document 34.

11. Irwin to Okkotsu, 15 January 1886, *AH Bureau Misc. Files,* document 1.

12. Nacayama to Gibson, Premier and Minister of Foreign Affairs, 26 October 1886, *AH Bureau Misc. Files,* document 9.

13. Taylor to King, 29 October 1895, *AH Bureau Letters* (1893–1897), p. 169.

14. Taylor to Frank H. Cooper, 27 August 1895, *AH Bureau Letters* (1893–1897), p. 163. Cooper was in charge of the immigration depot until 31 August 1895, when it was turned over to the Board of Health.

15. Samuel Parker, Minister of Foreign Affairs, to Consul General Masaki Taizō, 26 January 1892, *JFMAD 3.8.2.5 Bessatsu zatsu no bu* vol. 2. The doctor in question was Satō K.

16. Taylor to King, 5 October 1896, *AH Bureau Letters* (1893–1897), p. 231.

17. Commissioner of Labor, *Third Report,* p. 65.

18. For information on the history of some of the more prominent sugar planters, see Adler, *Sprekels;* Krauss and Alexander, *Grove Farm;* Taylor et al., *From Land and Sea;* and Vandercook, *King Cane.*

19. Commissioner of Labor, *Fifth Report,* p. 67.

20. Through W. G. Irwin and Company, Claus Spreckels at one time controlled the largest amount of land under sugar cultivation. See Adler, *Spreckels,* pp. 72–73.

21. Alexander and Baldwin was started in 1870 by Sam Alexander and Henry Baldwin, both children of missionaries. Captain Charles Brewer, a Boston seaman, joined James Hunnewell and established C. Brewer and Company in 1843. Castle and Cooke's founders were Samuel Castle, a storekeeper, and Amos Cooke, a schoolteacher, both of whom worked for the American Board of Commissioners for Foreign Missions. Theophilus H. Davies was an Englishman who came to the islands in 1857. Henry Hackfeld was a German sea captain who arrived in Hawaii in 1849 with his family. Both Davies and Hackfeld initially joined established companies which eventually became the basis for their sugar operations. See note 18.

22. Applications for Japanese laborers in a report by Taylor to the Board, 3 November 1898, *AH Bureau Letters* (1897–1900), pp. 82–83.

23. Okahata, *Japanese in Hawaii,* p. 277; Commissioner of Labor, *Third Report,* p. 11.

24. Commissioner of Labor, *Third Report,* p. 18.

25. Article, *Daily Bulletin,* 14 August 1885, *JFMAD 3.8.2.7.*

26. Consulate to the Foreign Ministry, 6 September 1910, *JFMAD 3.9.2.11.*

27. See internal foreign ministry memo, 4 September 1896, *JFMAD 3.8.2.60.* See also the exchange of letters between Consul General Shimamura Hisashi and Minister of Foreign Affairs Cooper, 17–18 September 1896 in the same volume.

28. Telegram from Saitō to Foreign Minister Katsura Tarō, 11 October 1905, *JFMAD 3.8.2.122,* vol. 5.

29. Printed circular from Saitō to the agents of the emigration companies, 18 September 1899, *AH Bureau Misc. Files,* document 35.

30. Commissioner of Labor, *Fourth Report,* p. 63.

31. See *JFMAD 3.8.2.256* and *3.8.2.266.*

32. See request received by the Foreign Ministry, 27 March 1912, *JFMAD 3.8.2.256;* 1 October 1913, *JFMAD 3.8.2.266;* a letter from Okayama prefecture to the Foreign Ministry, 22 September 1911, *JFMAD 3.8.2.266.*

33. See request, 12 February 1909, *JFMAD 3.8.2.256.*

34. Reports from the Consulate to the Foreign Ministry, 1902, *JFMAD 3.8.2.145,* vol. 4.

35. See *JFMAD 3.8.2.246.*

36. Reports on crimes in *JFMAD 3.8.7.16.* For other reports see *JFMAD 3.8.2.5 Bessatsu meibo,* vol. 4.

37. Chart attached to a letter from the Consulate to the Foreign Ministry, 5 May 1904, *JFMAD 3.8.2.195.*

38. Lists sent from the Consulate to the Foreign Ministry, 7 July 1922, *JFMAD 3.8.7.23 Bessatsu Hawai no bu,* vol. 1.

39. Reports from the Consulate to the Foreign Ministry, 1897, *JFMAD 3.8.2.88;* report from the Consulate to the Foreign Ministry, 25 July 1901, *JFMAD 3.8.2.88;* 11 March 1933, *JFMAD J.1.2.0 J 8–1,* vol. 2.

40. The only other personnel hired by the emigration companies were Japanese or Hawaiian lawyers who could provide legal advice and represent the companies in court. See Taylor to Sugawara T. O. , 12 February 1895, *AH Bureau Letters* (1893–1897), p. 128. Sugawara was an attorney who represented the Japanese Emigration Company of Hiroshima.

41. Information in this paragraph from Sōga, *Gojūnenkan,* pp. 101–102. This Jiyūtō or Liberal Party was founded in 1881 by Itagaki Taisuke and Gotō Shōjirō. It provided the main opposition to the new Meiji government.

42. C. A. Peterson, Inspector of Immigrants, to Alexander Young, President of the Board, 4 May 1900, *AH Bureau Misc. Files,* document 37.

43. Irie, *Imin kyūjūnen,* p. 93. Sōga, *Gojūnenkan,* pp. 112–113. Kawazoe, *Imin hyakunen,* pp. 149–150.

44. Kawazoe, *Imin hyakunen,* p. 150.

45. Letter from the eighteen emigrants to the Consul General in Vancouver, 9 May 1894, *JFMAD 3.8.2.36;* complaint filed with Kanagawa prefecture, 8 March 1905, *JFMAD 3.8.2.122,* vol. 5; Itō, *Issei* (English source), p. 25.

46. See 29 September 1901 *Japan Times* article reprinted in 17 October 1901 issue of the *Honolulu Republican, JFMAD 3.8.2.122,* vol. 5.

47. See *JFMAD 3.8.2.50,* vol. 1.

48. Itō, *Issei* (English source), p. 66. This report was sent by Ambassador Takahira Kogorō to Foreign Minister Komura Jutarō on 24 November 1908. The story of one person's confrontation with an emigration company can be found in Itō, " 'Morioka shōkai ni damasareta' to iki shōgen," pp. 53–57.

49. Gaimushō, *NGB,* vol. 42, pt. 1, p. 161. The original is in much more formal language than appears in my translation.

50. Printed circular from Saitō to the agents of the emigration companies, 18 September 1899, *AH Bureau Misc. Files,* document 35.

51. Commissioner of Labor, *Fourth Report,* p. 11. The figure 61,115 is given for 1900 in Fujii, *Dainippon,* pt. 1, p. 6.

52. Ibid.

53. The figures were compiled from Gaimushō tsūshōkyoku dai sanka, *Ryoken sankōsho,* p. 119.

54. Commissioner of Labor, *Second Report,* pp. 108–109. Many of the Japanese had borrowed misegane money, which is reflected in the $47.07 total.

55. Sekai kyōikushi kenkyūkai (ed.), *Sekai kyōikushi taikei 34 Joshi kyōikushi,*

p. 261. See also "Education in Japan," 26 March 1897, *Japan Times.* Nakamura (*Economic Growth,* p. 48) refers to one study which estimated that in 1868 43 percent of the males were literate and 10 percent of the females. Another indication of the educational level of the Japanese community in Hawaii is that between 1892 and 1922, a period of only thirty years, sixty-one Japanese language newspapers and periodicals were started in Hawaii. See Fujii, *Dainippon,* pt. 1, pp. 68–70.

56. Commissioner of Labor, *Third Report,* p. 118. The kerosene was for lighting purposes and not for heating. Boardinghouses for many single workers were staffed by other workers' wives.

57. This "Laborer's Balance Sheet" was sent with an open letter to W. O. Smith, Secretary of the HSPA, in January 1909. It is labeled "Exhibit K" and attached to a 30 January 1909 letter from the Consulate to Ishii Kikujirō of the Foreign Ministry. See *JFMAD 3.7.2.3,* vol. 1. Laundry was done for bachelors by workers' wives. Bath houses were built by the plantation companies and tended by individuals. The oil was for lighting purposes. "Send off money" refers to the custom of presenting a small amount of money to those leaving the plantations for other jobs or to those returning to Japan. In almost all cases, articles of clothing were sold by stores operated by the plantations.

58. See statement of Yamauchi Tsuru in Ethnic Studies Oral History Project, *Uchinanchu,* pp. 495–496.

59. Commissioner of Labor, *Report,* pp. 250–251.

60. Fujii, *Dainippon,* pt. 2., p. 6; Watanabe, *Hawai rekishi,* p. 441.

61. Commissioner of Labor, *Report,* p. 29 for information contained in this paragraph.

62. Ibid., pp. 83–84.

63. Ibid., pp. 139–187.

64. Commissioner of Labor, *Second Report,* p. 57.

Chapter 7
Emigration Companies in Hawaii: The Immigration Process

1. Taylor to Irwin, 27 May 1891, *AH Board Letters* (1891–1893), p. 37.

2. Article, *Hawai Shinpō,* 3 January 1902, *JFMAD 3.8.2.122,* vol. 3.

3. Report from the Consulate to the Foreign Ministry, 21 January 1903, *JFMAD 3.8.2.179.*

4. Telegram from Saitō to the Foreign Ministry, 16 July 1905, *JFMAD 3.8.2.122,* vol. 5.

5. President of the Bureau to Irwin, 3 April 1891, *AH Board Letters* (1891–1893), pp. 3–4. The eighteen-day quarantine requirement imposed on immigrants began on 14 April 1897 (see notice from the Board of Health, 14 April 1897, Gaimushō, *NGB,* vol. 30, p. 710). Before 1897 the period of quarantine was about one week; for example, the S.S. *Omi Maru* arrived in Honolulu on 29 March 1891 and its passengers were isolated until 3 April. In 1903 the quarantine period was shortened.

6. Sōga, *Gojūnenkan,* p. 8. A new immigration station was built at a cost of $30,000 and dedicated on 3 July 1905. See 4 July 1905 article, *Advertiser, JFMAD 3.8.2.122,* vol. 5.

7. "An Act Relating to the Landing of Aliens in the Hawaiian Islands," 1 March 1894, *JFMAD 3.7.1.2.*

8. See 6 November 1901 article from the *Honolulu Republican, JFMAD 3.8.2.122,* vol. 2.

9. Article, *Daily Pacific Commercial Advertiser,* 18 March 1897, *JFMAD 3.8.8.8,* vol. 1. See also Kawazoe, *Imin hyakunen,* pp. 172–175 and 13 April 1897 article, "The Hawaiian Question," *Japan Times.*

10. Article, "The Immigration Trouble in Hawaii," 12 April 1897, *Japan Times.*

11. Kihara, *Nipponjinshi,* pp. 486–487.

12. See correspondence between K. Ogura and Company (Ogura shōkai) and J. B. Castle, Collector of Customs, 18 March 1895–23 March 1895, Gaimushō, *NGB,* vol. 30, pp. 866–869.

13. Castle to K. Ogura and Company, 20 March 1895, Gaimushō, *NGB,* vol. 30, p. 868.

14. Consulate to the Foreign Ministry, 14 July 1905, *JFMAD 3.8.2.122,* vol. 5.

15. Nineteen volumes covering the 1885 to 1910 period under the title *Nyūkoku chōbo* are available in Hawaii.

16. Sōga, *Gojūnenkan,* p. 141.

17. See 1906 list, 20 August 1906, *JFMAD 3.8.2.122,* vol. 6, pt. 1 and Kawazoe, *Imin hyakunen,* p. 134 for these names and the rates at the boardinghouses.

18. Sōga, *Gojūnenkan,* p. 141.

19. Itō, *Issei* (English source), pp. 20–21.

20. Ibid., p. 24.

21. Ibid., p. 22.

22. Thurston to Nacayama, 23 April 1889, *AH Bureau Letters* (1888–1889).

23. Consulate to the Foreign Ministry, 6 September 1910, *JFMAD 3.9.2.11.*

24. See Moriyama, "1909 and 1920 Strikes" in Gee, ed., *Counterpoint,* pp. 169–180.

25. Wakukawa, *History,* p. 129.

26. Commissioner of Labor, *Fifth Report,* pp. 66–67.

27. Report from the Consulate to the Foreign Ministry, 5 February 1894, *JFMAD 3.8.2.41,* vol. 1. See also 26 January 1894 letter from Anton Cropp to Narita Gorō of the consulate in the same volume.

28. Itō, *Issei* (English source), p. 24.

29. Commissioner of Labor, *Fourth Report,* p. 18.

30. Letter from the Manager of Hawaii Coffee and Tea Company to H. A. Schaefer, 9 May 1892, *AH Board Letters* (1891–1893), pp. 212–215.

31. This type of wage scale was used in the earliest days of Japanese migration to the islands. A report sent by the consulate to the foreign ministry on 8 July 1886 mentioned the following average monthly wages (including food allowances) for different racial groups: Chinese, $19.19; Portuguese, $19.57; Japanese, $16.20; Norwegians, $19.00; Germans, $20.75; and South Sea Islanders, $15.93. See Gaimushō, *Hawai,* p. 27. This is a compilation of reports sent by the consulate in Honolulu between 20 April 1886 and 2 June 1887 on the subject of the Hawaiian sugar industry.

32. Commissioner of Labor, *Fourth Report,* p. 76 and Wakukawa, *History,* p. 176.

33. I have rearranged the original list in the order that they arrived at the plantation.

34. Report from the Consulate to the Foreign Ministry, 9 January and 27 April 1899, *JFMAD 3.8.2.143,* vol. 1.

35. Printed circular from Saitō to the agents of the emigration companies, 18 September 1899, *AH Bureau Misc. Files* (1868–1900), document 35.

36. Minutes of the Executive Council meeting, 13 July 1898, *AH Bureau Letters* (1897–1900).

37. Circular issued by William G. Irwin and Company for Kumamoto Emigration Company, January 1898. The circular is attached to a letter from Inoue Keijirō of Kumamoto Emigration Company to the Consulate, 14 May 1898, *JFMAD 3.8.2.84.*

38. Contract of Japanese Emigration Company of Hiroshima, 16 May 1898, *JFMAD 3.8.2.62,* vol. 4.

39. Ibid.

40. Certificate, 1902, *JFMAD 3.8.2.163.*

41. Report from Japanese Emigration Company of Hiroshima to the Consulate, 1 November 1897, *JFMAD 3.8.2.88.* The company had 497 women also under contract, but all were workers' wives.

42. Report from the Consulate to the Foreign Ministry, 31 January 1902, *JFMAD 3.8.2.152.*

43. Kihara, *Nipponjinshi,* p. 237.

44. Ōkubo et al., *Kindaishi,* pp. 300–301.

45. Gaimushō tsūshōkyoku, *Enkaku,* pp. 157–158.

46. See *JFMAD 3.8.2.152.*

47. Ōkubo et al., *Kindaishi,* pp. 300–301.

48. Ibid. Reports from the Consulate to the Foreign Ministry, 18 July 1903, 23 March 1905, 29 January 1906, 21 August 1907, 26 February 1908, and 25 March 1909, *JFMAD 3.8.2.152.*

49. Report attached to 10 January 1902 letter from Hiroshima prefectural officials to the Foreign Ministry, *JFMAD 3.8.2.152.*

50. Kodama, "Kaigai e" in Hiroshima-ken hen, *Hiroshima-kenshi kindai ichi,* pp. 1001–1002.

51. Report from the Consulate to the Foreign Ministry, 1898–1899, *JFMAD 3.8.2.152.*

52. Wakatsuki, "Japanese Emigration," p. 452.

53. Ibid., p. 451.

54. Sōga, *Gojūnenkan,* p. 173.

55. Shizuoka-ken kaigai ijū kyōkai, *Shizuoka-ken,* pp. 66–67.

56. Iwasaki, "Kii hantō," part 3, pp. 28–46.

57. Sōga, *Gojūnenkan,* p. 172.

58. Kihara, *Nipponjinshi,* p. 172.

59. Ibid., p. 178.

60. Wakukawa, *History,* p. 153.

61. Commissioner of Labor, *Third Report,* pp. 150–151.

62. Kihara, *Nipponjinshi,* p. 178.

63. Ibid.

64. Article, "Hopes for the Prosecuting Attorney in Japan," 1905, *Hawai Shinpō, JFMAD 3.8.2.93.*

65. Sōga, *Gojūnenkan,* p. 112. See also letter from Huntington Wilson, Secretary

of the Legation of the United States in Tokyo, to the Foreign Ministry, 16 January 1905, *JFMAD 3.8.2.198.*

66. Ibid.

67. Ibid., p. 113. The word for villa in Japanese is *besso.*

68. Commissioner of Labor, *Third Report,* p. 149.

69. Sōga, *Gojūnenkan,* p. 147.

70. Ibid., p. 99.

71. Announcement of the Central Japanese League, 30 November 1903, *JFMAD 3.8.2.198.* See also Wakukawa, *History,* p. 146.

72. Okahata, *Japanese in Hawaii,* p. 147.

73. See newspaper article, "No Labor Union This," undated, attached to a letter from the Consulate to the Foreign Ministry, 2 December 1903, *JFMAD 3.8.2.198.* See the attachment to 2 December 1903 letter from the Consulate to the Foreign Ministry, in the same file for a copy of the regulations of the League as "Chūō Nipponjinkai shuisho oyobi shokisoku."

74. Shiota Okuzō from Keihin Bank served as a director of the League. See announcement, 30 November 1903, *JFMAD 3.8.2.198.*

75. Wakukawa, *History,* p. 156.

76. Gaimushō ryōji ijūbu, *Waga kokumin* (honpen), pp. 150–151.

77. Wakukawa, *History,* p. 156.

78. Okahata, *Japanese in Hawaii,* p. 147.

79. Kihara, *Nipponjinshi,* p. 178.

80. Okahata, *Japanese in Hawaii,* pp. 147–148.

81. Ibid., p. 147.

82. Commissioner of Labor, *Fourth Report,* p. 51.

83. Commissioner of Labor, *First Report* for information concerning the 1900–1901 strikes.

84. Commissioner of Labor, *Third Report,* p. 144 for information concerning the 1903–1905 strikes.

85. Consul General Ueno Sen'ichi to Komura, 29 June 1909, *JFMAD 3.7.2.3,* vol. 1. The demand for "same wages" was an attempt by the workers to abolish the existing unequal wage scale.

86. The 1900–1910 statistics calculated from Commissioner of Labor, *Fourth Report,* pp. 60–61.

87. Watanabe, *Hawai rekishi,* p. 405.

88. Report from the Consulate to the Foreign Ministry, July 1904, *JFMAD 3.8.2.168.*

89. Commissioner of Labor, *Third Report,* pp. 21–22. The 20,641 "Orientals" leaving Hawaii included "300 Koreans and less than 75 Chinese."

90. Commissioner of Labor, *Fourth Report,* p. 60 for 1906–1909 figures.

91. Commissioner of Labor, *Fifth Report,* p. 64.

92. Commissioner of Labor, *Third Report,* p. 22. Original from the 22 March 1905 issue of *Hawaiian-Japanese Chronicle.*

93. Sōga, *Gojūnenkan,* pp. 227–228.

94. Commissioner of Labor, *Third Report,* p. 22.

95. Alex Center, General Agent, to H. Hackfeld and Company, Ltd., 1902, *JFMAD 3.8.2.168.*

96. Article, *San Francisco Chronicle,* 15 June 1902, *JFMAD 3.8.2.168.*

97. See 1902 list in *JFMAD 3.8.2.168.* See also *JFMAD 3.8.2.198.* The names in Appendix 15 are in addition to Yasuzawa and Egi Kyūjirō mentioned in the previous newspaper advertisements. Egi may be a misreading of Iki N. Negoro went on to play an important role in the 1909 sugar plantation strike. Tōyō Bōekigaisha was located in Seattle.

98. See 1903 list, *JFMAD 3.8.2.168.* There also seems to have been some recruitment done by non-Japanese agents but on a smaller scale. See for example the Hawaiian newspaper clipping of 3 December 1903 in the same volume. The article read in part "J. P. Ball, a local attorney, recently arrived from the mainland who is said to be acting here for some big mills around Seattle and Portland, and for whom he is recruiting Japanese laborers in these islands."

99. Okahata, *Japanese in Hawaii,* p. 161.

100. See letter from Alex Center, General Agent, to H. Hackfeld and Company, Ltd., Agents for Pacific Mail Steamship Company, 1902, *JFMAD 3.8.2.168.*

101. See advertisements, 1905, *JFMAD 3.8.2.198.* One set of advertisements can be found attached to 2 February 1905 letter from the Consulate to the Foreign Ministry. Another set is attached to a 1 March 1905 letter from the Consulate to Envoy Extraordinary Takahira Kogorō.

102. Commissioner of Labor, *Third Report,* pp. 41–42.

103. F. M. Swanzy, President of the HSPA, to Saitō, 18 April 1905, *JFMAD 3.8.2.168.*

104. A copy of this can be found attached to a letter from the Consulate to the Foreign Ministry, 8 May 1905, *JFMAD 3.8.2.168.*

105. Ishikawa, "Okinawa-ken," p. 60.

106. Ibid., p. 61.

107. See statement of Tamashiro Baishiro in Ethnic Studies Oral History Project, *Uchinanchu,* p. 364.

108. Notice issued by Yamanashi prefectural authorities, October 1905, *JFMAD 3.8.2.168.*

109. See notices in English and Japanese issued by the Consulate, 16 March 1903, *JFMAD 3.8.2.168.*

110. Commissioner of Labor, *Second Report,* pp. 97–106.

111. Okahata, *Japanese in Hawaii,* p. 201.

112. Gaimushō, tsūshōkyoku, *Ryoken kafusū,* pp. 190–204.

113. Ibid.

114. Compiled from lists in *JFMAD 3.8.2.283, Bessatsu Hawai no bu,* vol. 1.

115. Ishikawa, "Setonai chiiki kara no (shutsu) imin," p. 60.

116. See statement by Yamauchi Tsuru in Ethnic Studies Oral History Project, *Uchinanchu,* pp. 488–489.

117. Consulate in San Francisco to Hart H. North, Commissioner of Immigration in San Francisco, 17 February 1905, *JFMAD 3.8.2.122,* vol. 6.

118. Rice to the Commissioner of Immigration, 2 May 1899, U.S. Congress, House, *Treasury,* p. 15.

119. Commissioner of Labor, *Second Report,* pp. 108–109.

120. Fujii, *Dainippon,* section 2, pp. 68–70.

121. Commissioner of Labor, *Second Report,* p. 109.

122. Okahata, *Japanese in Hawaii,* p. 225.

Chapter 8
The End of the Emigration Companies

1. Gaimushō tsūshōkyoku, *Ryoken kafusū,* pp. 156–159.
2. Ibid., pp. 142–181.
3. *JFMAD 3.8.2.50,* vol. 1.
4. William M. Morgan, "Strategic Factors," (unpublished Ph.D. dissertation), pp. 131–132.
5. Department of the Treasury to the Collectors of Customs in Honolulu, 12 August 1902, *JFMAD 3.8.2.122,* vol. 3. This type of restriction continued over the years. One of the laws passed in the 1929 session of the Hawaii Territorial Legislature read in part, "It is hereby declared unlawful for any person not a citizen of the United States, or eligible to become a citizen, to take, kill or pursue any fish, turtle or squid in any of the waters within the jurisdiction of the Territory of Hawaii by means of any spear, arrow gun and/or hook attached to any spear." See attachment to 30 January report 1934 from the Consulate to the Foreign Ministry, *JFMAD J.1.1.0 J/X1-U3.*
6. "Specifications for Filling a Portion of Waikiki Road," in 15 September 1902 letter from the Consulate to the Foreign Ministry, *JFMAD 3.8.2.122,* vol. 3.
7. "An Act to Provide a Government for the Territory of Hawaii," 30 April 1900, *JFMAD J.1.1.0 J/X1-U3.*
8. Foreign office notice, 22 April 1896, attached to a letter from the Consulate to the Foreign Ministry, 23 April 1896, *JFMAD 3.7.1.2,* vol. 1.
9. Secretary of the Executive Council to King, 14 August 1899, *AH Board Minutes* (1879–1899), p. 8.
10. Untitled newspaper article, 13 October 1887, *JFMAD 3.8.2.5 Bessatsu dekaseginin,* vol. 2. The survey was taken by C. N. Spencer. At that time, Japanese ranked third in number behind the Chinese and Portuguese on the plantations.
11. Statement presented by the HSPA to a United States Senate Committee, 12 September 1902, *JFMAD 3.8.2.122,* vol. 2.
12. For details of the attempt to reintroduce Chinese laborers into Hawaii, see Reinecke, *Feigned Necessity.*
13. Commissioner of Labor, *Third Report,* p. 321. See also "An Act to Provide a Government for the Territory of Hawaii," *JFMAD J.1.1.0 J/X1-U3.*
14. Adler, *Spreckels,* pp. 230–257.
15. Telegram message from Hayashi to Aoki, 3 December 1898, Gaimushō, *NGB,* vol. 31, pt. 2, p. 238.
16. Nacayama, Managing Director of Tōyō imin gōshigaisha, to Smith, 26 July 1898, *AH Bureau Misc. Files,* document 34.
17. Attachment to a letter from Nacayama to Smith, 26 July 1898, *AH Bureau Misc. Files* (1868–1900), document 34.
18. Ibid.
19. See 8 July 1893 letter from Consul General Chinda Sutemi (San Francisco) to Envoy Extraordinary Tateno Gōzō (Washington, D.C.) and 13 July 1893 letter from Chinda to the Foreign Ministry, *JFMAD 3.8.8.5,* vol. 1.
20. Report from the Office of the U.S. Commissioner of Immigration to the Commissioner General of Immigration (Washington, D.C.), 22 September 1897, *JFMAD 3.8.8.5,* vol. 1.

21. Ibid.

22. Office of the U.S. Commissioner of Immigration to the Commissioner General of Immigration (Washington, D.C.), 22 September 1897, *JFMAD 3.8.8.5,* vol. 1.

23. Gaimushō ryōji ijūbu, *Hyakunen no ayumi,* pp. 42–43.

24. My calculations. The remaining 8 percent were individual emigrants who traveled to Hawaii without using the companies. See Gaimushō tsūshōkyoku, *Ryoken kafusū,* pp. 142–181.

25. Directive from the Foreign Ministry to the emigration companies, 4 July 1901, *JFMAD 3.8.2.148.*

26. Report of the Foreign Ministry, 17 December 1902, *JFMAD 3.8.2.122,* vol. 4.

27. Report of the Foreign Ministry, 23 September 1903, *JFMAD 3.8.2.122,* vol. 4.

28. Reports of the Foreign Ministry, 17 December 1902 to 12 February 1907, *JFMAD 3.8.2.122,* vols. 4 and 5.

29. Telegram message from Saitō to Komura, received 13 June 1905, *JFMAD 3.8.2.122,* vol. 5.

30. Report attached to 13 June 1905 letter from the Consulate to the Foreign Ministry, *JFMAD 3.8.2.122,* vol. 5. The original plan to divide up the 600 emigrant slots was drawn up on 25 March 1905.

31. Contract agreement between Japanese Immigration Bureau and the McBryde estate, 16 May 1899, *JFMAD 3.8.2.84.* This Bureau was known in Japanese as *Nippon imin kyōkai. Kyōkai* is usually translated as "society" or "association." I have nonetheless decided to use the name the companies mentioned in their prospectus and contracts. See Appendix 5.

32. Ibid.

33. Contracts of Japanese Immigration Bureau, 11 May 1899 to 16 May 1899, *JFMAD 3.8.2.84.*

34. Contracts of Japanese Immigration Bureau, 16 August 1899 to 21 August 1899, *JFMAD 3.8.2.84.*

35. Ibid.

36. The Japanese government retained the right to order the companies to form a guild as stated in Article 32 of the Regulations.

37. See the document attached to 9 October 1902 foreign ministry memo, *JFMAD 3.8.2.173.*

38. Ibid.

39. Ibid.

40. Report of the Metropolitan Police to the Foreign Ministry, 24 December 1907, *JFMAD 3.8.2.173.*

41. Kokusai kyōryoku jigyōdan, *Ijū tōkei,* pp. 66–67.

42. For evidence that Japanese illegally entered the United States by "jumping ship," see Itō, *Issei* (English source), pp. 55–64. For evidence of Japanese illegally crossing the Mexican border into the United States, see same source, pp. 64–73.

43. Rice to the Commissioner General of Immigration, 24 April 1899, U.S. Congress, House, *Treasury,* p. 9.

44. Gaimushō tsūshōkyoku, *Ryoken kafusū,* p. 142.

45. Ibid., p. 148.

46. U.S. Congress, Senate, *Reports,* vol. 1, pt. 25, p. 20.

47. Kokusai kyōryoku jigyōdan, *Ijū tōkei,* pp. 66–67.

48. Nishimukai, "Kaiungyō," pp. 67–119.

49. The number for 1898 is 1,039 in Kokusai kyōryoku jigyōdan, *Ijū tōkei,* pp. 66–67.

50. Evidence of early economic interest in the South Pacific by Japanese business can be found in David C. Purcell, Jr., "Japanese Entrepreneurs in the Mariana, Marshall, and Caroline Islands," in Conroy and Miyakawa, eds., *East Across the Pacific,* pp. 56–70.

51. Irie, *Hōjin hattenshi,* vol. 1, p. 128. See Kobayashi, *Nyūkaredoniatō no Nihonjin.*

52. Ishikawa, "Fijiishotō ni okeru Nihonjin keiyakuimin (1894–1895) ni tsuite," pp. 1–25.

53. Kodama, "Shoki," p. 21.

54. Gaimushō tsūshōkyoku, *Ryoken kafusū,* pp. 142–157.

55. Contract signed between Union Bank of Australia, Ltd., of Mourilyan, North Queensland, and Ichikawa Naosuke of Hiroshima, 17 June 1901, *JFMAD J.1.2.0 J 3–4.*

56. Takeda, "Hakugō seisaku no seiritsu to Nihon no taiō," p. 23.

57. Ono, "Problem," p. 46.

58. Kuroyanagi, "Firipin," pp. 50–61.

59. Gaimushō tsūshōkyoku, *Ryoken kafusū,* pp. 152–155. See also Kuroyanagi, "Firipin."

60. Wakayama-ken, *Iminshi,* p. 278. See also Kuroyanagi, "Firipin."

61. Kokusai kyōryoku jigyōdan, *Ijū tōkei,* pp. 66–67.

62. Ibid.

63. Itō, *Issei* (English source), p. 66.

64. See *JFMAD 3.8.1.1.*

65. See *JFMAD 3.8.1.6.*

66. Gaimushō tsūshōkyoku, *Ryoken kafusū,* p. 144.

67. Irie, *Hōjin hattenshi,* vol. 1, pp. 345–346.

68. Kokusai kyōryoku jigyōdan, *Ijū tōkei,* pp. 66–67.

69. Ibid.

70. Gaimushō tsūshōkyoku, *Ryoken kafusū,* pp. 142–189.

71. Ibid.

72. Ishikawa, "Imingaisha," p. 31.

73. Ibid. See also Gaimushō tsūshōkyoku, *Ryoken kafusū,* pp. 142–189. This company was apparently well financed. An article in the *Japanese Advertiser* referred to this company as a "concern which is backed by many of the biggest Japanese industrial concerns. . . ." See *Japanese Advertiser,* 19 August 1926 article, *JFMAD 3.8.1.11,* vol. 1.

74. Kokusai kyōryoku jigyōdan, *Ijū tōkei,* pp. 66–67.

Chapter 9
The Legacy of the Emigration Companies

1. Ishikawa, "Kuchida-son."

2. Ishikawa, "Jigozen-son."

3. Ishikawa, "Kuga-son."

4. Shizuoka-ken, *Shizuoka-ken,* pp. 66–67.

5. See Fukutake, ed., *Amerika mura;* Tsurumi, *Sutebusuton monogatari;* and Gamō, ed., *Umi.*

6. Kodama, "Dekaseginin," pp. 37–38; Gotō, ed., *Hiroshima-ken no chimei,* p. 619.

7. Ibid., p. 31.

8. Information about Yamano Akizō and his family was obtained from his koseki.

9. Information on Yamano Akizō's departure from Japan can be found in *JFMAD 3.8.2.5 Bessatsu meibo,* vol. 2, and *JFMAD 3.8.5.8,* vol. 10.

10. Emigrant lists attached to 29 May 1888 letter from Kanagawa prefectural officials to the Foreign Ministry, *JFMAD 3.8.2.5 Bessatsu meibo,* vol. 2.

11. Information from Yamano Akizō's life after his arrival in Hawaii from a series of interviews with his daughter, Matsuno Yamaguchi (formerly Yamano).

12. Information about Moriyama Goichi and his family was obtained from his koseki.

13. Information on Moriyama Goichi's departure from Japan can be found in *JFMAD 3.8.2.38,* vol. 23, pt. 2, and *JFMAD 3.8.5.8,* vol. 101.

14. See *JFMAD 3.8.2.78, 3.8.2.97, 3.8.2.102* and *3.8.2.116.*

15. Information about Moriyama Goichi's life after his arrival in Hawaii is from a series of interviews with his son, Sadao Moriyama.

16. Information on Yamaguchi Masato and his family is from his koseki. I have used information from interviews with his widow, Matsuno Yamaguchi.

17. Information about Yamaguchi Masato's departure from Japan can be found in *JFMAD 3.8.2.38,* vol. 26.

18. See *JFMAD 3.8.2.156,* vol. 1.

19. Information about Yamaguchi Masato's life in Hawaii is from interviews with Matsuno Yamaguchi.

20. Information on Kuwashima Iseno is from her koseki and interviews with her son, Sadao Moriyama.

21. Information about Matsuno Yamaguchi is from her father's koseki and from a series of interviews.

Sources Cited

This section is divided into seven parts: Japanese Foreign Ministry Archival Documents (JFMAD); Japanese Sources, Books and Government Documents; Japanese Sources, Journals and Newspapers; Archives of Hawaii; Books, Government Documents, and Theses in English; Journals and Newspapers in English; and Interviews and Lectures. It should be noted that this section lists only sources cited in the text. Many standard works were consulted but were not quoted from and therefore not listed in this section. I have provided English translations of all Japanese-language source titles listed in the first three sections. These are not literal translations but shortened and simplified forms of them.

All of the JFMAD documents are held in the Gaikō shiryōkan (Diplomatic Record Office) in Tokyo. Although some researchers in Japan and America rely heavily on the *Nihon Gaikō Bunsho* series compiled by the Foreign Ministry, it should be noted that this series consists of selected materials from original JFMAD files and are but samples of holdings.

Almost all of the other Japanese language materials in the second and third sections are available at the National Diet Library in Tokyo. Some of these materials are in the Japanese American Research Project collection at the University of California, Los Angeles, although they do not include journal articles. A useful bibliography for this collection is *A Buried Past.*

The Archives of Hawaii is the major source for primary documents on immigration to Hawaii. A useful guide to other materials available in Hawaii is Mitsugu Matsuda's *The Japanese in Hawaii* (Honolulu: University of Hawaii Social Sciences and Linguistics Institute, 1975).

The Kuwashima Iseno, Moriyama Goichi, Yamaguchi Masato, Yamaguchi Seishirō, and Yamano Akizō family registers were also invaluable sources of information for this work.

Japanese Foreign Ministry Archival Documents (JFMAD)

3.7.1.2 "Hawaikoku ni okeru jiyū keiyaku rōdōsha ni kansuru jōrei happu ikken" (Documents on ordinances relating to free and contract workers in Hawaii). April 1894–February 1897.

3.7.2.3 "Zaihawai honpōjin dōmei higyō ikken" (Documents on union and strike activities by Japanese in Hawaii). 3 vols. February 1909–July 1915.

3.8.1.1 "Mekishiko iminchi tanken toshite Nemoto Tadashi hoka ichimei shutchō ikken, fusu tankenhi no ken" (Documents on the trip of Nemoto Tadashi to Mexico). June 1893–October 1894.

3.8.1.3 "Imin hogohō narabini shikō saisoku seitei ikken" (Documents on the establishment of the Emigrant Protection Law and its by-laws). 2 vols. November 1893.

3.8.1.4 "Iminhō oyobi ryoken jimu kankei zakken (uchiawase kaigai o fukumu)" (Miscellaneous documents relating to the Emigrant Protection Law and passports). February 1894–December 1916. 3 vols. Bessatsu ryoken narabini imin jimu toriatsukai sankōsho (Information on passports and other emigration matters). Separate volume.

3.8.1.5 "Imin hogokisoku jisshigo imin toriatsukai ni kansuru kunrei oyobi shirei zakken" (Documents relating to the Emigrant Protection Ordinance and its enforcement). April 1894–January 1896.

3.8.1.6 "Gaimuzoku Nemoto Tadashi nanbei chihō imin tanken no tame shutchō no ken" (Documents on the trip of Nemoto Tadashi to South America). July 1894–February 1895.

3.8.1.7 "Imin hogohō shikōjō no tetsuzuki oyobi ryoken kisoku toriatsukai kata ni kanshi seitei shitaru fukenrei naiki ikken" (Documents on city and prefectural rules concerning the Emigrant Protection Law and passport regulations). 2 vols. June 1896–February 1921.

3.8.1.8 "Imin hogohō oyobi dō shikō saisoku ni kansuru kunrei narabini ukagai tō zakken" (Miscellaneous documents relating to the Emigrant Protection Law and its directives). 5 vols. July 1896–February 1921.

3.8.1.9 "Heieki gimu o sakuru no mokuteki o motte kaigai ni tokō surumono no torishimari ni kansuru hōritsu seitei ikken" (Documents on the establishment of laws preventing people from going abroad in order to avoid military service obligations). February 1908–March 1908.

3.8.1.11 "Teikoku imin seisaku oyobi hōki kankei zakken" (Miscellaneous documents relating to the official policies, laws, and regulations on emigration). 2 vols. November 1915.

3.8.2.1 "Hawaikoku sōryōji 'Uen Ritto' mumenkyo honpō nōmin yōn'yū dōkoku e tokō ikken" (Documents on the case of Hawaiian Consul General Van Reed taking Japanese farmers to Hawaii without official permission). 3 vols. April 1868–December 1875.

3.8.2.2 "Imin kankei zakken" (Miscellaneous documents relating to emigration). 5 vols. October 1870–October 1914.

3.8.2.3 "Honpō imin Hawai tokō ikken" (Documents on Japanese workers going to Hawaii). 4 vols. labeled 5, 6, 7, and 8, March 1879–May 1901.

3.8.2.5 "Nipponjinmin Hawaikoku e dekasegi ikken (kankeiyaku)" (Documents on Japanese workers going to Hawaii). 43 vols. November 1884–November 1898. Bessatsu chōhei tekirei shobun no ken, saiban hōhō no ken, shusshō narabini shibō no ken (Information on conscription, court cases, and records of births and deaths). Separate volume. November 1884–July 1886.

3.8.2.5 "Nipponjinmin Hawaikoku e dekasegi ikken (kankeiyaku)" (Documents on Japanese workers going to Hawaii). 43 vols. November 1884–November 1898. Bessatsu dekaseginin kaiyaku kikoku no ken (Information on Japanese workers returning to Japan). Separate volume. June 1885–October 1892.

3.8.2.5 "Nipponjinmin Hawaikoku e dekasegi ikken (kankeiyaku)" (Documents on Japanese workers going to Hawaii). 43 vols. November 1884–November 1898. Bessatsu dekaseginin meibo no bu (Emigrant lists). 4 vols. 1885–1894.

3.8.2.5 "Nipponjinmin Hawaikoku e dekasegi ikken (kankeiyaku)" (Documents on Japanese workers going to Hawaii). 43 vols. November 1884–November 1898. Bessatsu muyakutei tokōsha torishimari no ken (Information on Japanese workers going to Hawaii without contracts). Separate volume. September 1885–March 1887.

3.8.2.5 "Nipponjinmin Hawaikoku e dekasegi ikken (kankeiyaku)" (Documents on Japanese workers going to Hawaii). 43 vols. November 1884–November 1898. Bessatsu niwari gobu hoka chokin no ken (Information on the 25 percent savings plan). Separate volume. November 1885–April 1889.

3.8.2.5 "Nipponjinmin Hawaikoku e dekasegi ikken (kankeiyaku)" (Documents on Japanese workers going to Hawaii). 43 vols. November 1884–November 1898. Bessatsu tōgyō hōkoku no ken (Information on the sugar industry). Separate volume. May 1886–January 1889.

3.8.2.5 "Nipponjinmin Hawaikoku e dekasegi ikken (kankeiyaku)" (Documents on Japanese workers going to Hawaii). 43 vols. November 1884–November 1898. Bessatsu zatsu no bu (Miscellaneous information). 2 vols. December 1884–November 1893.

3.8.2.6 "Kaigai dekaseginin torishimari no gi ni tsuki kaikō shijō narabini Hiroshima, Yamaguchi, Fukuoka, Shimane, Kagoshima kaku kenchiji e naikun ikken" (Documents on orders concerning emigrants sent to the open ports and prefectural governors of Hiroshima, Yamaguchi, Fukuoka, Shimane, and Kagoshima prefectures). July 1884–August 1887.

3.8.2.7 "Nipponjinmin Hawaikoku e dekasegi ikken, gaimuken shōshokikan Inoue Katsunosuke tokubetsuiin toshite Hawaikoku e tokō ikken" (Documents on Japanese workers in Hawaii and the investigative trip of Inoue Katsunosuke). September 1885–January 1886.

3.8.2.9 "Hawaikoku e honpōjin dekasegi zakken" (Miscellaneous documents on Japanese emigrants going to Hawaii). December 1885–April 1893.

3.8.2.23 "Kaigai imin dōshikai imin toriatsukai eigyō ikken (mikan)" (Documents on the business operations of Kaigai imin dōshikai). July 1891–May 1896.

3.8.2.27 "Yoshisa imin gōmeigaisha gyōmu kankei zakken" (Miscellaneous documents concerning the affairs of Yoshisa imin gōmeigaisha). 3 vols. August 1892–July 1908.

3.8.2.35 "Kaigai tokō kabushikigaisha gyōmu kankei zakken" (Miscellaneous documents concerning the affairs of Kaigai tokō kabushikigaisha). 6 vols. July 1893–April 1915.

3.8.2.36 "Yokohama imin gōshigaisha gyōmu kankei zakken" (Miscellaneous documents concerning the affairs of Yokohama imin gōshigaisha). August 1893–May 1895.

3.8.2.38 "Imin toriatsukainin o keiyuseru kaigai tokōsha meibo" (A list of those people going overseas using emigration companies). 54 vols. December 1893–November 1920.

3.8.2.40 "Yokohama kaigai shokumin gōshigaisha gyōmu kankei zakken" (Miscellaneous documents concerning the affairs of Yokohama kaigai shokumin gōshigaisha). February 1894–October 1894.

3.8.2.41 "Hawaikoku ni okeru honpō imin kankei zakken" (Miscellaneous documents concerning Japanese immigrants in Hawaii). 6 vols. February 1894–October 1921.

3.8.2.43 "Imin toriatsukainin Ogura [Kokura] Kō gyōmu kankei zakken" (Miscellaneous documents concerning the affairs of Ogura [Kokura] Kō). June 1894–May 1900.

3.8.2.44 "Kobe tokō gōshigaisha gyōmu kankei zakken" (Miscellaneous documents concerning the affairs of Kobe tokō gōshigaisha). 6 vols. June 1894–May 1915.

3.8.2.46 "Imin toriatsukainin Morioka Makoto gyōmu kankei zakken" (Miscellaneous documents concerning the affairs of Morioka Makoto). 5 vols. October 1894–November 1921.

3.8.2.50 "Teikoku imin hogohō ihansha shobun zakken" (Miscellaneous documents concerning the handling of those who violated the Emigrant Protection Law). 2 vols. May 1895–February 1918.

3.8.2.52 "Dainippon imin kabushikigaisha toriatsukai eigyō ikken (haigyō)" (Documents on the business affairs of Dainippon imin kabushikigaisha). November 1895–March 1896.

3.8.2.54 "Imin toriatsukaigyō shutsugan funinka zakken" (Miscellaneous documents concerning the rejection of applications to enter the business of sending emigrants abroad). April 1896–February 1906.

3.8.2.57 "Tokio imin gōshigaisha gyōmu kankei zakken" (Miscellaneous documents concerning the affairs of Tokio imin gōshigaisha). 3 vols. July 1896–June 1916.

3.8.2.58 "Kimoto Shunkichi imin toriatsukai eigyō ikken (kigen keika mukō)" (Documents on the business affairs of Kimoto Shunkichi). August 1896–March 1897.

3.8.2.59 "Chinzei imin kabushikigaisha gyōmu kankei zakken" (Miscellaneous documents concerning the affairs of Chinzei imin kabushikigaisha). August 1896–June 1897.

3.8.2.60 "Hawaikoku ni oite Nipponjin Shinajin inyū hirei kettei ikken" (Documents on the decision to import Japanese and Chinese into Hawaii). August 1896–December 1897.

3.8.2.61 "Nippon imin gōshigaisha gyōmu kankei zakken" (Miscellaneous documents on the affairs of Nippon imin gōshigaisha). 3 vols. August 1896–August 1908.

3.8.2.62 "Kaigai tokō kabushikigaisha toriatsukai imin tokō ninka hōkoku zakken" (Miscellaneous documents on the permission granted Kaigai tokō kabushikigaisha to send emigrants abroad). 10 vols. October 1896–September 1907.

3.8.2.63 "Tōyō imin kabushikigaisha (kyūmei Kumamoto imin kabushikigaisha) gyōmu kankei zakken" (Miscellaneous documents concerning the affairs of Tōyō imin kabushikigaisha). November 1896–July 1897.

3.8.2.64 "Imin toriatsukainin Koyama Yūtarō gyōmu kankei zakken, fusu imingaisha dōmei kiyaku no ken" (Miscellaneous documents relating to the affairs of Koyama Yūtarō and the agreement to establish an association of emigration companies). November 1896–April 1898.

3.8.2.65 "Nippon imin gōshigaisha toriatsukai imin tokō ninka hōkoku zakken" (Miscellaneous documents on the permission granted Nippon imin gōshigaisha to send emigrants abroad). 4 vols. November 1896–October 1900.

3.8.2.66 "Kobe yūsen imin kabushikigaisha imin toriatsukai eigyō ikken (haigyō)" (Documents relating to the business of Kobe yūsen imin kabushikigaisha). December 1896–March 1898.

3.8.2.69 "Imin toriatsukainin Morioka Makoto (nochi ni Morioka imin gōmeigaisha, Morioka imin kabushikigaisha to aratamu) toriatsukai imin tokō ninka hōkoku zakken" (Miscellaneous documents on the permission granted Morioka Makoto to send emigrants abroad). 7 vols. December 1896–November 1920.

3.8.2.70 "Chūgoku imin gōshigaisha imin toriatsukai eigyō ikken" (Documents on the business affairs of Chūgoku imin gōshigaisha). January 1897–February 1897.

3.8.2.71 "Tōyō imin gōshigaisha gyōmu kankei zakken" (Miscellaneous documents concerning the affairs of Tōyō imin gōshigaisha). 9 vols. January 1897–December 1917.

3.8.2.74 "Tokio imin gōshigaisha toriatsukai imin tokō ninka hōkoku zakken" (Miscellaneous documents on the permission granted Tokio imin gōshigaisha to send emigrants abroad). 4 vols. March 1897–April 1908.

3.8.2.76 "Imin toriatsukainin Koyama Yūtarō ni kakawaru imin tokō ninka hōkoku zakken" (Miscellaneous documents on the permission granted Koyama Yūtarō to send emigrants abroad). April 1897–May 1898.

3.8.2.77 "Nippon shokumin kabushikigaisha imin toriatsukai eigyō ikken (kigen keika mukō)" (Documents on the business affairs of Nippon shokumin kabushikigaisha). April 1897–June 1898.

3.8.2.78 "Teikoku imin gōshigaisha gyōmu kankei zakken" (Miscellaneous documents on the affairs of Teikoku imin gōshigaisha). May 1897.

3.8.2.84 "Hawaikoku keiyakuimin inyū ninka hōkoku zakken" (Miscellaneous documents on the permission to send workers to Hawaii). July 1897–October 1899.

3.8.2.88 "Keiyakuimin no kikoku funachin chokin mimoto hoshōkin tsuki yokin tō no yokindaka torishirabe ikken" (Documents on emigrant bank accounts holding return passage fare and personal guarantee money). October 1897–August 1903.

3.8.2.90 "Imin toriatsukainin ni yorazaru imin ni taishi tokō ninka o ataetaru mono no seimei tsuki hyō keishichō fu ken yori hōkoku ikken" (Documents on information relating to those emigrants who did not use private companies to go abroad). 22 vols. October 1897–July 1915.

3.8.2.93 "Hawaikoku 'Honoruru' fu kaisetsu no Keihin chokin ginkō shiten ni oite honpō imin no henkin yokin toriatsukai ikken" (Documents on emigrant repayments and deposits in Keihin Bank in Hawaii). April 1898–November 1906.

3.8.2.95 "Kumamoto imin gōshigaisha gyōmu kankei zakken" (Miscellaneous documents concerning the affairs of Kumamoto imin gōshigaisha). 3 vols. April 1898–March 1909.

3.8.2.96 "Kumamoto imin gōshigaisha toriatsukai imin tokō ninka hōkoku zakken" (Miscellaneous documents on the permission granted Kumamoto imin gōshigaisha to send emigrants abroad). 4 vols. May 1898–May 1906.

3.8.2.97 "Teikoku shokumin gōshigaisha gyōmu kankei zakken" (Miscellaneous documents on the affairs of Teikoku shokumin gōshigaisha). 5 vols. June 1898–June 1909.

3.8.2.99 "Kumamoto imin gōshigaisha toriatsukai imin tokō ninka torikeshi hōkoku ikken" (Miscellaneous documents on the cancellation of the permission granted Kumamoto imin gōshigaisha to send emigrants abroad). January 1899–March 1900.

3.8.2.102 "Teikoku shokumin gōshigaisha toriatsukai imin tokō ninka ni kansuru zakken" (Miscellaneous documents on the permission granted Teikoku shokumin gōshigaisha to send emigrants abroad). March 1899–July 1900.

3.8.2.103 "Tokio imin gōshigaisha imin tokō ninka torikeshi ni kansuru zakken" (Miscellaneous documents on the cancellation of the permission granted Tokio imin gōshigaisha to send emigrants abroad). April 1899–March 1901.

3.8.2.104 "Tokio imin gōshigaisha narabini Nippon imin gōshigaisha ni oite Hawai imin no tokōhi tatekae ikken" (Documents on Tokio imin gōshigaisha and Nippon imin gōshigaisha's practice of advancing ship passage money to emigrants going to Hawaii). May 1899–July 1899.

3.8.2.105 "Imin toriatsukainin Morioka Makoto ni kakawaru imin tokō ninka torikeshi hōkoku ikken" (Documents on the cancellation of the permission granted Morioka Makoto to send emigrants abroad). May 1899–September 1903.

3.8.2.107 "Kyōdō imin gōshigaisha imin toriatsukai eigyō ikken (kigen keika mukō)" (Documents on the business affairs of Kyōdō imin gōshigaisha). June 1899–March 1900.

3.8.2.109 "Tōyō shokumin gōmeigaisha gyōmu kankei zakken" (Miscellaneous documents on the affairs of Tōyō shokumin gōmeigaisha). July 1899–August 1903.

3.8.2.113 "Nippon imin gōshigaisha toriatsukai imin tokō ninka torikeshi hōkoku ikken" (Documents on the cancellation of the permission granted Nippon imin gōshigaisha to send emigrants abroad). September 1899–May 1900.

3.8.2.114 "Taiheiyō imin gōshigaisha gyōmu kankei zakken" (Miscellaneous documents on the affairs of Taiheiyō imin gōshigaisha). September 1899–September 1903.

3.8.2.116 "Teikoku shokumin gōshigaisha toriatsukai imin tokō ninka torikeshi ni kansuru zakken" (Miscellaneous documents on the cancellation of the permission granted Teikoku shokumin gōshigaisha to send emigrants abroad). November 1899–December 1899.

3.8.2.117 "Kaigai tokō kabushikigaisha toriatsukai imin tokō ninka torikeshi hōkoku ikken" (Documents on the cancellation of the permission granted Kaigai tokō kabushikigaisha to send emigrants abroad). December 1899–February 1900.

3.8.2.120 "Niigata shokumin kabushikigaisha gyōmu kankei zakken" (Miscellaneous documents on the affairs of Niigata shokumin kabushikigaisha). December 1899–July 1900.

3.8.2.122 "Hawai e honpō imin dekasegi torishimari zakken" (Miscellaneous documents on the supervision of emigrants going to Hawaii). 8 vols. (There is no volume 1 or volume 8. Volume 6 is in two parts.) 1901–1919.

3.8.2.123 "Imin toriatsukainin Taniguchi Kaichi gyōmu kankei zakken" (Miscellaneous documents on the affairs of Taniguchi Kaichi). February 1900–July 1901.

3.8.2.124 "Fukuide [Fukuda] shokumin shōkai gyōmu kankei zakken" (Miscellaneous documents on the affairs of Fukuide [Fukuda] shokumin shōkai). February 1900–April 1902.

3.8.2.127 "Osaka tokō gōshigaisha gyōmu kankei zakken" (Miscellaneous documents on the affairs of Osaka tokō gōshigaisha). March 1900–July 1900.

3.8.2.128 "Shinobe Matsujirō imin toriatsukai eigyō ikken (haigyō)" (Documents on the business affairs of Shinobe Matsujirō). March 1900–September 1900.

3.8.2.129 "Shinjō [Shinsō] Rokyō imin toriatsukai eigyō ikken (kigen keika mukō)" (Documents on the business affairs of Shinjō [Shinsō] Rokyō). March 1900–October 1900.

3.8.2.132 "Murata Tamekichi imin toriatsukai eigyō ikken" (Documents on the business affairs of Murata Tamekichi). April 1900–October 1901.

3.8.2.135 "Taniguchi Kaichi toriatsukai imin tokō ninka hōkoku zakken" (Miscellaneous documents on the permission granted Taniguchi Kaichi to send emigrants abroad). May 1900–July 1900.

3.8.2.138 "Osaka tokō gōshigaisha toriatsukai imin tokō ninka hōkoku zakken" (Miscellaneous documents on the permission granted to Osaka tokō gōshigaisha to send emigrants abroad). June 1900–July 1900.

3.8.2.140 "Ōkura Kihachirō imin toriatsukai eigyō ikken (kigen keika mukō)" (Miscellaneous documents on the business affairs of Ōkura Kihachirō). July 1900–February 1901.

3.8.2.142 "Shinoda Saburobē imin toriatsukai eigyō ikken (kigen keika mukō)" (Documents on the business affairs of Shinoda Saburobē). August 1900–March 1901.

3.8.2.143 "Tōbō imin hōkoku zakken" (Miscellaneous documents on emigrants who deserted [the plantations]). 2 vols. August 1900–February 1918.

3.8.2.145 "Hawaikoku dekasegi honpōjin shibō zakken" (Miscellaneous documents on the deaths of Japanese immigrants in Hawaii). 10 vols. January 1901–December 1916.

3.8.2.148 "Imin kazoku no Hawai tokō ninka ni kanshi chō fu ken yori rinsei ikken" (Documents on the petitions from local officials concerning the permission for emigrant families to travel to Hawaii). July 1901–September 1902.

3.8.2.149 "Imin toriatsukainin Ōno Den'ei gyōmu kankei zakken" (Miscellaneous documents on the affairs on Ōno Den'ei). 2 vols. July 1901–October 1906.

3.8.2.151 "Imin toriatsukainin Senda Ichijūrō gyōmu kankei zakken" (Miscellaneous documents on the affairs of Senda Ichijūrō). September 1901–December 1902.

3.8.2.152 "Zaihawai honpō rōdōsha yori sōkingaku torishirabe hōkoku ikken" (Documents relating to the money sent back by Japanese workers in Hawaii). October 1901–April 1909.

3.8.2.153 "Bōchō imin gōshigaisha gyōmu kankei zakken" (Miscellaneous documents on the affairs of Bōchō imin gōshigaisha). 2 vols. October 1901–April 1911.

3.8.2.154 "Hiroshima imin gōmeigaisha gyōmu kankei zakken" (Miscellaneous documents on the affairs of Hiroshima imin gōshigaisha). 2 vols. October 1901–June 1915.

3.8.2.156 "Imin toriatsukainin Morishima Hisao gyōmu kankei zakken" (Miscellaneous documents on the affairs of Morishima Hisao). 2 vols. November 1901–May 1915.

3.8.2.157 "Tōhoku imin gōshigaisha gyōmu kankei zakken" (Miscellaneous documents on the affairs of Tōhoku imin gōshigaisha). December 1901–April 1903.

3.8.2.159 "Imin toriatsukai tesūryō ninka hōkoku zakken" (Miscellaneous documents concerning emigration companies and their permission to collect commissions). 13 vols.; begins with volume 2. 1901.

3.8.2.160 "Imin toriatsukainin Shibuya Kinshirō gyōmu kankei zakken" (Miscellaneous documents on the affairs of Shibuya Kinshirō). January 1902–November 1902.

3.8.2.162 "San'yō imin gōshigaisha gyōmu kankei zakken" (Miscellaneous documents on the affairs of San'yō imin gōshigaisha). 2 vols. February 1902.

3.8.2.163 "Hawai imin tsumitatekin kaishi kata ni kanshi zai 'Honoruru' sōryōji yori seikun ikken" (Documents on the reserve fund system for immigrants in Hawaii). March 1902–July 1902.

3.8.2.164 "Tosa imin kabushikigaisha gyōmu kankei zakken" (Miscellaneous documents on the affairs of Tosa imin kabushikigaisha). April 1902–November 1903.

3.8.2.165 "Imin toriatsukainin Kaneo Masatoshi gyōmu kankei zakken" (Miscellaneous documents on the affairs of Kaneo Masatoshi). April 1902–November 1908.

3.8.2.168 "Hawai imin Beikoku tenkō kinshi ikken" (Documents on the ban on immigrants' travel to the United States mainland from Hawaii). May 1902–July 1913.

3.8.2.171 "Imin toriatsukainin Mitsunaga Kyūta gyōmu kankei zakken" (Miscellaneous documents on the affairs of Mitsunaga Kyūta). September 1902–March 1904.

3.8.2.173 "Imin toriatsukai rengō jimusho setchi ikken" (Documents on the establishment of the Alliance of Emigration Agents office). October 1902–January 1908.

3.8.2.177 "Taiheiyō shokumingaisha gyōmu kankei zakken" (Miscellaneous documents on the affairs of Taiheiyō shokumingaisha). December 1902–April 1903.

3.8.2.178 "Chūgai shokumin gōshigaisha gyōmu kankei zakken" (Miscellaneous documents on the affairs of Chūgai shokumin gōshigaisha). December 1902–September 1903.

3.8.2.179 "Hawai 'Honoruru' kō ni oite ganbyō no honpō imin jōriku kyozetsu ikken" (Documents relating to the rejection of Japanese emigrants at Honolulu because of eye diseases). December 1902–September 1904.

3.8.2.182 "Nippon shokumin kabushikigaisha gyōmu kankei zakken" (Miscellaneous documents on the affairs of Nippon shokumin kabushikigaisha). 2 vols. December 1902–February 1906.

3.8.2.186 "Bansei imin gōshigaisha gyōmu kankei zakken" (Miscellaneous documents on the affairs of Bansei imin gōshigaisha). 2 vols. January 1903–August 1910.

3.8.2.188 "Suō imin gōshigaisha gyōmu kankei zakken" (Miscellaneous documents on the affairs of Suō imin gōshigaisha). April 1903–July 1908.

3.8.2.194 "Tairiku shokumin gōshigaisha gyōmu kankei zakken" (Miscellaneous documents on the affairs of Tairiku shokumin gōshigaisha). 5 vols. September 1903–July 1921.

3.8.2.195 "Saikin jūnenkan imin tōkeihyō chōsei sōfu kata zai 'Honoruru' sōryōji hoka yon ryōji e mōshi susumu no ken" (Documents on the request to the Honolulu consulate for statistical charts on emigrants for the last ten years). October 1903–February 1905.

3.8.2.196 "Kōkoku shokumin kabushikigaisha gyōmu kankei zakken" (Miscellaneous documents on the affairs of Kōkoku shokumin kabushikigaisha). October 1903–March 1906.

3.8.2.198 "Hawai zairyū honpō dekaseginin torishimari no tame Chūo Nipponjinkai setsuritsu ikken" (Documents on the establishment of the Central Japanese League). November 1903–April 1905.

3.8.2.223 "Meiji shokumin gōshigaisha gyōmu kankei zakken" (Miscellaneous documents on the affairs of Meiji shokumin gōshigaisha). 3 vols. September 1906–June 1918.

3.8.2.226 "Imin toriatsukainin Takemura Yoemon gyōmu kankei zakken" (Miscellaneous documents on the affairs of Takemura Yoemon). 2 vols. October 1906–January 1914.

3.8.2.231 "Meiji imin gōshigaisha gyōmu kankei zakken" (Miscellaneous documents on the affairs of Meiji imin gōshigaisha). March 1907–March 1917.

3.8.2.237 "Imin unsōsen kankei zakken" (Miscellaneous documents on ships carrying emigrants). 9 vols. July 1907–May 1919.

3.8.2.246 "Zaigai honpōjin no kinpin taishaku ni kansuru jiko zakken" (Documents on the problems concerning the money lent to and borrowed by overseas Japanese). January 1908.

3.8.2.256 "Hawaikoku e dekasegi honpōjin jūsho seishi torishirabe zakken" (Miscellaneous documents relating to addresses, births, and deaths of Japanese in Hawaii). February 1909–October 1916.

3.8.2.263 "Hoku-Bei gasshūkoku Hawai oyobi Eiryō Kanadatō ōkan senkyakuinsū chihōkan yori hōkoku ikken" (Documents concerning the number of ship passengers going to Hawaii, Canada, and other countries). October 1909–November 1910.

3.8.2.266 "Hawaikoku e dekasegi honpōjin kikoku matawa sōkin setsuyu zakken" (Miscellaneous documents on Japanese immigrants returning to Japan and their remittances). December 1909–April 1918.

3.8.2.283 "Ryoken kafu shutsugan ni yōsuru zaigai kōkan hakkyū kakushu shōmeisho kōfu jinmeihyō ikken" (Tables of names together with certificates necessary for passport applications). 67 vols. January 1912–. Bessatsu Honoruru no bu (Information from Honolulu). 11 vols. April 1912.

3.8.2.360 "Hawaikoku e honpōjin dekasegi zakken (daiichi kankeiyaku)" (Miscellaneous documents on Japanese in Hawaii). 1887.

3.8.4.15 "Hawai seifu ni oite honpō jōyō ishi kaiko ikken" (Documents on the dismissal of Japanese doctors employed by the Hawaiian government). January 1897–February 1897.

3.8.5.8 "Kaigai ryoken kafu (fuyo) hennōhyō shintatsu ikken (fukumu fuyo meisaihyō)" (Documents and tables on passports and numbers of people returning to Japan). 238 vols. January 1879–December 1921.

3.8.7.16 "Hawai zairyū honpōjin no mibun tōroku bo no gi ni kanshi zaihonpō Beikoku rinji dairi kōshi yori mōshiide ikken" (Documents on the American proposal concerning the registration of Japanese in Hawaii). February 1909–June 1909.

3.8.7.23 "Zaigai honpōjin mibun kankei zassan" (Miscellaneous documents on identification matters concerning Japanese living overseas). 18 vols. February 1911–. Bessatsu Hawai no bu (Information on Hawaii). 6 vols. January 1922.

3.8.8.3 "Zaigai teikoku shinmin gaikoku seifu no hogo irai ikken" (Documents on the protection of Japanese citizens by foreign governments). August 1884–August 1900.

3.8.8.5 "Amerikakoku Sōkō ni oite dōkoku imin nyūkokuhō teishoku moshikuwa kengi no kado o motte honpōjin jōriku kyozetsu zakken" (Miscellaneous documents concerning immigration laws in San Francisco and the rejection of Japanese landing there). 2 vols. July 1893–April 1916.

3.8.8.8 "Hawai ni oite honpō imin no jōriku kyozetsu ikken" (Documents on the rejection of Japanese emigrants in Hawaii). 21 vols. March 1897–December 1898.

3.9.1.1 "Beikoku imin torishimari jōrei Beikoku kōshi yori sōfu ikken" (Documents on American regulations concerning immigration). March 1876.

3.9.2.11 "Hawai ni okeru gaikokuimin kankei zassan" (Miscellaneous documents concerning foreign immigrants in Hawaii). August 1909–July 1921.

J.1.1.0 J/X1-U3 "Gaikoku ni okeru hainichi kankei zakken (Miscellaneous documents on anti-Japanese matters in foreign countries). 43 vols. June 1920–April 1942. Bessatsu Hawai no bu (Information on Hawaii). Separate volume. September 1920–.

J.1.2.0 J 3–4 "Honpō imin toriatsukainin kankei zakken (Miscellaneous documents on emigration agents). Tōyō imin gōshigaisha. December 1917.

J.1.2.0 J 8–1 "Imin ni kansuru tōkei oyobi chōsa kankei zakken" (Miscellaneous documents containing statistics and surveys of emigrants). 2 vols. Imin nenpyō (Yearly charts on emigrants). 3 vols. January 1927–?

Japanese Sources: Books and Government Documents

Akiyoshi, Tatsujirō. *Tō-Beisha hikkei* (A handbook on travel to America). Tokyo: n.p., 1908.

Araki, Ryōzō. *Nanori jiten* (A dictionary of names). Tokyo: Tōkyōdō, 1959. 2d ed. 1976.

Doi, Yatarō. *Hawai iminshi: Yamaguchi-ken, Ōshima-gun* (A history of emigration to Hawaii: Ōshima county, Yamaguchi prefecture). Tokyo: Matsuno shoten, 1980.

Fujii, Hidegorō. *Dainippon kaigai ijūminshi dai ippen Hawai* (A history of Japanese emigration, part 1: Hawaii). Osaka: Kaigai chōsakai, 1937.

Fukutake, Tadashi, ed. *Amerika mura* (America village). Tōkyō: Tokyo daigaku shuppankai, 1953.

Gaimushō. *Hawai tōgyō hōkoku* (On the Hawaiian sugar industry). Tokyo: Gaimushō, 1888.

———. *Nihon gaikō bunsho* (Papers relating to the foreign relations of Japan). Vol. 27, part 2 (1894). Tokyo: Nihon kokusai rengō kyōkai, 1953.

———. *Nihon gaikō bunsho* (Papers relating to the foreign relations of Japan). Vol. 29 (1896). Tokyo: Nihon kokusai rengō kyōkai, 1954.

———. *Nihon gaikō bunsho* (Papers relating to the foreign relations of Japan). Vol. 30 (1897). Tokyo: Nihon kokusai rengō kyōkai, 1954.

———. *Nihon gaikō bunsho* (Papers relating to the foreign relations of Japan). Vol. 31, part 2 (1898). Tokyo: Nihon kokusai rengō kyōkai, 1954.

———. *Nihon gaikō bunsho* (Papers relating to the foreign relations of Japan). Vol. 35 (1902). Tokyo: Nihon kokusai rengō kyōkai, 1957.

———. *Nihon gaikō bunsho* (Papers relating to the foreign relations of Japan). Vol. 42, part 1 (1909). Tokyo: Nihon kokusai rengō kyōkai, 1959.

Gaimushō gaikō shiryōkan. *Nihon gaikōshi jiten* (A historical dictionary of Japanese foreign relations). Tokyo: Nihon gaikōshi jiten hensan iinkai, 1979.

Gaimushō hyakunenshi hensan iinkai hen. *Gaimushō no hyakunen* (The 100 years of the foreign ministry). Tokyo: Hara shobō, 1969, 2d ed. 1975.

Gaimushō ryōji ijūbu. *Kaigai ijū hyakunen no ayumi* (One hundred years of overseas emigration). Tokyo: Gaimushō ryōji ijūbu, 1968.

———. *Waga kokumin no kaigai hatten (honpen)* (The expansion of our people overseas [text]). Tokyo: Gaimushō ryōji ijūbu, 1971.

———. *Waga kokumin no kaigai hatten (shiryōhen)* (The expansion of our people overseas [data]). Tokyo: Gaimushō ryōji ijūbu, 1971.

Gaimushō tsūshōkyoku. *Imin toriatsukainin ni yoru imin no enkaku* (A history of emigrants who went abroad using private companies). Tokyo: Gaimushō tsūshōkyoku, November 1901.

———. *Ryoken kafusū oyobi imin tōkei* (Statistics on passports granted and emigrants). Tokyo: Gaimushō tsūshōkyoku, 1921.

Gaimushō tsūshōkyoku dai sanka. *Ryoken imin jimu sankōsho* (A reference book on passports and emigration). Tokyo: Gaimushō, 1920.

Gamō, Masao, ed. *Umi o watatta Nihon no mura* (The Japanese village that crossed the ocean). Tokyo: Chūōkōronsha, 1962.

Gotō, Yōichi, ed. *Hiroshima-ken no chimei. Nihon rekishi chimei taikei.* (Place names in Hiroshima prefecture). Vol. 35; eventually 50 volumes. Tokyo: Heibonsha, 1982.

Hawai Nihonjin iminshi kankō iinkai. *Hawai Nihonjin iminshi* (A history of Japanese immigrants in Hawaii). Honolulu: Hawai nikkeijin rengō kyōkai, 1964.

Hiroshima-ken hen. *Hiroshima-kenshi kindai ichi* (The history of Hiroshima prefecture [Modern period, part 1]). Hiroshima: Hiroshima-ken, 1980.

Hosoi, Wakizō. *Jokō aishi* (The sad history of factory girls). Tokyo: Iwanami shoten, 1954.

Irie, Toraji. *Hōjin kaigai hattenshi* (The history of Japanese overseas expansion). 2 vols. Tokyo: Ida shoten, 1942. Reprint, 1981.

———. *Imin kyūjūnen* (Ninety years of emigration). Tokyo: Gaimushō ijūkyoka, 1958.

Itō, Kazuo. *Hoku-Bei hyakunen zakura* (Hundred-year old cherry blossoms in North America). 2 vols. Seattle: Hoku-Bei hyakunen zakura jikko iinkai, 1969.

Kaigai ijū jigyōdan. *Kaigai ijū jigyōdan jūnenshi* (The ten-year history of Kaigai ijū jigyōdan). Tokyo: Kaigai ijū jigyōdan, 1973.

Kajinishi, Mitsuhaya, Sadayo Tatewaki, Toshio Furushima, and Kenzō Oguchi. *Seishi rōdōsha no rekishi* (The history of silk mill workers). Tokyo: Iwanami shoten (Iwanami shinsho, No. 218), 1955.

Katayama, Sen. *To-Bei annai* (Guide to America). Tokyo: To-Bei kyōkai, 1901.

Kawazoe, Zen'ichi (also as Kenpū). *Imin hyakunen no nenrin* (One hundred years of immigration). Honolulu: Imin hyakunen no nenrin kankōkai, 1968.

———. *Ishokuju no hana hiraku* (Blossoming flowers from transplanted trees). Honolulu: Ishokuju no hana hiraku kankōkai, 1960.

Keizai kikakuchō chōsakyoku tōkeika. *Nihon no keizai tōkei.* (Statistics on the Japanese economy). Vol. 1 of 2 volumes. Tokyo: Shiseidō, 1964.

Kihara, Ryūkichi. *Hawai Nipponjinshi* (A history of the Japanese in Hawaii). Tokyo: Bunseisha, 1935.

Kimura, Yoshigorō and Tatefumi Inoue. *Saikin seikaku Hawai tokō annai* (A current and accurate guide to Hawaii). Tokyo: Hakubunkan, 1904.

Kobayashi, Tadao. *Nyūkaredoniatō no Nihonjin* (The Japanese of New Caledonia). Tokyo: Karuchā shuppansha, 1977.

Kokusai kyōryoku jigyōdan. *Kaigai ijū tōkei* (Statistics on overseas emigration). Tokyo: Kokusai kyōryoku jigyōdan, 1980.

Mitsunaga, Akira. *Konnichi no Hawai* (Today's Hawaii). Yamaguchi: Mitsunaga shoten, 1904.

Miyaoka, Kenji. *Shōfu—kaigai rurōki*—(Prostitutes: Accounts of overseas wanderers). Tokyo: San'ichi shobō, 1968.

Morisaki, Kazue. *Karayukisan* (Those going to China). Tokyo: Asahi shinbunsha, 1976.

Nagai, Matsuzō, ed. *Nichi-Bei bunka kōshōshi, dai-gokan: Ijū-hen* (A history of Japanese-American cultural relations, volume 5: Emigration). Tokyo: Yōyōsha, 1955, 1981.

Naramoto, Tatsuya and Keiji Misaka. eds. *Yamaguchi-ken no chimei, Nihon rekishi chimei taikei* (Place names in Yamaguchi prefecture). Vol. 36; eventually 50 volumes. Tokyo: Heibonsha, 1980.

Ōkawahira, Takamitsu. *Nippon iminron* (On Japanese emigration). Tokyo: Bunbudō, 1905.

Ōkubo, Toshiaki, Shōji Imai, Katsumi Usui, Keiji Ushiyama, and Masaomi Yui. *Kindaishi shiryō* (Materials for modern history). Tokyo: Yoshikawa kōbunkan, 1965. Reprint 1968.

Ōnishi, Ringorō. *Jitsuyō teikoku chimei jiten* (A practical dictionary of place names). Tokyo: Bunken shuppan, 1901. Reprint 1979.

Ono, Takeo. *Gendai Nippon bunmeishi, dai-kyūkan: nōsonshi* (A cultural history of present day Japan, volume 9: The history of agriculture). Tokyo: Tōyō keizai shinpōsha, 1942.

Saotome, Mitsugu. *Okei.* 2 vols. Tokyo: Asahi shinbunsha, 1974.

Sekai kyōikushi kenkyūkai. *Sekai kyōikushi taikei 34 Joshi kyōikushi* (The history of education in the world, volume 34: The history of education for women). Tokyo: Kōdansha, 1977.

Shizuoka-ken kaigai ijū kyōkai. *Shizuoka-ken kaigai ijūshi* (The history of overseas emigration from Shizuoka prefecture). Shizuoka: Shizuoka-ken kaigai ijū kyōkai, 1970.

Sōga, Yasutarō. *Gojūnenkan no Hawai kaiko* (Reflections on fifty years in Hawaii). Tokyo: Gojūnenkan no Hawai kaiko kankōkai, 1953.

Tōgō, Minoru. *Nippon shokuminron* (On Japanese colonization). Tokyo: Bunbudō, 1916.

Tsurumi, Kazuko. *Sutebusuton monogatari* (The story of Steveston). Tokyo: Chūōkōronsha, 1962.

Tsurutani, Hisashi. *Amerika seibu kaitaku to Nihonjin* (Japanese and the opening of the American west). Tokyo: Nihon hōsō kyōkai, 1977.

Wakayama-ken. *Wakayama-ken iminshi* (A history of emigration from Wakayama prefecture). Wakayama-shi: Wakayama-ken, 1957.

Watanabe, Shichirō. *Hawai rekishi* (A history of Hawaii). Tokyo: Ōtani kyōzai kenkyūjo, 1930.

———. *Hawai rekishi* (A history of Hawaii). Rev. ed. Tokyo: Kōgakkai kyōikubu, 1935.

Yamagishi, Takashi. *Beikoku Hawai tokō mondō* (Questions and answers about travel to Hawaii). Tokyo: Hōbunkan, 1902.
Yamamoto, Shigemi. *Aa nomugi tōge* (Oh! Nomugi pass). Tokyo: Asahi shinbunsha, 1968.
Yamashita, Sōen. *Gannen mono imin Hawai tokōshi* (A history of the voyage of the gannen mono to Hawaii). Tokyo: Beifu jihōsha, 1956.
Yamazaki, Tomoko. *Sandakan hachiban shōkan* (Sandakan prostitute house number eight). Tokyo: Bunshun bunko, 1975.
———. *Sandakan no haka* (The graves of Sandakan). Tokyo: Bunshun bunko, 1977.
Yōbi, Tenko (?). *Hawai kikō* (A traveler's account of Hawaii). Ōita: n.p., 1889.

Japanese Sources: Journals and Newspapers

Asahi Shinbun. Article, 15 December 1906.
Bōchō Shinbun. Article, 30 November 1884.
Hawai Nichi Nichi Shinbun. Editorial, 22 June 1905.
Hawai Shinpō. Articles, 3 January 1902 and 1905.
Imai, Teruko. "Kindai Nihon saisho no shūdan kaigai ijū to sono hamon" (The first group of emigrants in Japanese modern history and its consequences). *Ijū kenkyū,* no. 17 (March 1980), 1–11.
Irie, Toraji. "Meiji gannen no Hawai imin" (The first year emigrants to Hawaii). *Gaikō jihō,* vol. 77, no. 6 (1936), 158–167.
———. "Senkakusha no keifu" (The lineage of the pioneers). *Kaigai ijū,* no. 268 (1 October 1969), n.p.
———. "Senkakusha no keifu" (The lineage of the pioneers). *Kaigai ijū,* no. 270 (1 December 1969), n.p.
Ishikawa, Tomonori. "Fijiishotō ni okeru Nihonjin keiyakuimin (1894–1895) ni tsuite" (Japanese contract immigrants in the Fiji islands [1894–1895]). *Ijū kenkyū,* no. 14 (July 1977), 1–25.
———. "Hawai ni okeru shoki Okinawa-ken imin issei no rekishi-chirigakuteki kōsatsu" (A social-geographical study of first generation Okinawa immigrants in Hawaii). *Shigaku kenkyū,* no. 136 (June 1977), 59–84.
———. "Hiroshima-ken nanbu Kuchida-son keiyakuimin no shakai-chirigakuteki kōsatsu" (A social-geographical study of Japanese contract emigrants from Kuchida village in Hiroshima prefecture). *Shigaku kenkyū,* no. 99 (February 1967), 33–52.
———. "Hiroshima-wangan Jigozen-son keiyakuimin no shakai-chirigakuteki kōsatsu" (A social-geographical study of Japanese contract emigrants from Jigozen village in Hiroshima prefecture). *Jinbun chiri,* vol. 19, no. 1 (February 1967), 75–91.
———. "Okinawa-ken Kunigami-gun Kin-son ni okeru shutsuimin no shakai-chirigakuteki kōsatsu" (A social-geographical study of emigrants from Kin village in Okinawa prefecture). *Ryūkyū daigaku hōbungakubu kiyō,* shigaku chirigaku hen, no. 19 (March 1976), 55–92.
———. "Nihon shutsuiminshi ni okeru imingaisha to keiyakuimin ni tsuite" (The place of emigration companies and contract emigrants in the history of Jap-

anese emigration). *Ryūkyū daigaku hōbungakubu kiyō,* shakai hen, no. 14 (1970), 19–46.

———. "Nishiindo Futsuryō Gādorūputō ni okeru Nihonjin keiyakuimin (1894–1900) ni tsuite" (Japanese contract immigrants on the island of Guadaloupe). *Ijū kenkyū,* no. 20 (March 1983), 113–137.

———. "Setonai chiiki kara no (shutsu) imin" (Emigrants from the Inland Sea region). *Shigaku kenkyū,* no. 126 (April 1975), 54–71.

———. "Yamaguchi-ken Ōshima-gun Kuga-son shoki Hawai keiyakuimin no shakai-chirigakuteki kōsatsu" (A social-geographical study of Japanese contract emigrants going to Hawaii from Kuga village in Yamaguchi prefecture). *Chiri kagaku,* no. 7 (June 1967), 25–38.

Itō, Kazuo. " 'Morioka shōkai ni damasareta' to iki shogen" (I was cheated by the Morioka immigration company). *Kaigai nikkeijin,* no. 6 (October 1979), 53–57.

Iwasaki, Kenkichi. "Kii hantō minami kaigan ni okeru kaigai dekasegiimin no kenkyū," (Research on emigrants from the south coast of the Kii peninsula). *Chirigaku hyōron,* vol. 12, no. 7, pt. 1 (1936), 1–23.

———. "Kii hantō minami kaigan ni okeru kaigai dekasegiimin no kenkyū," (Research on emigrants from the south coast of the Kii peninsula). *Chirigaku hyōron,* vol. 13, no. 3, pt. 2 (1937), 1–18.

———. "Kii hantō minami kaigan ni okeru kaigai dekasegiimin no kenkyū," (Research on emigrants from the south coast of the Kii peninsula). *Chirigaku hyōron,* vol. 14, no. 4, pt. 3 (1938), 28–46.

Kodama, Masaaki. "Dekasegiimin no jittai" (The actual conditions of emigrants). *Hiroshima-shi kōbunshokan kiyō,* no. 3 (March 1980), 31–53.

———. "Imingaisha ni tsuite no ichi kōsatsu" (Some thoughts on emigration companies). *Kibi chihōshi kenkyū,* no. 128 (October 1980), 12–25.

———. "Imingaisha no jittai" (The actual conditions of emigration companies). *Shigaku kenkyū,* gojusshūnen kinen ronsō, Nihon hen (October 1980), 459–484.

———. "Meijiki Amerika gasshūkoku e no Nihonjin imin" (Japanese emigrants going to America in the Meiji period). *Shakaikeizai shigaku,* vol. 47, no. 4 (December 1981), 73–100.

———. "Shoki imingaisha no imin boshū to sono jittai" (The early recruitment of emigrants by emigration companies). *Hiroshima-kenshi kenkyū,* no. 3 (March 1978), 20–44.

Kuroyanagi, Toshiyuki. "Firipin ni okeru hōjinmin" (Japanese emigrants in the Philippines). *Ijū kenkyū,* no. 18 (March 1981), 50–61.

Matsunaga, Hideo. "Hawai imin 'gannen mono' no Yokohama shuppatsu" (The departure from Yokohama of the gannen mono emigrants). *Kaijishi kenkyū,* no. 7 (1966), 98–110.

———. "Hawai imin to Mitsui Bussan" (Mitsui Bussan and emigrants going to Hawaii). *San'yū Shinbun,* 12 parts (3 December 1964–1 April 1965).

Miyamoto, Tsuneichi. "Shima no kurashi to dekasegi" (Island living and working away from home). *Tenbō,* no. 88 (April 1966), 136–150.

Nippu Jiji. Article, 4 December 1908.

Nishimukai, Yoshiaki. "Senzen no imin yusō to wagakuni no kaiungyō" (Prewar emigrant shipments and Japan's shipping industry). *Keizai keiei kenkyū,* no. 18 (1967), 67–119.

———. "Senzen no imin yusō to wagakuni no kaiungyō horon" (Prewar emigrant shipments and Japan's shipping industry). *Keizai keiei kenkyū nenpō,* no. 19 (1968), 147–167.

———. "Senzen no imin yusō to wagakuni no kaiungyō saihoron" (Prewar emigrant shipments and Japan's shipping industry). *Keizai keiei kenkyū nenpō,* no. 20 (1970), 103–120.

Ogawa, Hitoshi. "Hiramatsu Shinpachi shōden" (The biography of Hiramatsu Shinpachi). *Ijū kenkyū,* no. 18 (March 1981), 43–49.

Osaka Asahi Shinbun. Editorial, 1902.

Oshimoto, Naomasa. "Imingaisha to funagaisha" (Emigration companies and shipping companies). *Ijū kenkyū,* no. 18 (March 1981), 74–91.

Sasa, Hiroo. "Imingaisha to chihō seito" (Emigration companies and rural political parties). *Kokushikan daigaku bungakubu jibun gakkai kiyō,* no. 15 (January 1983), 61–80.

Takeda, Isami. "Hakugō seisaku no seiritsu to Nihon no taiō" (The establishment of the "White Australia" policy and Japan's response). *Kokusai seiji,* no. 18 (1981), 23–43.

Tanaka, Masahiro. "Tōhoku sensō ni katsuyakuseru Suneru no sujō" (The history of Edward Schnell and his participation in the Tōhoku war). *Kokugakuin zasshi,* vol. 74, no. 5 (May 1975), 14–27.

Watanabe, Kimiko. "Nikkei 'gannen mono' no imintachi" (First year emigrants from Japan). *Rekishi to jinbutsu* (July 1976), 109–119.

Yagisawa, Zenji. "Hawai ni okeru Nippon iminshi no issetsu" (Another version of the history of Japanese immigration in Hawaii). *Shakaikeizai shigaku,* vol. 4, no. 5 (August 1934), 41–61.

Yoshida, Hideo. "Meiji shoki no Hawai dekasegi, part 1" (Japanese workers going to Hawaii in the early Meiji period). *Takushoku ronsō,* vol. 3, no. 2 (October 1941), 253–305.

———. "Meiji shoki no Hawai dekasegi, part 2" (Japanese workers going to Hawaii in the early Meiji period). *Takushoku ronsō,* vol. 3, no. 3 (December 1941), 447–480.

Archives of Hawaii (AH)

Board of Immigration Minutes (1879–1899).

Bureau of Immigration, Misc. Files, "Immigration—Japanese" (1886–1900).

Board of Immigration Letters (1 April 1891–February 1893).

Bureau of Immigration Letters (1893–1897).

Bureau of Immigration Letters (1897–1900).

Department of the Interior—Miscellaneous Files, Immigration: Japanese (1868–1900).

Foreign Office Letter Books, Diplomatic and Miscellaneous, Japan (1873–1900).

Books, Government Documents, and Theses in English

Adler, Jacob. *Claus Spreckels.* Honolulu: University of Hawaii Press, 1966.

Aller, Curtis. "The Evolution of Hawaiian Labor Relations: From Benevolent Paternalism to Mature Collective Bargaining." Unpublished Ph.D. dissertation, Harvard University, 1958.

Beasley, W. G. *The Meiji Restoration.* Stanford: Stanford University Press, 1972.

Bureau of Commercial Affairs. *Japanese Laws and Ordinances Relating to Emigration, Passports and Regulations.* Tokyo: Bureau of Commercial Affairs, Department of Foreign Affairs, 1912.

Commissioner of Labor. *Report of the Commissioner of Labor on Hawaii, 1901.* Washington: Government Printing Office, 1902.

———. *Second Report of the Commissioner of Labor on Hawaii, 1902.* Washington: GPO, 1903.

———. *Third Report of the Commissioner of Labor on Hawaii, 1905.* Washington: GPO, 1906.

———. *Fourth Report of the Commissioner of Labor on Hawaii, 1910.* Washington: GPO, 1911.

———. *Fifth Report of the Commissioner of Labor on Hawaii, 1915.* Washington: GPO, 1916.

Conroy, Hilary. *The Japanese Frontier in Hawaii, 1868–1898.* Berkeley: University of California Press, 1953.

Conroy, Hilary, and T. Scott Miyakawa, eds. *East Across the Pacific.* Santa Barbara: Clio Press, 1972.

Ethnic Studies Oral History Project, University of Hawaii and United Okinawan Association of Hawaii. *Uchinanchu: A History of Okinawans in Hawaii.* Honolulu: Ethnic Studies Program, University of Hawaii, 1981.

Gee, Emma, ed. *Counterpoint.* Los Angeles: UCLA Asian American Studies Center, 1976.

Glick, Clarence. *Sojourners and Settlers.* Honolulu: Hawaii Chinese History Center and the University Press of Hawaii, 1980.

Hane, Mikiso. *Peasants, Rebels, and Outcasts.* New York: Pantheon Books, 1982.

Hanley, Susan B., and Kozo Yamamura. *Economic and Demographic Change in Preindustrial Japan, 1600–1868.* Princeton: Princeton University Press, 1977.

Harrison, John A. *Japan's Northern Frontier.* Gainesville: University of Florida Press, 1953.

Ichioka, Yuji, Yasuo Sakata, Nobuya Tsuchida, and Eri Yasuhara, comps. *A Buried Past.* Berkeley: University of California Press, 1974.

Itō, Kazuo. *Issei.* Translated by Shinichiro Nakamura and Jean S. Gerald. Seattle: Executive Committee for Publication of Issei, 1973.

Johannesson, Edward. *The Hawaiian Labor Movement: A Brief History.* Boston: Bruce Hunphier, Inc., 1956.

Krauss, Bob, and William P. Alexander. *Grove Farm Plantation.* Palo Alto: Pacific Books Publishers, 1965.

Kuykendall, Ralph S. *The Hawaiian Kingdom, Vol. 3, 1874–1893.* Honolulu: University of Hawaii Press, 1967.

Liebes, Richard. "Labor Organization in Hawaii: A Study of the Efforts of Labor to

Obtain Security Through Organization." Unpublished M.A. thesis, University of Hawaii, 1938.

Lind, Andrew. "Economic Succession and Racial Invasion in Hawaii." Unpublished Ph.D. dissertation, University of Chicago, 1931.

Morgan, Theodore. *Hawaii: A Century of Economic Change, 1778–1876.* Harvard Economic Studies, vol. 83. Cambridge: Harvard University Press, 1948.

Morgan, William M. "Strategic Factors in Hawaiian Annexation." Unpublished Ph.D. dissertation, Claremont Graduate School, 1980.

Nakamura, Takafusa. *Economic Growth in Prewar Japan.* Translated by Robert A. Feldman. New Haven and London: Yale University Press, 1983.

Norman, E. H. *Japan's Emergence as a Modern State.* New York: Institute of Pacific Relations, 1940.

Ogawa, Gotaro. *Conscription System in Japan.* New York: Oxford University Press, 1921.

Okahata, James H. *A History of the Japanese in Hawaii.* Honolulu: United Japanese Society of Hawaii, 1971.

O'Neill, P. G. *Japanese Names.* New York: John Weatherhill, Inc., 1972.

Ono, Giichi. *War and Armament Expenditures of Japan.* New York: Oxford University Press, 1922.

Reinecke, John. *Feigned Necessity: Hawaii's Attempt to Obtain Chinese Contract Labor, 1921–23.* San Francisco: Chinese Materials Center, Inc., 1979.

Rosovsky, Henry. *Capital Formation in Japan, 1868–1940.* Glencoe: Free Press, 1961.

Smith, Thomas. *Political Change and Industrial Development in Japan: Government Enterprise 1868–1880.* Stanford: Stanford University Press, 1955.

Suzuki, Teiiti. *The Japanese Immigrant in Brazil.* 2 vols. Tokyo: University of Tokyo Press, 1969.

Taylor, Frank J., Earl M. Welty, and David W. Eyre. *From Land and Sea.* San Francisco: Chronicle Books, 1976.

Taylor, William Henry. "The Hawaiian Sugar Industry." Unpublished Ph.D. dissertation, University of California, 1935.

U.S. Congress. House. *President's Message Relating to the Hawaiian Islands.* 53d U.S. Cong., 2d sess., 1893. Doc. 47.

———. House. *Letter from the Secretary of the Treasury.* 56th Cong., 1st sess., 1900. Doc. 686.

———. Senate. *Reports of the Immigration Commission.* 61st Cong., 2d sess., 1910. Doc. 633. 3 vols., 25 pts.

Vandercook, John W. *King Cane.* New York and London: Harper and Brothers Publishers, 1939.

Wakukawa, Ernest. *A History of the Japanese People in Hawaii.* Tokyo: Toyo shoin, 1938.

Waswo, Ann. *Japanese Landlords: The Decline of a Rural Elite.* Berkeley, Los Angeles, London: University of California Press, 1977.

Watanabe, Shinichi. "Diplomatic Relations Between the Hawaiian Kingdom and the Empire of Japan, 1860–1893." Unpublished M.A. thesis, University of Hawaii, 1944.

Yamato, Ichihashi. *Japanese in the United States.* New York: Arno Press and the New York Times, 1932. Reprint 1969.

Journals and Newspapers in English

Daily Bulletin. Article, 14 August 1885.

Daily Pacific Advertiser. Articles: 27 February 1885, 18 March 1897, 4 July 1905, and 2 July 1906.

Daniels, Roger. "American Historians and East Asian Immigrants." *Pacific Historical Review,* vol. 43 (November 1974), 449–472.

———. "Westerners from the East: Oriental Immigrants Reappraised." *Pacific Historical Review,* vol. 35 (November 1966), 373–383.

Hawaiian-Japanese Chronicle. Advertisements, 22 March 1905.

Honolulu Republican. Articles, 17 October and 6 November 1901.

Honolulu Star-Bulletin. Article, 18 July 1916.

Hori, Joan. "Japanese Prostitution in Hawaii During the Immigration Period." *Hawaiian Journal of History,* vol. 15 (1981), 113–124.

Ichioka, Yuji. "Ameyuki-san: Japanese Prostitutes in Nineteenth Century America." *Amerasia Journal,* vol. 4, no. 1 (1977), 1–21.

Ike, Nobutaka. "Taxation and Landownership in the Westernization of Japan." *The Journal of Economic History,* vol. 7, no. 2 (November 1947), 160–182.

Japan Times. Articles: 22 March 1897, 27 March 1897, 12 April 1897, 13 April 1897, 2 September 1901, 1904 (?).

Japan Weekly Gazette. Article, 11 April 1891.

Japanese Advertiser. Article, 19 August 1926.

Mundle, Sudipto, and Kazushi Ohkawa. "Agricultural Surplus Flow in Japan, 1888–1937." *The Developing Economies,* vol. 17, no. 3 (September 1979), 247–265.

Ono, Kazuhiro, "The Problem of Japanese Emigration." *Kyoto University Economic Review,* vol. 28, no. 1 (April 1958), 39–59.

Rowland, Donald. "The United States and the Contract Labor Question in Hawaii, 1862–1900." *Pacific Historical Review,* vol. 2, no. 3 (September 1933), 249–269.

Russ, William A. Jr. "Hawaiian Labor and Immigration Problems before Annexation." *Journal of Modern History,* vol. 15, no. 3 (September 1943), 207–222.

San Francisco Chronicle. Article, 15 June 1902.

Shindo, Motokazu. "The Inflation in the Early Meiji Era." *Kyoto University Economic Review,* vol. 24, no. 2 (October 1954), 39–59.

Staniford, Philip. "Nihon ni itemo sho ga nai: The Background, Strategies and Personalities of Rural Japanese Overseas Immigrants." Undated. Mimeo.

Wakatsuki, Yasuo. "Japanese Emigration to the United States, 1866–1924: A Monograph." *Perspectives in American History.* Edited by Donald Fleming. Vol. 12. Harvard University: Charles Warren Center for Studies in American History, 1979.

Interviews and Lectures

Moriyama, Sadao. Waipahu, Hawaii. December 1978, August 1980, and August 1981.

Murakawa Yōko. Tokyo, Japan. November 1982 and January 1983.

Oshimoto Naomasa. Emigration Service Department, Japan International Cooperation Agency. Tokyo, Japan. July 1981.
Yamaguchi, Matsuno. Wahiawa, Hawaii. December 1978–January 1979.
"To-Bei Annai: Japanese Emigration Guides to America, 1885–1905." International Conference of Orientalists in Japan. Tokyo, Japan. 8 May 1981.
"Imingaishashi kenkyū no ichi hōhō" (One method of researching the history of emigration companies). Ryūkoku University. Kyoto, Japan. 4 July 1981.

Index

Production Notes

This book was designed by Roger Eggers. Composition and paging were done on the Quadex Composing System and typesetting on the Compugraphic 8400 by the design and production staff of University of Hawaii Press.

The text and display typeface is Compugraphic Bembo.

Offset presswork and binding were done by Vail-Ballou Press, Inc. Text paper is P & S Offset, basis 50.